SOURCES OF THE APOSTOLIC CANONS

SOURCES OF THE
APOSTOLIC CANONS

WITH A TREATISE ON

THE ORIGIN OF THE READERSHIP AND OTHER
LOWER ORDERS

By PROFESSOR ADOLF HARNACK

TRANSLATED BY LEONARD A. WHEATLEY

WITH AN INTRODUCTORY ESSAY ON
THE ORGANISATION OF THE EARLY CHURCH
AND THE EVOLUTION OF THE READER

By the Rev. JOHN OWEN

AUTHOR OF 'EVENINGS WITH THE SKEPTICS'
'THE SKEPTICS OF THE ITALIAN AND FRENCH RENAISSANCE'
'VERSE MUSINGS ON NATURE, FAITH, AND
FREEDOM,' ETC. ETC.

WIPF & STOCK · Eugene, Oregon

Wipf and Stock Publishers
199 W 8th Ave, Suite 3
Eugene, OR 97401

Sources of the Apostolic Canon
with a Treatise on the Origin of the Readership and Other Lower Orders
By Harnack, Adolf
ISBN 13: 978-1-60608-280-5
Publication date 11/24/2008
Previously published by Adam and Charles Black, 1895

TRANSLATOR'S PREFACE

THERE is no need of apology in bringing before our readers a work of Professor Harnack's. His fame is now in 'all the Churches,' and by his writings a great light has been thrown on early Church History. In the German title the expression 'so-called' occurs; this I have omitted, as I can hardly imagine that any one will think that by using the phrase 'Apostolic Canons' I believe them to be of Apostolic origin. Dr. Harnack in the present work gives little attention to them, referring his readers to his edition of the *Didaché*. This work was out of print at the time our translation was made, so it was considered necessary to have some introduction, and the Rev. John Owen kindly consented to write one. I regret that his continued ill-health, which all must deplore, prevented his accomplishment of the task until now.

I take this opportunity to sincerely thank Mr. Frederic Norgate and Mr. Archibald Constable for much assistance and advice.

L. A. W.

CONTENTS

	PAGE
INTRODUCTORY ESSAY	ix
CHAP. I. WORK OF THE EDITOR	2
CHAP. II. THE SOURCES FORMING THE BASES OF CHAPTERS 16 TO 18 OF THE APOSTOLIC CANONS REVIEWED AND EXPLAINED	7
CHAP. III. THE CHURCH GOVERNMENT ACCORDING TO SOURCE A OF THE APOSTOLIC CANONS—	
1. The Order of Rank of the Offices . .	28
2. The Government of the Congregation : the Bishop and College of Presbyters . .	28
3. The Reader	38
4. The Deacons . . . - . .	39
5. The Widows	41
CHAP. IV. HISTORICAL CONTENTS OF SOURCE B . . .	43
CHAP. V. THE SOURCES SERVING AS A BASIS TO DOCUMENTS A AND B WITH SPECIAL CONSIDERATION OF THE PASTORAL EPISTLES	46
CHAP. VI. THE DATE OF THE COMPOSITION OF DOCUMENTS A AND B	52
SUPPLEMENT ON THE ORIGIN OF THE READERSHIP AND OF THE OTHER LOWER ORDERS	54

INTRODUCTORY ESSAY ON
THE ORGANISATION OF THE EARLY CHURCH
AND THE EVOLUTION OF THE READER

INTRODUCTION

IF it were required to describe in one word, cumulative and comprehensive, the prevailing and characteristic energy of the nineteenth century, it would be difficult to find a better or more descriptive term than *Disintegration*. Every human institution, political or religious; every scheme of thought, philosophical, theological, or scientific; every fabric of long-accredited belief, or tradition; whatever product of human reason or practical exigency, in short, that can claim apparently or really characteristics of growth and fixity, has either undergone or is in process of undergoing the most searching investigation and vivisection. These solvent energies are, of course, of the most diversified kind. Heterogeneous in origin and object, they differ no less in modes of application. Where they chiefly resemble each other is in sharing a kind of mutual affinity—a contagiousness of opportunity—by means of which activities of varying kinds seem dominated by a concurrence, more or less accidental and unaccountable, of times and seasons.

Now it is obvious that disintegration must have been preceded by a prior process—that of integration: the accretion and gradual consolidation of the varying elements and materials which resulted in the ultimate formation. It is not less obvious that this integration may—nay in some cases must—have been a long and protracted process; that, like certain geological processes—*e.g.*, the accumulation of globigerina ooze in the bed of the Atlantic—human growths and beliefs of a certain type have taken centuries for their evolution and formation. This fact has, it is needless to observe, an important bearing on subsequent processes of disintegration and analysis. Not unfrequently integration implies stagnation. It may even mean the plethora which betokens and announces *disease*. The fabric which it has taken centuries to build may be constructed, at least in part, of the hay, stubble, and other facile but unworthy materials which go to the formation of so many human erections. Besides, disintegration does not necessarily imply destruction. It may mean only reconstruction. Probably there have been few movements in human history—few examples, *i.e.*, of disintegration and reintegration—in which what seemed the best and most durable materials of the old dismantled and demolished structure have not been utilised for the new building.

Confining our attention to special forms and directions of this disintegrating energy we note its activity and extreme importance in two departments of human inquiry.

1. It is impossible not to be struck by the disintegration—the relaxing of cohesive elements and ties of all kinds—which has manifested itself in Christian theology,—I mean *the accredited and traditional body of Christian doctrine and belief* which has obtained in most Christian churches since the time of the Reformation.

2. Allied with this, yet only partially dependent upon it, has, been the corresponding upheaval in traditional and commonly accepted beliefs as to *the organisation of the early church*. This has been so great as to create almost a reversal of the ecclesiastical theory once current among all the great churches of Christendom.

Two characteristics are common to these two movements.

1. Both are in the direction of freedom, liberty of doctrinal thought and of ecclesiastical action,—freedom in the expression of Christian truth, freedom in the choice and arrangement of those external forms best adapted for its diffusion.

2. Both have been, though not originated, yet largely quickened and sustained, by a continuous current of documentary and similar discoveries. In no age since the formation of the New Testament Canon have so many original writings, new versions and recensions of older documents, etc., come to light. The importance of this fact is further enhanced by their indisputable genuineness. They form a series of unimpeachable witnesses unexpectedly called to give evidence in a difficult and long tried case, and, though differing in age, origin, and character, uniting in a testimony more or less corroborative and consentient.

Now whether we regard it as a mere historical coincidence, or as a kind of providential " pre-established harmony," it is undeniably true that similar epochs of intellectual excitation —the vehement energising of opposed but mutually interacting forces—have been marked by a succession of events foreign and extraneous in origin, and stimulating in character and tendency. Thus in the great revival of Hellenic thought that marked and glorified the " age of Pericles," the intellectual excitation that pulsated and throbbed in Athenian life was due in no small measure to the succession of foreign teachers and thinkers that came from Elea or other Greek colonies, and roused the best Athenian intellects to a fermentation destined to mature in noble effort, and with results on the speculation of civilised humanity conterminous only with its existence. Or again, in the religious upheaval which marked, and humanly speaking caused, the founding of Christianity, no small place must be assigned to the continuous appeal to Messianic hopes and aspirations fostered by a succession of "false Christs and false prophets," many of whom were extraneous in origin, while nearly all were sudden and unexpected in time and circumstance. Again, the great regenerating upheaval which is worthily named the Renaissance—especially as it came into being and power in Italy—was first largely vitalised, and afterwards sustained, by a succession of foreign stimuli. When, *e.g.*, Greek teachers and grammarians in their flowing Oriental robes, or caskets of precious woods, whose perfumed interiors were the worthy receptacles of priceless Greek or Latin manuscripts, were among the ordinary imports which the Florentine or Pisan merchant—himself probably imbued with the prevailing taste for classicalism—landed from his Levantine traders on the quays of either of those great sea-port towns, we may imagine the excitement produced among scholars, students, and dilettanti, whose blood already ran high with the fever of Pagan revivalism. Once more, it was a succession of political events and coincidences, most of which were wholly strange and unexpected, that made the German (Lutheran) Reformation both possible and successful. Whatever therefore might be said of the astronomical theory which makes the sun's heat the effect of the never-ceasing impact of such foreign bodies as meteorites, we may certainly say that the most marked periods of human inquiry and intellectual excitation have been created or promoted by a succession of foreign agencies and contributory forces of a stimulating kind. Our present revivalism in the matter of early Christian history, though not originated, may be said to have been quickened and accelerated, by the discovery of the *Didache*

—the most significant document in its bearing on primitive doctrine and practice which eighteen centuries of Church history has yet revealed to us. This discovery was followed, as my readers are probably aware, by a succession, which is nothing less than marvellous and phenomenal, of similar discoveries. Among them, but including for the sake of completeness other Apocrypha previously known, may be enumerated:—*The Apology of Aristides, Tatian's Diatessaron, The Apocalypse of Peter, The Gospel according to the Hebrews, The Gospel according to the Egyptians, The Gospel according to Peter, The Protevangelium, The Gospel of the Infancy of Mary, The Gospel of Nicodemus or Acts of Pilate, The Acts of Paul and Thecla, The Apocalypse of Moses*, etc., ending, *inter alia*, with the fragments or recensions of the Apostolic Canons which have furnished material for the following instructive monograph of Dr. Harnack's, a translation of which is herewith presented to the English reader and student of ecclesiastical history.

So far as we may judge from the literary intelligence which at this very moment is creating excitement among Biblical scholars, viz., the discovery of a new Syriac recension (completer than that of Cureton) of the four Gospels, these fresh " finds," or, reverting to the simile I have already employed, these new and unexpected stimuli, motor influences, or accelerative impacts on our progressing and fruitful fermentations, are not as yet exhausted.[1] Those of my readers who would know, if only approximately, the nature, amount, and significance of these new and startling additions to our early Christian literature, must, I fear, be referred, at least as yet, to

---

[1] See by all means vol. ii. No. 3 of the Cambridge *Texts and Studies* (edited by J. Armitage Robinson), APOCRYPHA ANECDOTA, by M. R. James, especially the Preface and enumeration of contents.

that illustrious succession of Biblical scholars and inquirers—
I would fain include also publishers and booksellers—which
has long raised Germany to the foremost rank in point of
learning and enlightenment among the nations of Europe.
For example, Dr. Harnack, in the last and splendid edition
of his *Dogmengeschichte*, 1892, has partly commented on,
partly with keen prophetic glance has anticipated and fore-
shadowed, the reflected light, which such discoveries as, *e.g.*, the
Didache have shed both on the doctrine and discipline of the
early church, while a work of still more significance, treating
each of these discoveries as it occurs with the amplest possible
research, and thus covering—so far as it is hitherto completed
—the whole area of additional knowledge and elucidation
furnished by all of them collectively, is that noble series of
volumes now issuing from the Hinrichs press, under the
editorship of Doctors von Gebhardt and Harnack, and bearing
the general title of *Texte und Untersuchungen zur Geschichte
der altchristlichen Litteratur.* It is the fifth part of the second
volume of this most important series that my friend, the
translator of the following pages, has resolved—most judiciously
and fittingly in my opinion—to submit to the judgment of
English scholars. The ancient fragments—to be described
later on—on which the accompanying monograph is based,
may be said to have been *doubly* edited by Dr. Harnack, inasmuch as that scholar first devoted pp. 193-241 of his celebrated
edition of the *Didache*[1] to their description and elucidation,
while in the following treatise, under the title of *Die Quellen
der sogenannten apostolischen Kirchenordnung, nebst einer Un-
tersuchung über den Ursprung des Lectorats und der anderen
niederen Weihen*, he again deals with these fragments of

---

[1] This work forms parts 1 and 2 of vol. ii. of the *Texte und Untersuchungen.*

Christian antiquity. The present monograph, however, manifests a somewhat ampler knowledge of the general subject of ecclesiastical organisation—or rather the want of it—as it existed in the early church, and besides has the more special object of bringing its teachings to bear on the hitherto little known subject of the inferior or lesser orders in the early Christian communities. Particular light is thus thrown on the office and duties of the Reader, and incidentally on the importance—at least among some churches—of the purely didactic, as distinct from the sacerdotal, mission of the Church. More than one reason may be assigned for the ampler treatment of this subject, and consequently more than one justification might be alleged for introducing it to the notice of the English reader. Omitting minor causes and considerations, I will here insist only on the following prime reasons for regarding Dr. Harnack's monograph as both opportune and useful.

The general question of the organisation of the early Church, the chief orders in its ministry and their functions, are, of course, subjects which, for a variety of reasons, have always been esteemed of the very highest importance. To say that their importance has been exaggerated at different periods and for particular purposes is to enounce a statement so trite and commonplace that it might well be classed as trivial. Repeatedly in the history of the Christian Church have the discussions and arguments as to its official organisation assumed the character and claimed the recognition of cardinal questions, *articuli stantis aut cadentis ecclesiae*—the criteria of a standing or falling church. It is, indeed, one of the many anomalies in the history of Christianity, that a scheme not so much of belief as of ethical energy and action—that a prescribed relation of man to God which acknowledges his individual freedom and independence as a primary fact—that a mission which distinctly subordinated the messenger or minister, in point of authority and importance, to the message he was commissioned to deliver, should have evolved tendencies and taken directions so perversely opposed to those that might naturally have been anticipated. Certainly—as we shall shortly see—there was nothing in the teaching of Christ, nor in the attitude He Himself voluntarily assumed before men, that rendered the questions of the consolidation of an ecclesiastical society, the official order or ministerial régime that might best subserve its hierarchical purpose of supreme importance. But, however these anomalies may be solved, the fact remains indisputable. The ecclesiastical and traditional theory of a threefold order in the Christian ministry—the assumption that such an order was of Divine institution, that it obtained among and was recognised by all Christian churches alike from the very dawn of Christianity—have now been long rejected by all ingenuous scholars. In England no small share in the final consummation of this rejection must be assigned to the historical labours and ingenuous, truth-loving disquisitions of two eminent divines—Bishop Lightfoot and Dr. Hatch, the former of whom, by his well-known excursus on "The Christian Ministry," in his *Commentary on St. Paul's Epistle to the Philippians*, the latter by his Bampton Lectures, and articles furnished to the last edition of the *Encyclopædia Britannica* and Smith and Wace's *Dictionary of Christian Antiquities*, may claim to have set the question at rest. At the same time there remained undiscussed and unsettled subsidiary questions or phases pertaining to the main issue. We find, *e.g.*, not only in St. Paul's Epistles, but in the Apostolic Fathers, and generally in the early Christian literature, genuine and spurious, of the first two centuries, different enumerations of subordinate officials as they existed in different churches or Christian communities. Now, whether we consider these enumerations as they occur in their first informal and incidental, but evidently most genuine, shape in the Acts of the Apostles or the Epistles of St. Paul, or, again, in such purposive and tendential writings as the Ignatian Epistles, or, once more, as they are duly elaborated and arranged by ecclesiastical antiquaries and historians, every impartial student must be struck by the fact of their heterogeneousness both in nomenclature and function, while a conclusion of almost equally far-reaching importance is suggested by the correlated fact of their being for obvious reasons, as we shall soon see, distinctive and individualistic—nay, even largely disparate—each from the rest. Taking, *e.g.*, the Corinthian church in that fermentative stage which every large and well-founded Christian community necessarily underwent, and which is so graphically described in the First Epistle to the Corinthians, the question at once suggests itself, What was the precise difference between the *Prophet* and the *Interpreter*? Which of the twain came nearest in function to the office of the Reader? That the two χαρίσματα might conceivably exist in the same person, or at all events might be claimed by him as co-equally his endowments, is evident, while not less evident is the fact that both "gifts" were regarded as sharing an instructive or didactic purpose. St. Paul, with his well-known preferential appeal to the reason and understanding of his converts, and his distrust of emotions which might be unregulated or eccentric, made no secret of his own comparative estimate of their value for ministerial purposes. He preferred, for his own part, the office of *Reader* or *Interpreter* to the voluble but vague utterances of his enthusiastic converts; or, putting the alternative in another form, he would rather speak five words dictated by reason (διὰ τοῦ νοός μου) and aimed directly at the edification of the hearers, than a thousand words prompted by the gift of tongues, but not necessarily adapted to convey instruction to their hearers (1 Cor. xiv. 19). The difficulty of St. Paul's position, and the need of his determined stand against the doctrinal and devotional extravagances of his more enthusiastic converts, are capable of large historical illustration. All the sober-minded leaders of every great religious movement have found the need of restraining the mischievous excesses, and regulating even the more innocent divagations, of an impulsive and unreasoning inspiration. Luther, Calvin, St. Cyran and the Jansenist leaders, the Quaker Barclay, John Wesley, etc., all preferred, like St. Paul, the "gift" of *interpretation* as distinct from and superior to that of *prophecy*; and all applied that gift to restrain the exuberant prophetical zeal of their followers. The scenes that were inevitably enacted in some of those early Christian assemblies before the ferment of conversion and fresh religious enthusiasm had sobered down into the gravity of a calm reason-guided persuasion are not difficult to imagine. We may, *e.g.*, picture a church of St. Paul's founding—at all events imbued with his principles on the subject of Christian worship—wherein the Reader or Interpreter—possibly the Apostle himself (1 Cor. xii.)—exercised his vocation. We can readily imagine the tact, the sound common sense, the calm, judicial discrimination—combined, however, with caution in not too severely repressing enthusiasms and energies which might be turned into other and more useful directions—which the Apostle would have employed on such an occasion. We can realise how fittingly such an Interpreter would have endeavoured to reduce to a solid residuum of edification and practical common sense the frothy declamation or devotional rapture of some young and fanatical convert. Like the severe impartiality of some eminent judge following on the reckless and *ex parte* rhetoric of an unscrupulous advocate, his reading and interpretation would be directed to extorting what amount of logical coherence and sound sense might haply exist in the impassioned utterances on which it was his duty to comment.

We shall have to return to this subject later on, as a characteristic of churches either founded by St. Paul or accepting his free teaching as to the organisation of Christian communities and his entire indifference both as to officials and to ritual, provided only that his first precept on these subjects was duly observed: Πάντα δὲ εὐσχημόνως καὶ κατὰ τάξιν γινέσθω.

Turning now to those causes and precedent considerations which gave the Reader, with other officials discharging allied functions, the importance which they clearly enjoyed in most of the early Christian communities, we note first:

THAT THE TRUE STARTING-POINT OF THE CHRISTIAN MINISTERIAL OFFICE MUST BE LOOKED FOR IN THE MISSION AND CHARACTER OF CHRIST HIMSELF.

One advantage in the restoration of the historical Christ, in the gradual disentanglement of His person and offices from the hierarchical prepossessions with which ecclesiasticism has invested them, in the stress on the essential attributes of His teaching which mark the age in which we live, is that it renders a direct appeal to Himself, to His work and mission, inevitable. With the lessened stress on ecclesiastical and dogmatic development now extending itself among thoughtful and reasonable men, we are able to ask, not what names, offices, and functions the church ordained, when towards the end of the second century a kind of dogmatic homogeneousness began to assimilate the creeds and organisations of the various Christian communities, but what offices were *a priori* likely to be fitting and acceptable *for the primary purpose of Christ's mission*. The issue thus raised can be solved in more than one way. Thus it might be asked whether Christ in His original beneficent activity was most a Bishop, or Priest, or Deacon; in other words, whether his *rôle* of self-enjoined duties resembled in any *especial* manner that discharged by any one of these functionaries. Curiously enough, one of the first representations of Him in any public capacity is as a Reader in the ordinary service of the synagogue, while references to the Mosaic law, to the Prophetical and other writings of the Old Testament, and to the necessity of their study occur more than once in His parables. Perhaps the true answer might be that Christ united in His own functions the more humane semi-secular and kindly aspects of the three offices. At any rate— and this is a point beyond question or controversy—Christ put Himself in a position of entire equality with His Apostles, and taught them to cherish similar democratic and fraternal relations with those whom they instructed. This was one distinction between the Apostles and the seventy disciples as commissioned by Him and the teachers of and rulers over the Gentiles, that the latter arrogated an authority which the former were forbidden to claim. Their office and functions were ministerial, beneficent, self-sacrificing and subordinate. Their official designation, whose signification survives as well in the *Servus Servorum Dei* of Popes as in the plain *Minister* of Presbyterian and Congregational churches, started with a connotation of equality, and this, moreover, not of a mere levelling kind, but one that implied subordination and subservience, self-sacrifice and self-effacement. The method and warrant of the Teacher's office as laid down by Christ in precept and example was the experiential persuasion or conviction by which every sane or wise man conceives himself qualified to guide those less sane or wise than himself. It postulated a training into doctrines of a certain import and vitality, and an insight by continued personal communication into a particular spirit and life. Similarly the power and authority of the Healer presupposed a recognition of the *Evil* which presented itself now as a spiritual ailment, now as a physical infirmity, as well as some power to counteract its maleficent agency in either case. In short, during the earlier and by far the greater half of Christ's mission-work—the portion to which the sending out of the twelve and the subsequent mission of the seventy clearly belong, the conception of ministerial authority was allied with ministerial fitness, and the sole position claimed by Christ with His fellow missionaries was fraternal. This indeed was the tie which bound together not only Christ and His ministers, but all the early Christian missionaries and their hearers; for it was no mere rhetoric or figure of speech that was conveyed by the words, 'Whosoever shall do the will of God, the same is my brother and sister and mother.' If tradition records a subsequent period, when Christ was addressed by His disciples and followers by titles of reverence implying an authority extrinsic and independent of considerations of fitness, etc., the fact may be explained in connection with the correlated and increasing conviction of the Apostles that their master was the Messias, and was thus entitled to those distinctive titles and appellations by which that great and mystical potentate was commonly described by the Jews in the time of Christ.

We are now in a position to summarise what may be most fittingly described as partly the *missionary rôle*, partly the *Royal Messianic claims*, of Jesus of Nazareth; and, basing our inferences on what we described as two successive stages of the same spiritual energy, we seem compelled to conclude that Christ's mission was rather to establish a kingdom than to found a church, to construct or set moving, on the lines and with the spontaneous self-determining impulses of reasoning men, an *Ethico-Religious* society. The object of his labour was in other words not to gather men—first of all, His nation, and secondly, the portions of outlying humanity that might be reached by the Jews—into an ecclesiastical society having special laws or distinctive marks or badges of a doctrinal kind, but into a self-constituted community, owning no other ties or duties than those proceeding from righteousness and mutual benevolence. The watchword of His mission—the informal condition of entry into His kingdom —was REFORM YOURSELVES ($\mu\epsilon\tau\alpha\nu o\epsilon\hat{\iota}\tau\epsilon$), which implies much more than the sentiment of penitence or repentance, besides connoting the exercise of volitional energy, which rendered equally superfluous reliance on extraneous powers or ministrations as well as on any sanctions or considerations of religious or ritualistic acts. Doubtless it had, with other significations, especial reference to the requirements of Messianic times, for it seems to have been employed largely to indicate the permanent change and amelioration of Thought, which according to the best Rabbinical teaching was to mark the advent of the Messias. The sway of a Potentate whose claims to sovereignty were based on justice and righteousness presupposed similar moral conditions on the part of those whom he claimed to rule. Indeed the gradual substitution of ethical for racial and national virtues—such as we find indicated in the later prophets—is one of the most significant marks of progress in the later evolution of Messianic aspiration. But there was nothing in these qualities which imparted a distinctive, ecclesiastical or sectarian condition of membership or citizenship, so to speak, to those who possessed them. The requirements were not Jewish or national in any exclusive sense of the term. They were conditions pertaining to humanity rendered obligatory by the elementary needs of social and political life. The requirement, *e.g.*, that men should do to others as they would have others do to them, though obviously transcending the enforcement or compulsion of secular political systems, had nothing of a religiously sectarian character. The brotherhood—the just reciprocity of human interests and duties of which it formed the principle—was the largest and most profoundly grounded of all the motives to human conduct. It was that of man to man, not of Jew to Jew, still less of religionist to religionist, or sectarian to sectarian.

Nor again were these requirements of such a kind as to render necessary an hierarchical guarantee or sacerdotal consecration. Many have regarded with a wonderment falling but a little short of consternation the little stress which in the ministry of Christ is placed upon common worship, or ritual, or any other tie of a religious or doctrinal kind. The prayer He inculcated was the private devotion which harmonised so well with the immediate personal relation which He similarly advocated as that existing between man and God, between the child and his father. It seems doubtful even, whether the knowledge or use of it was common among the twelve, or that it was ever employed by them as either a private or public ritual. The only religious service, so far as we have any record, in which Christ and His Apostles joined together, was the Hymn with which they concluded their celebration of the Passover, though this was probably no more than the chanted Psalms with which the Paschal feast was concluded in every Jewish household. But it is evident that such an ignoring of congregational union, of doctrinal and devotional bonds, rendered the intervention of ministers or superintendent officers less needful. Christ Himself taught assembled crowds in the open air by the sea shore, or on the mountain side, just as opportunities presented themselves, and we are justified in supposing that the same informal means of instruction were adopted by the Apostles. Indeed it would seem that just as Christ's own method was largely individualistic, so the beginnings of Christian teaching on the part of the Apostles were neither ecclesiastical nor congregational. It was the teaching of separate households, or rather of that person or those members of the family whom the missionary Apostle might judge to be most worthy of his efforts.

But if Christ's own *rôle* and ministry, and that committed by Him to his Apostles, had nothing of the constituent elements of sacerdotalism—was wholly, *i.e.*, free from the ideas and tendencies which are involved in and are likely to develop into systematic ecclesiasticism—the same conclusions are forced upon us by a consideration of the main teachings and methods which are commonly summarised as Christ's ministerial work. At some risk of intruding a subject which a few may deem desultory, while most will regard it as trite, it may be well to glance briefly and comprehensively at the nature of Christ's mission. Nothing less than this seems needed, in order to determine the place and functions which the Reader and similar officials might claim to possess in a community supposed to be founded and organised by Christ.

Taking, then, the constituent elements of that work in what we may reasonably regard the order of their importance, we may say that the primary object of His teaching was the inculcation of those qualities and virtues especially needed by the ethical monarchianism which He proclaimed. With the insight of the genuine Reformer into the thought-tendencies, the aspirations, political, religious, or social, of those who needed reforming—the raw material, so to speak, of the passionate enthusiasm which craved not so much suppression as guidance—He took possession of the more vehement impulses of His nation and time, and remoulded and directed them into the motive energies of His own cause. The method He employed, the conditions of its employment, were like those adopted by other great religious teachers—*e.g.*, St. Francis and the great Friar movement, Luther, and Wesley. Here also we find a stir and commotion, based upon a widely diffused and profoundly implanted feeling, which it only needed a prophet or inspired teacher to rouse into action. What the general terror of Christendom at the apprehended nearness of the end of the world effected for the coming of the Friars— what the anti-Papal enthusiasm of Germany did for Luther's mission, and the Pietistic reaction of England against the cold secularism of the eighteenth century accomplished for the work of Wesley and his evangelical allies—that the popular Messianic hope and excitation did for the missionary work of Christ. How strong that hope was, how fervently that aspiration glowed, is indirectly demonstrated in the pages of Josephus. The passionate intensity that culminated in the blind and ruthless fanaticism therein recorded is but the religious hopes and national aspirations to which Christ appealed in the synagogues and popular assemblies of Galilee perversely evolved and too narrowly circumscribed. It is to this large mass of theocratic and patriotic sympathy that we must look for whatever amount of popularity that attended Christ's own preaching and teaching—the spontaneous parable or discourse, and the comment on accepted traditional texts from Psalms and Prophets, which He compares to the wise steward's "bringing forth from his treasury things new and old." Doubtless, the first aim of His mission work was the spiritual awakening which, based upon ethical and humane duties, imparted to the founding of the new Messianic kingdom a fresh semi-secular stimulus, altogether new in its concentrated emphasis, to Jewish religious culture. His was no appeal to those principles and motives of religious and moral duty which came into force and rapid maturity after the close of the Maccabaean epoch—the intense and fanatical patriotism, *e.g.*, fostered by the ambitious and rival dynasties of high-priests; the appeal to a Mosaism which had either become a narrow and intolerant ecclesiasticism, or, taking the *Law* at earlier stages of its development, laid stress only on its ritual and sacrificial aspects. The reliance on a prophetical call and authority which left little room for individual independence in the sphere of religion or ethics—in a word, all those principles of popular Judaism which aimed mainly at the fixing of some extraneous arbitrary authority, some intervention between the human conscience and its Author, were deliberately and emphatically laid on one side. For the first time as an article of popular Jewish religionism, the subject and the worshipper were placed in immediate juxtaposition with the supreme object of their allegiance and adoration. That such a position had been achieved by many a psalmist and prophet may be granted; but this was probably an unusual exotic product of rare individual predispositions cultivated and matured into a culmination of the highest spiritual excellencies. The new standpoint laid down by Christ is evidenced by His new teachings of God and Moses, and by the antagonism of those teachings to the doctrines then current. Probably not the least ineffective method of inferring the main drift of Christ's teachings in cases where direct information might seem inadequate would be to collect and arrange all the propositions, principles, motives, rules of conduct, etc., antithetical to the Pharisaism—the creed of the high-priests, Mosaic legists, and scribes—then current. Thus a summary of all the main points of Christ's teaching might be readily compiled by a juxtaposition of the Sermon on the Mount and the chief of the parables with the animadversions, *e.g.*, of the twenty-third chapter of St. Matthew. No one who has made such an experiment can fail to be struck by the vigorous, persistent denunciation of all principles, ideas, and dogmas which are the natural and inevitable outgrowths of absolutism in politics and sacerdotalism in religion. Never in the sacred interests of human freedom and equality was there a more explicit and emphatic definition of man's rightful position before God and his fellow-man. Children of a common Father—the very idea proclaimed an equality of relation which rendered hierarchical rule on the one hand, or spiritual subordination on the other, sheer impossibilities. Similarly the spiritual enlightenment gradually accruing to the disciples of the New Faith, and through them to the world at large, by personal contact with the thought and life of Jesus of Nazareth, was a force which, experience has demonstrated, was not only capable of indefinite advance, but contained in itself the germs of a diversiform and prolific fruitage.

The Future of Christ's Christianity.

Little is said in the best authenticated teachings of Christ of His own anticipations of the future of His religion. Apart from the mystical, strangely and profoundly suggestive significance of some of His rarer utterances—especially the need of His baptism of fire, or His final lifting up before the gaze of all men—utterances which stood in the same relation to His discourses as the Transfiguration scene did to the ordinary incidents of life—apart also from the spiritualised Messianic form and spirit of His kingdom, we have little to indicate the ultimate shaping and brilliant crystallisation of His Gospel. He seems to have been almost indifferent to every merely external outcome of His teaching regarded as a product of pre-arranged plan and organisation. He never considers the effect of His doctrines on the various creeds and nationalities among which they were destined to circulate. He is wholly unanxious as to connecting links and ties of an external and formal kind by which the Divine and spiritual brotherhood of Christians—sons of a common Father—might be formed and sustained. The tree being in its very nature good, its bearing of leafage and fruitage, as well in the present as the future, was unalterably fixed and imperishably perfect. A common collocation of all that was simply noble and ethically great from the first consecration of humanity to God, which was the truth intended to be taught by the call of Abraham and the homely anthropomorphic devotion of the patriarchs, constituted what He especially recognised as the main history of the past; while a common *sederunt* of all ethically and religiously disposed men of every race and creed with the same Jewish patriarchs was His simple forecast of and aspiration for the future of Christianity. The traditional consecration of the Jewish nation in Abraham and Moses indicated His view of the religious commencement of TIME; the final reunion of humanity in a broader spiritualised and Messianised religious and moral culture furnished His conception of ETERNITY.[1]

It is partly the result of this commingled simplicity and severity—the spiritual depth and purity of Christ's Gospel combined with its instinctive insight into the essential needs of mankind—that, though it has already come into contact with forms of civilisation, of ethical, philosophical, and religious systems of every conceivable type, its natural effect has been not so much to destroy, to contravene, to antagonise and falsify what had originally been born of human ideas and instincts, as to reconstruct and re-establish that moiety of them which might justly claim to be heaven-born and Divine, to transform and hallow what was corrupt, to strengthen and corroborate what was weak, to terrestrialise what was ethereal, to humanise what was transcendental; in a word, to affiliate human wishes ideas, and interests to what had hitherto been conceived as exclusively and altogether Divine and celestial—a kind of κένωσις of the *universal Divine* into the *universal Human*.

It is instructive to note that this conception of the universal regeneration of the world through Christianity closely assimilates its object to the divine task of philosophy as that was

---

[1] Something of this kind seems also to have been the opinion of St. Paul with reference to the final renovation of Judaism as the ultimate *consummation of all things*. See below.

conceived and defined by the great teacher of ancient Greece—I mean Socrates—who described the true object of human knowledge and research as the bringing down philosophy from heaven to earth. So far as this object has been energised for, whether by pagan philosophers or Christian teachers, so far has the great aim of philosophical and religious culture—the object of truth inquiry—rightly asserted itself as its noblest, divinest consecration; and it is because men of either type, philosophers or religionists, scientists or Christians, have forgotten or neglected this true end of their mission, that they have deviated from their true course, and misinterpreted the reasons and conclusions of which they claimed to be the masters and teachers.

On the other hand, this accepted and unquestionable fact supplies us with grounds for hope that the God-given task of Christianity in the past gives us an earnest of its best work in the future. We must remember that the correlation of causes and effects is unaffected, other things being equal, by differences in time or variations in space. As a condition of mental evolution, of progressive change, the latitude and longitude of Palestine have no advantages over those of Italy or Greece. Regarded as a primary law of matter, of light *e.g.*, the phenomena presented by its varied manifestations must needs be ever and always the same. Let us suppose, for example, that in the gradual processes of creation, of the different manifestations of light—sun, moon, and starlight—each was at first only occasional and temporary, observers would have to determine its qualities and results by inferring ulterior and probable effects from those already experienced, to conclude, in other words, future results from those actually and finally ascertained of the past. Such an inductive observation would soon determine that the *nature* of light, in relation, let us say, to the visual organs of sentient creatures, was necessarily always and ever the same. Similarly the nature and energy of Truth, or the religious and spiritual enlightenment of humanity, as to which Christ's Gospel might be comprehensively defined as its supreme culminating point, manifested itself ever as possessing the same form and growth, the same nature and essential characteristics.

There are, however, some remarks deserving notice in our present consideration of Christ's actual Revelation in relation—

I. to the Christianity of the past—that commonly identified with and historically described as the Christianity of the Church; and

II. to whatever modifications, ecclesiastical or mainly secular, it may appear likely to undergo in the future.

I. Summarising the evolution of the Gospel in relation to its organisation, official character, and Divine intention, by estimating the result of its activities and operations from the standpoint of Christ Himself, we must allow that it was not successful; that it failed to fulfil, in a straight, undeviating course, the anticipations of Christ Himself. Doubtless, an organisation founded on a community of belief and aspiration—belief in the speedy evanishment of the present age Judaism; aspiration for the new world and dynasty of the Messias—gradually evolved itself. A *church*, if we can only divest the term of most of its ecclesiastical connotations, came into being. A centre point, with centrifugal and centripetal forces, like one of our solar planets, assumed a position of fixity, around which circulated fitfully and irregularly new life and thought and energy; and it would be worse than foolish to suppose that these slowly engendered activities operated irrespectively of the natural laws that govern the world. They were conditioned and stimulated by causes which, in all such periods of religious excitation, come to the forefront of speculation. There is, in short, an undeniable commixture of what is ordinary, natural, and commonplace, and what is marvellous and mysterious, in the origin of the Christian Church. Nominally a kingdom has become founded, with the opportune advantages, at such a critical period, of ideas and institutions which harmonised with all that was dearest to Jewish thought and feeling. The kingdom, *e.g.*, must have a king. Its qualifications are permanently religious and spiritual on the one hand, broadly and humanely ethical on the other. As long as these primary conditions are observed, nothing more is required. The form of the universal monarchy is purposely left free. Its detailed organisation is a matter of small importance; the act of worship, the religious rite, the verbal form of prayer, are matters of no importance. The spread of its doctrine, its influence and power—all are left to its own self-determination, and to the forces in natural operation at the time, moving along the *line of least resistance.* Its best teachers are charged to bring forth from their treasury things new and old. The world-history will, in other words, furnish examples and illustrations in ample number of the wholesome effect of freedom and tolerance in the domain of thought and belief. By the selfsame principles the world of humanity will become regenerated. A new heaven and a new earth will gradually disclose and mould themselves on the ruins of the old. The apocalypse towards which Christianity has been advancing for twenty centuries will by degrees unfold its varied glories, its perennial beauty and majesty, and, more than aught else, the calm and serenity which comes from the conviction that mankind has attained finally and for ever the supreme altitude of devout piety, the conviction of the noblest human duty of which it is, by reason of its highest instincts and energies, rendered capable of reaching.

II. We may hence conclude that whatever progress thought or speculation is destined to make in the future, whatever extent of amplitude, expansion, and profundity may await physical science or metaphysical philosophy, this will remain unaffected by the relation which the primary principles and precepts of Christianity have always borne to extraneous departments of human speculative theory and practical conduct.

The constitution of the universe on the one hand, and of man's faculties, broadly interpreted, on the other, can never be nullified, nor indeed can they be even modified so as to alter their mutual relations. The duties men owe to the eternal beneficent Power which they entitle God, as well as to those immovably suggested by their spiritual instincts and the voice of conscience, must ever remain in essentials permanent and indestructible, and the fundamental basis of Christianity must for the self-same reason be regarded as Eternal.

The fuller recognition, the ampler expansion, of this Truth will form the coming of Christ's Kingdom. Such a recognition in the future development as in the earliest youth of the Gospel will be independent of any particular organisation or official arrangement of the Christian churches. The Christian world is becoming, let us say, too old and grey-headed to be moved by questions which concern only the expediency of adopting one kind of organisation or one set of officials instead of another. Controversies on the subject of bishops, priests, and deacons are becoming almost as antiquated as those on the solar systems of Ptolemy and Copernicus. But the position of the Reader in the early Christian church will ever retain some portion of interest for those "on whom the ends of the world are come." Since Christianity as long as it is a creed, as long as it is connected by ties of the most tenacious kind with the history of the past, must always need an instruction, there may, for that reason, be in the office of Reader and Preacher—in the instruction which it is their primary object to convey—a resuscitation of an earlier state of things, and the primary duty of the Christian teacher may become—more in the future than what it has been in the past—a vast and varied instruction, truthfully and impartially selected from every field of human knowledge, science, and intelligence, so that the Christian teacher will be exercising his highest functions when he draws from a treasury, growing with appalling speed and opulence into something like an Immensity, things new and old.

THE COMMISSION OF THE TWELVE AND ITS RELATION TO THE SUBSEQUENT OFFICIAL ORGANISATION OF THE CHURCH, ESPECIALLY TO THE OFFICE OF READER.

Returning now to our historical survey, and assuming for the time being that a part of Christ's mission work was an arrangement of officials or ministerial functionaries adapted for its continuance and extension, it is important to ascertain the direction of qualification—the disposition and temperament, intellectual, moral, and social, which commended itself to Christ as especially suitable for His purpose. Here, it is obvious, our starting-point must be the call of the Twelve, and the charge of grace and duty committed to their keeping. Such a charge must, we may feel well assured, have been preceded by some measure of preliminary training. The method and substance of Christ's own teaching had to be reproduced by the Apostles. What they had seen Him do when He took part in the religious services of the synagogue in Galilee and elsewhere they must imitate. Especially the office of the Reader had to be discharged. Favourite texts and passages from the Psalms, the Deutero-Isaiah, the later prophets, most of them with a traditionally Messianic significance, were adduced after the manner of their Master. Emphasis had to be laid on the new acceptation of God's relation to man. The Universal Father instead of the Theocratic Ruler of the Jews; the equality and fraternity of men of every race; the near approach of the new kingdom based on the fundamental truth of this new brotherhood, together with the initial mark of individual fitness—" Be self-reformed, for the kingdom of heaven is at hand "—constituted a starting-point and stimulus common to the Twelve as to their divine Teacher. The humane and semi-secular character of Christ's own work was reflected in the mission of the apostolate as well as signified in the charge by which that mission was authoritatively assigned. In point of fact, Christ's own description of His mission as given to the Baptist is, almost word for word, a recapitulation of His charges to the twelve apostles and the " seventy others ": " The blind receive their sight, the lame walk, the lepers are cleansed and the deaf hear, the dead are raised up and the poor have the Gospel preached to them," the principal difference being the especial power Christ bestowed on the Twelve of casting out unclean spirits—the exorcism which formed so large a part of Jewish therapeutics. In all these charges and descriptions we discern .

1. The true character of the ministry of human beneficence of the highest type.

2. The revelation incidentally made of the dual source of man's health and general well-being, and the capacity of promoting by the self-same sanitary measures the health of body as of mind and spirit.

No words could better describe the mission of the Twelve than the homely, pithy account of Christ's own work and its inspiring source: "He went about doing good, for God was with Him." The activity thus implied was the imparting, by means of persuasive power and spiritual vigour and earnestness, a conviction founded on the double grounds of reason and feeling, and inducing a calm and yet stern spirit of self-determination and equanimity. Without such stable foundations the advice to self-reformation, the preparation for the citizenship of the Messianic kingdom, would have been nugatory and idle. We may assent to this without forgetting that the fervid yearning for the expected kingdom as a terrestrial dominion in which patriotism and the warm glow of national feeling varied occasionally with the lurid flames of religious exclusiveness and intolerance, was in most cases the doubtful motive to which the twelve apostles were forced to appeal. In the passionate intensity of Messianic hopes, stimulated by the perpetually increasing dread of foreign subjugation, every principle or motive impulse that stirred the mind from its lethargy was found to be efficacious, no matter how extravagant or ideal were the objects held out before it as of possible attainment.

Regarded as a question of official organisation, the mission of the Twelve is important for more than one reason : (1) it proves beyond question or cavil the semi-secular character of the first missionaries of Christianity. All their appeals to their authority founded on the name of Christ, as well as their

INTRODUCTION xxxvii

methods of instruction, were removed as far as might be from those of sacerdotalism as it was presented either by the well-matured development of the Jewish synagogue or by the still more formidable ritual of the Christian Church of the second century. We have no record of any system of doctrinal teaching employed by the twelve, nor of any forms of liturgical or Christian worship adopted in their popular ministrations. We are not even certain, as already remarked, whether the Lord's Prayer was ever used on public occasions;—indeed, it would almost seem, both by the terms in which its use was enjoined, together with the stress generally laid on private prayer, that this especial form was limited to the disciples just as a similar model of devotion was taught by the Baptist to his own private circle of followers. But in the absence of any prescribed authoritative or exclusive usages, whether in the way of teaching or acts of worship, the function of the Twelve becomes essentially non-ecclesiastical, and the office in the Jewish synagogue and among the earlier communities of Christianity to which it chiefly approximates is that of the Reader, *i.e.*, not the original teacher, but the commentator on already prepared and received texts and teachings. The apostles were also applied to in all cases of infirmity in the fullest sense of the term. Powerlessness, torpidity, whether moral or physical,—incapacity, in short, of whatever kind, or from whatsoever cause arising,—was the weakness or inability for good which these physicians essayed to convert into virile vigour and ethical manliness, the new spiritual health and sanity of those who hitherto had been diseased. No distinction was recognised, such at least as would have required an entire difference of treatment between the mental and spiritual ailment on the one hand and the physical disease on the other. A spirit of infirmity was a feebleness which might possess and weaken either mind or body. Indeed, if the possession of an unclean or decrepit spirit was diagnosed, it mattered little whether its presence and the resultant need of exorcism was expressed in terms of matter or in terms of spirit. The spirit of infirmity, *e.g.*, which had for many years bound down a victim to debility, was but the physical synonym of Satan, who had manifested his customary malevolence against a daughter of Abraham for the same period. Exorcism as practised by Jewish *medici*, who in this respect were imitated by the Christian apostles, was resolvable into one single indivisible operation. The casting out of the evil spirit, if it entailed a moral regeneration, a strange and mysterious new birth, was also attended by the repair of the physical defect, the renewal of the bodily senses which had been lost by disease. " When the devil was gone out the dumb man spake " is the authenticated report of a case which is described as the casting forth of a deaf and dumb spirit. Conversely, leprosy, blindness, palsy, lunacy, etc., were names of diseases manifested by physical symptoms but reputed to be spiritually curable by exorcism. All nervous diseases or ailments characterised by debility, torpor, defective vitality, etc., were the supposed malign energies of evil spirits, and undoubtedly formed the sphere of therapeutics in which the Christ-trained activities of the Twelve were most actively employed. " Raise the dead " was the most remarkable injunction in the apostolic charge, and if there were only one well attested instance of the success of such a thaumaturgic commission the Evidences of Christianity would have occupied a very different position to-day from that in which they are placed by reasonable and thoughtful men. But this notorious absence of any one such instance, combined with the metaphorical usage of the word "death" for all kinds of spiritual torpidity (exemplified especially in the words " Let the dead bury *their dead* ") reflects a flood of light not only on this particular passage but on the generally metaphorical method of describing the beneficent wonder-working of the twelve apostles.

This, however, does not exhaust the whole of the semi-secular activity of the twelve apostles. Besides their labours of healing, especially their task of imparting new mental and spiritual strength to those who had need, they exercised their office of direct instruction. We may assume, without fear of contradiction, that this function consisted largely in reproducing the teachings of their Master. The parables, the λόγια they had heard him deliver in the synagogues, the reproductions of Messianic texts, together with His own comments on them, and especially the spiritualising of their sensuous content and meaning,—in short, the function of the Twelve, both in their first mission and in any subsequent mission of which we have no record, was closely akin to that of the Reader in the Jewish synagogue, and the same office as it became gradually differentiated in the Christian communities during the latter half of the second century. We shall see a little further on how much the diaconate contributed to this differentiation by its own semi-secular character—by that aspect of Christian beneficence which gave particular attention to the sick and needy, as well as by that feature of Christian instruction which was content to interpret already received texts and traditions rather than require spontaneous and perpetual novelties in Christian doctrine.

Briefly, so far as the mission of the Twelve may be regarded, *exceptis excipiendis*, as affording a precedent for the official organisation of the church in after times, the standpoint of office, the analogies of interests and duties, point to the official status and occupations of the Reader much more closely than to those of the Overseer, the Sacrificing Presbyter, the Prophet or Inspired Teacher, or any other among the various offices which different Christian churches and communities evolved for the satisfaction of their different needs.

The Mission of the "Seventy Others."

Few incidents in the traditional life and teaching of Christ —especially in reference to its missionary character—are more puzzling than the sending forth of the seventy disciples, the "*seventy others*," as they are called—perhaps more in subordination of rank than of any other kind of distinction from the twelve. Independently of the fact that the passage occurs nowhere else in the Synoptics, and that there is no overt allusion to it in the Acts of the Apostles, the alleged event is surrounded by difficulties of the most formidable kind. These are, generally speaking, indirect and circumstantial. Given the whole of the *data* in the amplest possible manner, and with as great an approach to exactitude as would be attainable in the most bewildering complexity of various and inconsistent probabilities and semi-likelihoods—and we are no nearer historical truth, attained by the customary laws of historical evidence, at the end of a long investigation than we were at starting. Given, *e.g.*, Christ's own ministerial activity from His baptism, the environment in the way of popular culture and Messianic enthusiasm which formed the seed-plot of His Gospel, the opposition which the spiritualisation of Mosaism would work among the more educated classes ; the appeal which Christ had for that very reason been compelled to make to the uneducated and half-superstitious, etc. etc.,—to discover, train, discipline and establish some eighty-two teachers (twelve apostles plus seventy others) competent to instruct the rude denizens of Galilean villages and country towns in the rudiments of a system of ethics and religion capable of becoming by natural evolution and expansion the sublimest scheme of culture—divine and human—which had ever been presented for the consideration and acceptance of mankind. We may imagine in some supposed given instance the coming of a pair of these itinerant preachers, like a brace of Franciscan monks some centuries afterwards; or like a couple of Quaker ministers or Methodist 'locals' in still more modern times placidly confronting the excitable natives of an English village in the Midlands somewhere about the middle of the eighteenth century. If the fame of Jesus of Nazareth had preceded them, they would have found their task easier. That there was an active circulation of rumours when these pertained to religious and political topics is abundantly shown by Josephus, and on no subject was the hearing of the Jewish or Roman patriot more acute than the reported rising of a new claimant to Messianic honour and power. Any fresh arrivals from among the seventy might therefore make sure of a good audience who announced their intention of introducing to their notice the new and superior claims of this same Jesus of Nazareth, whose wonderful cures and exorcisms had long been the objects of country-side gossip. Granted the possibility of this large body of more or less trained teachers, the difficulty of finding audiences—multitudes that pressed upon them to hear the 'Word of God'—would not have been very great. The indebtedness of Christ to fame and rumour, notwithstanding His own injunctions to preserve His marvellous works in the

d

strictest secrecy, forms a remarkable feature of His mission work. But this concession of eighty-two itinerant advocates of the Messianic claims of Jesus Christ and the genuinely miraculous character of His works involves us in difficulties so great as to be wellnigh insuperable. It seems therefore not unreasonable to look about us for some theory that would at least help to lessen the strain on probability that it must be said to entail. In harmony with similar exegetical adjustments which have been successfully applied to meet corresponding difficulties in the Old Testament, we might even venture to suggest that we have here a retrospective reference to the Acts of the Apostles and to the account there given of the institution of the *Seven Deacons*. That the two books came from the same pen has always been an undenied acceptance of Ecclesiastical History. That the books manifest traces of a mutual relation, and occasionally of a mutual adjustment and dove-tailing of incidents, statements, etc., partially correspondent each with the other, has also been admitted by later critics. Hence there is the less difficulty in conceding that the mission of the seventy in the Gospel is *not the primary* but the secondary form of the crude bare assertion that the Diaconate with its seven members was an institution founded in the lifetime of Christ himself with—*as the customary numerical enhancement so common to the Jews—the multiplication of the original number by ten.* The latter increase was further suggested and facilitated by the fact that the sum thus obtained brought up the total number of the seventy disciples of Christ to the seventy or seventy-two which had long since become a kind of *sacred sum total* in the case of any aggregate of remarkable personages or assemblies.

We must, however, bear in mind that the suggestion thus

indicated need not be taken for more than it stands for. It merely sets forth as a possible hypothesis that the narrative of the mission of the seventy as we find it in St. Luke may be a retrospective evolution of or allusion to the early story of the institution of the Diaconate. After some kind of organisation had been established in the early church with something like a subordination of functionaries, it was only natural to search for a lower office which should constitute the first step in the ministerial order as *supposedly* arranged by Christ. This could only have been an inferior grade of disciples, such as the disciples, and especially the seventy, ostensibly was. A crude distinction of this kind seems hinted at in the difference continually suggested between the apostles and the unqualified disciples, as well as in the overt assertion that the apostles were *chosen* from the general mass of the disciples, and that they had in especial cases certain names conferred upon them typifying qualities or functions. The subsequent stress upon these names, as, *e.g.*, in the case of Peter, must be accepted with caution, both as being inconsistent with contemporaneous circumstances, and as indicating tendential attributes and designs too markedly ecclesiastical to be received without circumspection.

What is however to be noted in reference to this mission of the seventy, and which will again reappear when we come to the formal institution of the Diaconate and similar subordinate grades in the ministerial organisation of the church, is that the functions of the seventy were of a semi-lay character; that these disciples did not exercise sacerdotal or priestly functions of any kind; that their duties were rather of a didactic instructive kind; that, in other words, their duties were largely those of *Readers*, whether in the synagogue or in the early Christian churches. They would not have presumed to start new doctrines or formulate new liturgical usages. They were merely commentators on traditional texts, or books or forms. The Master's injunction, especially the cardinal precept: "Reform yourselves, for the kingdom of heaven is at hand," constituted itself the prime condition of admission. When this was accompanied by every needed kind of general beneficence or charity, forming a general tie of goodness, gratitude, and reciprocity among men, and a profound and devout acknowledgment towards God as the Universal Father of all men, every condition of thought and activity seemed satisfied on which a man's Christianity could be made to depend. No more elaborate organisation of ministers, no greater or fuller systematisation of dogmas, no mere æsthetic artistic symbolism of liturgical forms, no other moulding or shapement of word or thing, earthly or heavenly, human or divine, could be set forward as the highest possible conception of the supremest religion. What the future of Christianity might have been, with only the starting points of the missions of the twelve and the seventy to give it vitality and sustaining power, it is not worth while guessing, but with these germs naturally developed, as we might in imagination conceive them, we should have escaped some of the dire evils to which an elaborate sacerdotalism consigned Christendom for some centuries of its greatest perversion and darkness.

The Post-Resurrection Commission of Hierarchical Supremacy on the One Hand and Submission on the Other.

No consideration of the institution of the Christian ministry would be complete that did not take into account the well-known injunction, "Go ye into all the world," etc. etc. Its importance consists in the liturgical and dogmatic additions to the general precept of preaching the Gospel, a commandment which we dare not say includes more than the injunction to reformation in preparation for the kingdom of Christianity. But in regarding the passage as a whole, and bearing in mind (1) the stress that sacerdotalists have in every age of Christianity placed upon it as containing the central principle of their faith; and (2) the strange, ominous, and even fatal contrast between its spirit and the general spirit of the thought and teaching of Christ, we seem suddenly confronted by a dilemma of the most startling kind : viz., either the injunction is genuine and its mode of presentation authentic, or the teaching of Christ as contained in the other portions of the Synoptics is false and inconsistent in the highest possible degree. The change, *e.g.*, from some notable passages in the Synoptics is like that which we experience when we pass from the cool breezy hillside of a Scotch mountain to the heated sickly clammy atmosphere of a house built for the forcing of exotics. No doubt the spirit of the post-resurrection commission is one that we are destined to meet in subsequent years of Church History; but it is one which we discover when Ecclesiasticism has grown rampant, when the neglect, however inadvertent, of some ritual usage is marked with punishment of the most cruel kind—the death accorded to the unbaptized in the decisions of all patristic Rhadamanthuses being always eternal. It is difficult to express in language of adequate strength the absolute unqualified contradiction between the spirit of extreme intolerance, the reliance upon a superficial rite as a condition of salvation, and on a state of non-belief in Christian doctrines as involving a penalty of eternal damnation,—in short, the essential principles of sacerdotalism, and the generous tolerance and forbearance which accepted moral conduct, and virtual belief in all forms of goodness (*i.e.* Christianity)—in brief, the genuine articles of the best creed of cultured non-sacerdotal humanity. So great, indeed, is the contradiction, so overpowering the difficulty, of allowing these utterances of one human voice or exponents of one ostensibly single human life-conduct to remain in such flagrant dissonance, that the suggestion has been made more than once to get rid of the incompatibility by destroying its most aggressive member. Here again we have only to read the after history of the Christian Church *into* its alleged contemporaneous record. We have only to bear in mind the sacerdotalism of the second or third centuries—and earlier than this we cannot trace our Gospels as connected documents—to enable us to recognise in the supposed post-resurrection commission a law of a church dominated by ecclesiasticism, where the due confession of faith preceded in every case the initiatory rite, where the non-acceptance of the Christian creed involved eternal damnation, where the ritual act was held to override the conduct or the life of the Christian, and where the authority of the priest was absolute over the life and death of the people.

At all events, and this we must deem to be a matter of congratulation, less and less stress is now being laid on this post-resurrection commission and the unqualified authority it is supposed to commit to the Christian ministry either in the way of formulating creeds or in promulgating authoritative ecclesiastical punishment for the non-acceptance, or only partial acceptance, of the creeds in the way that Church authorities or Councils have thought fit to impose them. Gradually the contradiction between the thought and tendencies which animated the work of Christ, and those which permeate this alleged commission, is disclosing itself, and at last men feel that there is an irrconcileable discrepancy between the unconsciously revealed spirit of the life and a tradition biassed by hierarchical evolution between the Christism of the Founder and the ecclesiasticism of the Church.

THE ACTS OF THE APOSTLES AND THE PAULINE EPISTLES ON THE MINISTERIAL ORGANISATION OF THE EARLY CHURCH.

The critical value of a book or document is often obscured by its excessive familiarity. Although it is known to have a function of enlightenment, its illustrative power is the less because too great for the organs or uses employing it. On the question, *e.g.*, of ministerial organisation in the earliest Christian communities, the New Testament books which transcend in importance all the rest are the Acts of the Apostles and the chiefest and best accredited of the Pauline epistles, and yet it is but rarely that these are referred to—at least with a full recognition of their authority—as decisive of the question. Hence, supposing that all Christendom knew of ecclesiastical history, especially in reference to the official organisation of the Christian Church, had been the period covered by the church councils, what a curious revulsion of feeling would be caused by the discovery of some document embodying the church history of the Acts of the Apostles and the mission work of St. Paul! Instead of finding a pre-ordained threefold order of ministers which had from the beginning been established by Christ and held rule in the Church, we should discover only one order which could in any legitimate manner claim to be instituted by Christ, *i.e.* the apostolate of the twelve. This had no other or diviner control than might be implied in the providential rule over such terrestrial chances as casting lots. Doubtless we might believe in a divine consummation of terrestrial events when the data for their accomplishment are more or less of a gambling kind, and the choice of the earliest successor to Judas by casting lots might have as strong an element of chance as any of the other gambling methods by which his later successors have been chosen—as, *e.g.*, the political party that happened to be in power—when some bishop of the English Church had to be appointed. Besides *the Twelve*, the other order was that of the Diaconate. Seven were chosen for lay or mixed duties in connection with the Church—not improbably, as we have already suggested—with an eye to the seventy disciples of St. Luke. Probably the duties of the Reader, as they afterwards came to be defined, belonged more to the functions of the Twelve than to those of the Seven, *i.e.*, the ministry of the word and prayer, though there is an obvious danger of dogmatising on the point. The offices of the Reader's attendance on and instruction of the sick made the reading of and commenting on certain passages duties of primary importance. But the chief point of general diagnosis in this general conspectus is the entire absence of anything like an universally accepted order or arrangement of Christian ministers. The traveller bent on investigating the chief centre points of Christian growth or progress such as they existed in the churches of Palestine, Syria, Asia Minor, and Upper Egypt, might journey from one rising Christian community to another without scarcely a single reminder that there was anything like a systematising either of Christian doctrines, or modes of worship, or ministerial order. Damascus, Antioch, Jerusalem, Joppa, Tyre,

Sidon, Corinth, Ephesus, Athens, Rome, Alexandria, etc., were in each case independent centres of Christian thought and Christian life. The only points of contact were: (1) a community, often vague and vacillating, of Christian tradition; (2) some recognised association with one of the twelve; (3) a persuasion more or less lively of the approach of the Messianic kingdom and of the expectation that Jesus himself would shortly come to judgment; (4) a feeling largely derived from the oral and traditional teachings of Christ of primary Christian truths, such as, *e.g.*, the universal fatherhood of God, his equal acceptance of all goodness as constituting a claim on His fatherly regard, the need for all men of repentance and self-reformation—such teachings as, in a word, we know to have been retailed from one church to another, just, as in point of fact, St. Paul's epistles were similarly transmitted until in due process of sifting and collection each main church had its own especial anthology, its own choice selection of *logia*, oral sayings, parables, discourses, and sentences, which became its own ethical and doctrinal basis, and constituted its contribution to one or other of the Synoptic Gospels when these came to be arranged in a documentary form. There was thus, as we may readily see, a free interchange of opinion on all points connected with Christianity, whether regarded as a doctrinal scheme or a tradition of history. Further, room was left for the expansion of Christian opinion on most points of doctrine in harmony with peculiarities and idiosyncrasies of individual churches. Thus, to take the most prominent example of all: the Palestinian churches remained until after the fall of Jerusalem and the dispersion of the Jews under the influence if not actual domination of the twelve. Some of the Syrian churches were similarly allied with those of Palestine for reasons of community of race, language, or commerce. On the other hand, the Christian churches which were surrounded and influenced by Gentile opinion as, *e.g.*, Rome, Athens, and Corinth, assimilated those elements in Christian tradition which were less removed from ideas which they had already discovered in their Gentile training. As an example of this freedom of Christian teaching as well as an illustration of the autonomy and self-dependence of early Christianity in the arrrangement of its officials, we have the striking instance of St. Paul. Unconnected with the twelve; knowing nothing of the seven deacons but as objects and partial victims of his fanatical and murderous hatred; unversed in Christian teaching whether at the lips of Christ or of His apostles; instructed only in just those elements of Pharisaic Judaism which were most opposed to the characteristic teachings of the gospel, Paul had all the qualities of spontaneity and self-centred freedom that any man could have. So far, indeed, as human external authority was concerned, or conformity to a pre-arranged system of ministerial order or gradation, nothing could be further from him than a submissive recognition of either. It is impossible to overestimate the value of a precedent like St. Paul on the side of freedom, of religious activities in vigorous automatic operation, and strong individual idiosyncrasies acting *proprio motu* without any human coercive influence from without, especially when dogmatic forces were exercising an unduly hardening power over the religious thought and life. St. Paul, as has often been pointed out, is the compeer of those self-impelled eccentric spirits whose spontaneous energies have from time to time given new life to Christianity—however perverted that life may have occasionally been—such men, *e.g.*, as Ignatius Loyola, St. Benedict and St. Francis, Luther, George Fox, and

Wesley. Especially great is St. Paul's influence on the question of the Christian ministry. We have already glanced at this point, without however doing more than touching the fringe of the subject.

Self-impelled as St. Paul was, at least in respect of human and objectively cognoscible agencies, it is easy to see that there was in reality no limit to the freedom he was prepared to grant in respect of the ministerial order of the Church. From his own standpoint of Christian liberty, and with his final standard of expediency and utilitarianism, there was no unbending rule in the names and functions of officials, in the order they were required to maintain, in their mutual agreement as respects modes of worship, etc. The only mode of government which he recognised was congregational—each church consisting of a community of Christians, most of them baptized, but including a number of catechumens and candidates who shared only a general agreement with the worship and government of the church. With these ideas of *essentials* in respect of church government and discipline, we cannot be surprised to find, as already remarked, different catalogues of ecclesiastical officers and functions, each list being mainly determined, so far as we can see, by circumstances and conditions of a special and local kind. The cosmopolitan susceptibilities which rendered the apostle on the intellectual and spiritual side of his character so ready to become " all things to all men if by any means he might gain some " found a point of support and alliance in the physical temperament which so largely prompted his missionary enterprise. It is rare that the genuine geographer, in whom universalist instincts and foreign humanitarian sympathies have been fully aroused, permits the induration or limitation of one side or aspect of his "travelled heart." The enlightenment of half-secular sensibilities and a generally informing culture refuse to exclude the religious attributes and spiritual affinities from the sum total of geographical information. Conversant as St. Paul was with the race, history, development of Athens, Rome, Ephesus, it was inevitable that he should compare points of general interest, for purposes of harmony or the reverse, with the salient features of the nascent Christianity. What doctrines or characteristics in the new creed, *e.g.*, would be especially acceptable to men who had been nurtured on such different phases of Gentile culture as would have been presented, to take a few selected instances, from such well-known types as Rome, Corinth, and Antioch? Not only would there be preferences or repulsions with respect to intellectual aptitudes and idiosyncrasies, but varieties of æsthetic, artistic, and sentimental tastes would have to be consulted and provided for. In other words, not only would the essentials of Christ's teaching—or doctrines that were so understood by St. Paul—have to be considered, allocated, and adjusted with reference to already existing differences and intellectual specialisations, but even the petty externalities, the lightly woven fringe of delicate outward adornment, as presented in the modes and graces of liturgical forms and usages, the gradations, dress, and vessels of duly appointed officials, were arranged in accordance with recognised proclivities partly inherent partly acquired. It is needless to add that whether considered in reference to doctrine, to official organisation and arrangements, to liturgical usages and forms of worship, there was no definite limit, no rigid rule in theoretical fittingness or customary practice, which gave to one ministerial order or function any essential superiority over the rest. In all the Pauline churches—those that were founded by St. Paul or some one of his confidential ministers, or lastly, those which could claim to be ruled by the principles laid down in a recognised epistle of the great apostle of the Gentiles, there existed therefore an absolutely unrestricted liberty in respect of grades of ministers and forms and rules of worship, while the sole restriction left—that in doctrinal teaching—was conceived in such a form, with a wholesome stress on ethical rather than on purely speculative requirements, that the general result was to impart to his interpretation of Christianity a harmony sometimes strange and unexpected with certain aspects of Gentile teaching. Indeed the analogies and affinities between certain of the ideas and aspirations of the apostle, and the more penetrative and profounder conceptions —intellectual and spiritual—of the best Greek thinkers from Plato to Plotinus, are among St. Paul's most remarkable characteristics, and even now await a much ampler investigation than has hitherto been bestowed upon them. Confining ourselves to our special subject—St. Paul's relation to ministerial or official organisation as it existed in the Christian communities of his time we may bear in mind:—

I. The apostle's own idiosyncrasy. The basis of his mental character was intellectual and spiritual idealisation; the motive-force of his mental energy was a direct *vis viva* of mystical religious insight. Inwardness and introspection were the criteria of every system or scheme of thought that presented itself for his criticism or acceptance. Christianity thus came before him less as a narrative of historical facts observing historical sequence than as a golden thread on which were suspended gems and precious stones of spiritual sentiment, thought and aspirations. Conceived largely as a scheme Judaic and national in its starting-point, and world-embracing in its objects, he regarded it less as a, systematisation of dogmas in the sense of beliefs, than as a perennial source of inspiring reformative energy. Christ was less Jesus of Nazareth than the Divine centre—at once the point of starting and concentration—of all religious and moral energy. The Church was not a corporation held together by ties formal and external in their origin and operation, but a spiritual body based upon the freedom which pertains inherently to all spiritual activities and aspirations. Nothing could be further from such a scheme than a system, dead, mechanical and formal, of hierarchical domination. When each individual member was a centre, possibly, of spiritual enlightenment and inspiration, nothing could be more deadening than a pre-arranged order of teachers and ministers, sometimes exercising the function of instructors in thought and knowledge, at others of ministers taking the lead in sacrificial or ritual worship. We have already seen that the threefold order of bishops, priests, and deacons, even granting its existence under certain circumstances and in certain fitting localities, was never regarded by him as anything else than an accidental arrangement, determined wholly by convenience. The arrangement was no more a fixity than any prescribed form or routine of liturgical rite. To have laid stress upon such an order as existing by means of a divine and prescribed guarantee, such as would, *e.g.*, have been presented by a distinct institution by Christ Himself, would have been little else than a forfeiture of that grace of selection by which he claimed to have been appointed an apostle. The supreme authority of Christ, the omnipotency of that divine influx of grace or the Holy Spirit which was the one source of goodness or divine power, would have been directly invalidated by an external ordinance or a mechanical conveyance of a supposed spiritual power. The argument operated the more irresistibly on account of the dissensions among the apostles themselves. From the Apostolic conclave at Jerusalem, and especially from its confessed leaders, St. Peter and St. James, St. Paul stood for the greater part of his life in a serene and determined aloofness. The principles and guarantees on which they relied as conveying the mark of their apostleship he not only ignored, but partially even despised. Probably the privilege on which most stress was laid by the earliest apostolic society was the claim of having seen and conversed with Jesus both before and after His resurrection. In the election, *e.g.*, of Matthias it was made a *sine qua non* on the part of the candidates that they were men who had gone in and out among the apostles during the lifetime of Jesus, beginning at John's baptism ; but even this personal converse was claimed by St. Paul on more than one occasion, and this with the greater confidence, because the apostle claimed a converse as with a visible being with the first resurrection form of Jesus. In a word, all his own experiences, all the guarantees of his mission, all the spiritual influences and sentiments by which he was so readily and profoundly moved united in inducing a disregard for a systematic organisation of a Christian society such as subsequent evolution and gradual consolidation under other and different influences imparted to the Church.

II. In harmony with these idiosyncrasies, intellectual and spiritual, were the influences arising from Paul's own education, and his long acquaintance as an earnest Jewish Pharisee with the religious services of the synagogues. If the former rendered him regardless of a formal hierarchical organisation among Christian churches, the latter could not but have had the tendency of laying stress on the office and function of *the*

Reader. In the synagogue service this was certainly an office of prime importance. The very fact that the religious instruction of the Jews consisted of the Law, the Hagiographa, the Prophets, etc., together with the comments of Rabbis and other duly attested expositors of these sacred writings, imparted to the Reader an authority which no other minister of the synagogue durst claim. Not only was a common Lectionary employed, so that, among the Palestinian and Babylonian synagogues at least, a certain community of scriptural lessons, etc., was in use, but even the stated sermons appointed for certain seasons and days were directed to be read. Now, bearing in mind the use which the Christian apostles made of the Jewish synagogues, and how closely they copied the order of their teaching and worship, it is evident that, whether assigned or not to a minister duly set apart for the office, the function of the Reader must have found a place very early in the history of the Christian Church. It is true, and the argument must be allowed its fair weight, without permitting it to minimise, still less to ignore altogether, the influence of the synagogue worship on the usages of the Christian churches, that the Christian teacher was not possessed of that affluence of scriptural records which the Jewish Reader possessed. We shall, perhaps, not be wrong in supposing that the traditional sayings and parables of Christ (such collections of λόγια as were, *e.g.*, ascribed to St. Matthew), were employed as Haggadah to comment upon the reading of a selected portion, *e.g.*, of the LXX. Still, with due allowance made for the sources of the Law and the Gospel, there was a sufficiency of Hagiographical and Prophetical writing extant, and claiming a quasi-divine authority, among Christians, to allow for and justify the functions of Readers in most Christian communities. Moreover, in addition to these distinctively Jewish records there were among the literary treasures of various Palestinian churches, especially those wherein the leading Judaeo-Christians happened to be wealthy, a greater store than usual of genuine and well authenticated Christian records. Such were, *e.g.*, translations of parts of the LXX. to the Syro-Hebraic of North Palestine, collections of λόγια, or sayings of Jesus, which certain itinerant members of the Church had brought together from some of the Christian centres of South Palestine. These were mostly identified by the names of the Christian communities to which they belonged, as, *e.g.*, the λόγια of the church at Joppa, Capernaum, Antioch, Tyre. Besides, there were certain letters of apostles or men of apostolic rank, as, *e.g.*, of Peter, Apollos, Barnabas, and Paul, addressed either as private letters to prominent members of the Church or encyclical letters addressed to the Church. Then, again, there were visions of an apocalyptic kind communicated to the separate churches for purposes, as it would seem, of attestation. In short, the materials at the disposal of the Reader in Pauline churches, in which translations of portions of Hagiographa, expositions of Hebrew prophet, or Rabbi law doctor, spontaneous and impulsive deliverances of prophecy, deliberate narrations of sacred visions especially in relation to the coming day of the Lord, were set forth without any prescribed order, the sole obligations being deference to the Presbyter, Reader, Apostle, or Prophet who had been chosen to rule the proceedings, and observance of the universally recognised Pauline rule:—Πάντα δὲ εὐσχημόνως καὶ κατὰ τάξιν γενέσθω.

III. But there remains one more consideration in the evolution of Pauline culture which would make the apostle's deference to Jewish usages and his sympathy with Jewish aspirations all the more natural. The consummation of all things to which he looked and for which he laboured was, in a large sense of the term, Jewish. This alone would induce him to regard Jewish worship and the usages thereunto pertaining with a peculiar tenderness and consideration. The function of Reader—to take a single but important example—imported a continuity of office, didactic purpose, unhierarchical significance, which established the usages of Jewish worship, their methods of imparting and receiving religious instruction, which so far was a propaedeutic of the same usages and methods, to be restored at the ultimate consummation of all things. For St. Paul, we must remember, never left for any length of time out of the purview of his religious foresight and the earnest craving of his Judaeo-Christian aspiration the ultimate destiny of the great universal ISRAEL OF GOD. Lord Beaconsfield once said, in reference to the great heroes of his race, that an arrest of decay was more realisable as an object of patriotic energy than a furtherance of development. It is certain that this formed the especial object of the most discriminating patriotism of the noblest Jewish patriots. "*If thou hadst known, even thou, at least in this thy day, the things which belong to thy peace,*" is an utterance which might be paired off as possessing an identity of outlook and aspiration with such objects as "THE HOPE OF ISRAEL," *until the fulness of the Gentiles be come in, and so all Israel shall be saved*, etc. It would not be difficult to realise this magnificent apocalyptic vision as it practically disclosed itself to the vivid imagination and impassioned feeling of the great universalist Judaeo-Gentile apostle. The central standpoint of the apostle was the sublime reunion in the person and work of Christ of all the great teachings, all the sublimest exemplars of the continuous revelation with which God had blessed humanity. How high the Reader, the inspired instructor, the most highly qualified teacher, or the imparter of religious and moral truth, must needs have stood in every such scheme need not here be insisted on. St. Paul could not have laid emphasis on such a scheme without a wise disregard of the organisation of the Church and its entire uniformity in every example, nor without acknowledging the importance for teaching purposes, and with the object of a free liberal expansion in every direction of Christian liberty, of any such office as the Reader.

A Typical Lord's Day Service at a Pauline Church in the North of Palestine, about the end of the First Century.

Τί οὖν ἐστιν, ἀδελφοί; ὅταν συνέρχησθε, ἕκαστος ὑμῶν ψαλμὸν ἔχει, διδαχὴν ἔχει, γλῶσσαν ἔχει, ἀποκάλυψιν ἔχει, ἑρμηνείαν ἔχει. Πάντα πρὸς οἰκοδομὴν γενέσθω.

It was the early morning of a fair spring day in one of the later years of the last decade of the first century. As yet the sun had not surmounted the hill-tops on the other side of the Sea of Galilee, which accordingly projected their shadows more than half-way across the Sea. The town of Bethsaida had not yet recovered itself from the devastations of the Jewish War, but it was one of the first of the cities bordering the Sea of Galilee to do so. Especially it became the home of a colony of Judaeo-Christians, whose place of worship was a disused synagogue on the western side of the town. This morning the congregation had already assembled, as indeed it usually did as soon as it was light, and when the Christian worshippers on their way to prayer met only a few straggling fishermen returning home after the toil of the preceding night, or shepherds driving forth their flocks to pasture, or vine-dressers starting to work in the vineyards, which were as yet only the growth of the few years that had elapsed since the cessation of the Jewish War.

The Christian church at Bethsaida was typical of such communities. It was supposedly founded by Apollos under the auspices of St. Paul. Its organisation, which had frequently undergone modification, was marked by simplicity. At this time there was a Presbyter Sylvanus, who had been formally installed into his office by the laying-on of hands of Apollos. There were, besides, some two or three elders whose functions seemed to have been to fill up any temporary vacancies among the office-bearers of the church. Next was the Reader Theophilus, who also had the duties of translating parts of the LXX. for the edification of the community, and who interpreted when certain other of the brethren were seized with the ecstatic inspiration which was termed the Gift of Tongues. There were besides two prophets, Matthias and John, whose duties consisted in preaching, in a wild, spontaneous, rhapsodical manner, sermons which all pointed to the immediate coming of Christ, and the signs they supposed themselves to have seen and felt of the second coming of the Messias to judgment.

Like all the other communities in Palestine, and so far controlled by the order of worship and doctrinal teaching customary in Jewish synagogues, there was no regular or universally prescribed arrangement in the different portions of the service. At the same time, a certain superintendence of the proceedings was exercised by one of the elders who was appointed for the occasion *ad hanc rem*; but this again depended altogether on the attendance of the congregation, and how far those who chanced to be present had exercised official duties on any former occasion. It would seem therefore, that, so far as the order of the meeting was concerned, it bore no small resemblance to the meetings of the early Methodists or Quakers in England, in which the chief performers had to wait upon inspiration.

On the occasion we are endeavouring to recall, the service began by prayers on the parts of the presbyter and one of the elders. When these were concluded, another elder announced that he had provided himself with two translations of two Psalms, one from the LXX., another from the Hebrew text of the Old Testament, both being rendered into the Syro-Hebraic, which was the common language in the district surrounding the Sea of Galilee. The reading of these Psalms gave occasion to various comments, most of them turning on the point how far they could be regarded as Messianic. At this point the service became largely conversational. Different opinions being set forth on the authorship, meaning, etc., of the Psalms, the point in which most agreed was the resolve to find prophecies of future events.

The Bethsaidian church at the time we are speaking of did not possess a Reader of its own; but a minister, the Reader Theophilus, who came originally from Antioch, but had long been quartered at Bethsaida, discharged the functions commonly assigned to the Reader. He, as soon as the Psalms were ended, opened a roll and read therefrom certain portions of the prophets, adding to most passages some short comments, after the manner of the Rabbis in the neighbouring school, *e.g.*, of Tiberias. That the officiating minister was a disciple of St. Paul's was evident from the persistency with which he made the universal Gentile world participants with and heirs of the promises made by Jehovah to the fathers. Then followed the interlude of a hymn, and then Theophilus again took his place at the Reader's desk, and commenced that portion of his functions which assimilated, in the words of Tertullian, the duties of Reader to those of an Evangelist. The director of the meeting handed him a roll of MS., in which was inscribed דְּבָרִים יְהוֹשֻׁעַ λογια 'Ιησοῦς THE WORDS or ORACLES OF JESUS.[1] This was the usual title of separate collections of the sayings, discourses, parables, etc., of Jesus, into which the oral teachings traditionally attributed to Him had by degrees become crystallised, preserved, *i.e.*, in a permanent form, and published as the sacred literature or *depositum* of different churches or Christian communities. In most cases each of these collections was assigned to an itinerant Apostle or Evangelist, though the grounds of the assignment might not *always* be conclusively established. Sometimes the titles of the collection varied. Among, *e.g.*, the Palestinian churches in which Jewish sympathies were especially prominent, it was probably not unusual to add to *the Oracles of Jesus* the more distinctive titles הַמָּשִׁיחַ or בֶּן־דָּוִד *The Messias* or *the Son of David*. Analogous marks denoted Ebionite or Gnostic tendencies, while the ordinary difference between Jew and Gentile was indicated by ῾Ελληνίστοι and ῾Εβραῖοι. It was only reasonable that each church or congregation took especial pride in its own collection of λόγια, partly from its traditional authorship, or authenticity, or the corroboration its own collection received when compared with the collections of other churches, though there might conceivably have been cases in which ἅπαξ λεγόμενα, single or

---

[1] Dr. Lightfoot admits that the earliest documents in the Christian Church were characterised by some such indefinite title as this, but he does not seem to perceive the clue which this gives to (1) the formation of different λόγια or Evangelistic Oracles in different churches; (2) the effect of this on the ultimate compilation of the four gospels as they were received by the church.

INTRODUCTION lxiii

unique narratives, formed the ground of boasting—as, *e.g.*, the last eleven verses of the Gospel according to St. Mark, or the narrative of the woman taken in adultery in St. John viii. 3-11. We may readily conceive the facility with which the collection of "Jesus λόγια" of one church was borrowed by another, or in some cases where exchanges of different collections might easily be made.

This explanation seems needful to explain the functions which the Reader Theophilus exercised on this occasion in the church of Bethsaida. Incidentally also it may help to show how readily collections of the various churches might be made under the direction of some leading mind, which should ultimately assume the forms of certain Gospels indicating tendencies as distinct as those exemplified, *e.g.*, by the Gospels of St. Matthew or St. John.

That there was a similar interchange of the Epistles of St. Paul or St. Peter or St. James, is shown by Colossians iv. 16. Indeed, at this very service we may readily imagine that, following closely on the reading of different λόγια or *Evangelistic Oracles*, followed supposedly the reading of two letters, one inscribed, τῇ Λαοδικέων Ἐκκλησίᾳ, and the other, τῇ ἐν Σαλαμῖνι Ἐκκλησίᾳ. These were letters which the church at Bethsaida had borrowed from the churches of Salamis and Laodicea—lending in return letters of Apostles treasured in their own depository.

While the Reader or "reading minister" was still perusing the passages of the Old and New Testament with which he had come especially provided, the director of the meeting, or *Ruler of the Christian Synagogue*, gave the service another direction. He had already noticed symptoms of disquiet in a prophet named Matthias, his excitement assuming an aggravated form at every mention of the Messias, and His expected return to judgment.

At last he seemed unable to control himself. With a trembling hand, but as noiselessly as he could, he unrolled and rolled again sundry manuscripts which he held in his hand. The director saw what he reverently regarded as the overmastering influx of inspiration, and made silent signs for the Reader to cease. Whereupon Matthias burst forth in language which at times seemed too passionate for distinct utterance, but struggled between incoherence of expression and the combined beauty and profundity of the language employed for its utterance. Thus he commenced in something like the following strain :—

"In truth, my brothers and sisters, the spirit of the Lord is upon me and the power of the Highest is overshadowing me. So great is that mystic force that I know not how to give it utterance. Methinks I am like to one of the blessed twelve on the first day of Pentecost, as I remember hearing when a child from one who was himself present at that festival of voiceful yet inarticulate rapture. I feel moved to say what I know not—yet know I that what I know not the Divine Spirit, source of all Divine knowledge, He knoweth what I cannot know ; so falleth it out that my utterance is the audible expression of a knowledge transcending mine own. Haply it may please the Divine goodness, through the grace of His Son Jesus Christ, to impart to you the interpretation of these marvels lately vouchsafed unto me. For not always are there given to one and the same minister both the gift of tongues and the interpretation of tongues, as Paul witnesseth in his letter to the Corinthians. Behold, therefore, my brothers —may God open the eyes of your understanding so that ye may see what I am bidden to disclose to you !—see, I say, the wondrous vision unrolled before my eyes. For no later than last night when I laid me down in peace on mine own housetop, wearied by a long day's work at vine-dressing and a long evening of net-fishing on our sea, that scarce so did it seem to me that mine eyelids had composed themselves to slumber than I heard the repeated cry of the parable contained in these 'words of Christ' which the Church of Nazareth lent us, and which we have now carefully stored in our own treasury of the sayings of Jesus. Ye well know the words I mean." [Here the prophet lifted up his voice into a kind of thrilling falsetto of excitement.] "'Lo! the Bridegroom cometh, go ye forth to meet him.' Again and again the same cry resounded, filling earth, sea, and sky with its penetrating power. At first, I confess, I was filled with fear. Fain would I, if I could, hide myself in my inner room; methought I was in my house when the cry saluted my ears, for what if it should be so! my lamp, which I had already prepared—for so I deemed—should have consumed all its oil. To rush frantically forth and inspect it was the work of a moment; I did so; and, to my horror, my lamp was not only untrimmed but oilless. I went to the oil-jar to get a fresh supply; but that too was empty, and still the cry resounded louder and louder: 'The Bridegroom cometh, go ye out to meet him.' Whither, to what purpose could I go? I dared not venture beyond the threshold of mine house. The new strange lights that flashed through door and windows as if the firmament were alight with some new fire,—it was not sunlight nor moonlight nor any other type of light such as we who live on earth are able to kindle from wood and oil and the like combustible things; and while I was thus stricken speechless and motionless with unutterable horror, methought I was no longer within the enclosure of four walls. Suddenly I stood upon the shore of the sea, and high above it I saw the Son of Man seated on a throne which was the centre of a light more blinding than that of the sun. Yea, brothers and sisters! the day was truly come at last. The Judge was seated on his throne, round about him on every side were thousands upon thousands of saints. The books were opened. Good and evil angels awaited in every case the judgment and the reward or punishment which it awarded. The sky was filled with the joyous shouts of the blessed, or—as the case might be—with the lamentations of the rejected. At last, methought I heard mine own name, at the which hastening forward, trembling and not able to reconcile the oilless condition of my lamp with the full persuasion that I had in truth both trimmed and replenished it with fresh oil. But the Son of Man, to my great wonderment, did not look at me with a frown; it was rather an indescribable glance of sympathy the while He said: 'Blessed be thou, good servant; thy lamp was left in truth ready for use, but an enemy poured out the oil and rendered it in other ways useless for burning. All therefore that thou art charged with is a negligence which, forsooth, thou couldest not well avoid.' . . . He spake other words to me, but what they were I do not correctly remember. . . . But what impressed itself most shrewdly and deeply on my mind was the reply which the Son of Man Himself made to the excuse, more than once alleged, that if they—the sinners placed at the tribunal—had but known the laws by which the final judgment was to be conducted, they would have taken the more heed. To which the Judge at once said: 'Have ye not read and received my judgments? Yea, times without number. What church is there, wherever My gospel is preached, which doth not possess in its repository some collections of my sayings? Know ye not that there be verdicts, decisions, and judgments? When I commended the poor in spirit, the meek, the peace-maker, full well might ye know how that these words are so many judgments given, as it were, from My judgment seat when I was upon earth. Trow ye that I might now give you a different judgment from that which I gave you so long ago?"

"But tell us, O prophet, what might the wondrous story of thy dream *tell of us*?"—such was the question that beset the enthusiastic speaker from his auditors on every side. To this he replied: "Methought that of you who are now here present I could not recognise one in the great crowd that thronged confusedly before the judgment seat; but truly that was not wonderful, so close was the press. Indeed, methought I stood —so far as concerned friends or acquaintances—entirely alone. Only two filled the dread scene before mine eyes. It was the Son of Man and myself. Together we filled, so it seemed, the Universe. Two minds, two souls, two eternal beings; there was no room for aught besides. The Judge and the Sinner, the Saviour and the Saved—what a feeling it was that then overpowered me! It seemed as if His being, His soul, His life absorbed mine, and that by that absorption I was judged. There was no more scope for anything like self. What I had regarded as an existence separate, alone, apart from all other existences, was gone. Nothing was left but Christ. I was in Him, He was in me, and both of us were in God." . . .

At this point the speaker made a short space; less however for want of matter than from want of breath. Of this, however, the director of the meeting took advantage by saying: "The day is waxing old, my brothers, and there are yet those who seem to signify their wish to speak; so as our brother

Matthias seems inclined to pause, I will, soliciting his forbearance, ask Sylvanus to address us." Whereupon the person addressed began to speak:—

"Most fitting was it, my brothers, that I should follow Matthias in his speech to you; for surely if Christians are to note the portents that crowd around us in our day dreams and our night visions, then nothing can be more certain than that the Day of the Lord is come, nay, that it is nigh, even at the doors. For to myself it also happened, even as unto our beloved brother Matthias, to be visited in the night season with a dream of the Day of the Lord. Methought—it was on the last Lord's day night when, as you remember, our thoughts and exercises at our meeting in this place were so greatly preoccupied with the same great day—that as I was winding my way across the hills from Nazareth to this place, suddenly there brake on mine ears the sound of a trumpet. It had a curious crashing effect, as if it broke up the bounds of the earth, the sea, the sky, all of which at once became commingled in a wild chaotic confusion. Suddenly amid the din of the tempest, caused by this clashing of the conflicting elements, methought I heard voices crying out everywhere the well-known cry in thrilling tones of our own hymn:

> '"The day of the Lord is nigh;"
> List to the heralding cry
> From human accents below,
> Piercing the heavens on high.'

And as I listened and looked with a dread sense of pain that sometimes overwhelmed me, methought at the very highest point of the sky I could discern the vision of the Son of Man. A form of incomparable grandeur was seated on a throne, which itself was placed on a cloud of blackness adorned and relieved by a moving border of bright coruscating lightness. This, I soon found out, was the Judgment Seat, where He sat surrounded by hosts of thousands of angels. Then was there a great commotion. The kings of the earth—the principalities and powers commonly honoured among men—all these came forward, and were briefly judged and summarily sentenced— some to blessedness, and others to woe everlasting. Ah, then did I witness, and rejoiced in witnessing, the vengeance of God on our enemies and persecutors. Then was there the penalty of blood for blood, torture for torture, life for life. The bloodthirsty Emperors, Proconsuls, and other officials who sentenced unoffending Christians to tortures worse than death, were now adjudged to endure torments worse than those which they had decreed to the followers of Christ." . . .

"Yea! but tell us of thyself," here interrupted the director of the meeting; "what hap befell thee when arraigned before the dread judgment seat?"

"That would I gladly do," was the reply, "if I but knew it; but, sooth to say, when I heard my name proclaimed and called for in a voice louder than thunder, a terrible dread overwhelmed me, and I trembled so vehemently that I awoke."

"I would we could place more reliance on dreams than we seem warranted in doing," said the director. "For my part, I have beheld the Day of the Lord in visions of the night about once a week or oftener for nigh upon the last ten years, indeed since the memorable time when I read the Apocalypsis of the Apostle John."

"It might be well, however," replied Matthias, "that we should not allow our hopes to grow cold, so that we become like unto those who seem even to deny that the Day of the Lord is at hand; so I propose that we now sing as usual our

Judgment-day hymn." Thereupon, to a tune, the liveliness of which was suggested by the rapid dactylic rhythm of the words, the congregation broke forth spontaneously into the following

EARLY CHRISTIAN HYMN.

Refrain—The Day of the Lord is nigh;
List to the heralding cry,
The blend of men's voices below
With the trumpet that rends the sky.

1. The Day of your Lord is nigh;
Lift, Christians, your gaze on high;
Greet aloud His Return to earth
With your loudest triumphal cry.

2. Fulfilled is now—what of old
The Oracles, Seers foretold—
Our great Shepherd is here, and we stand
Sole ingathering of His Fold.

3. Begun is Messias's reign,
Passed now is Expectancy's pain,
Our nation's long frustrated hope—
Turned to joy, thrilling heart and brain.

4. Above the high mountain's crest,
Whereupon earth's mirk clouds rest,
Now gleams a celestial glow,
As though earth in heaven's glories were drest.

5. So, smiting our long, dark night
We mark the sword-flash of Thy light;
We hail the long-watch'd-for dawn,
Thy DAYSPRING so cloudless and bright.

6. With a tense uplifting strain,
Each Christian now joys to gain
The heaven-born bliss of his Lord,
With all freedom from ill and pain.

7. Heaven's canopy, see, is aglow,
Earth's suns and heaven's stars alike throw
On the WHITE THRONE and Sceptre of Christ
All the glory each knows to bestow.

8. Be ye ope, golden gates of heaven,
   Iron barriers of hell, be ye riven;
   The two pathways opposed and trod
   By the pardoned or unforgiven.

9. The Day of the Lord is come:
   Whether mured ye be in the tomb,
   Or chained in Life's prison, come forth—
   Come forth to your Rest and your Home.

This hymn was sung in a wild eager kind of way, as by men intoxicated by some overpowering idea. It was followed by another hymn, which resembled the one already quoted, so far as it contained a reference to THE TWO WAYS of the *Didache*. This second hymn had as a refrain an Invocation to the Day of Judgment as the commencement of the *Millennial Reign of Christ*.

The singing of these hymns was followed by the celebration of the Eucharist—which, however, consisted of a fairly abundant meal of bread, milk, and wine, and other simple comestibles. This concluded the sacred part of the meeting. What was left referred to what might seem to deserve the name of business matters. Thus the elders and ministerial officials discussed informally the question of the variation between two λόγια or sayings of Jesus, one of which belonged to the church at Jerusalem, while the other they had borrowed from the church at Nazareth. There was also the question of St. Paul's Epistle to the church at Laodicea, and in what manner it might be best returned. Other questions related to the conduct of different members of the church, especially some Jews of Alexandria and the East, who had imported strange and immoral practices altogether opposed to the teaching of the gospel. The common recitation of the Lord's Prayer concluded the meeting.

CAUSES OF VARIETY OF ORGANISATION, OFFICIAL AND OTHER, IN THE EARLY CHURCH.

In the preceding paragraphs we have noticed incidentally various causes operating, in some cases obviously, in others with a certain amount of secrecy, but in both cases with a directness and imperative power which give them the character of being inevitable, in the direction of diversifying the organisation of the various Christian communities. In point of fact, each Christian congregation possessed an individual character, extending not only to ministerial organisation but to peculiarities of teaching, ritual observances, especially in the celebration of the Agapae, or the ministration of the sacraments, and in the collections of sacred literature—the materials which supplied the Reader, or the elder, presbyter, prophet, or other official who might for the time being exercise the function of Reader. The conditions which gave to these causes their peculiarity of character differed of course widely at different times, and under the stress of different circumstances. Thus, to take obvious examples, the methods and conditions of church-founding and establishing Christian communities must have differed widely according as they were instituted before the Fall of Jerusalem, and the events consequent upon the Diaspora—the dispersal of the Jews throughout the greater part of the Roman Empire. Some unifying causes, tending to assimilate the organisation and teaching of the various Christian churches, were in operation by means of their having been founded by one or other of the apostles who were especially deputed for this purpose by the apostles at Jerusalem, at least by some of them, for we have no example of a consentient voice of the whole number upon any question relating to the organisation of a church. *A priori*, one might suppose that Christian missionaries starting from a common centre would leave behind them Christian settlements or colonies possessed of similar ministers charged with similar duties; but in practice we know how largely this supposition was modified by accidental and spontaneous causes. St. Paul, *e.g.*, is a well-known example of an *unofficial* minister. His sudden outburst of new conviction is followed—not by submission to any of the twelve apostles (his deprecation of this is as boastful as it is practical and emphatic)—but by the acceptance of the advice and sympathy of a certain disciple of whose name as connected with the apostles we have no mention. The name and title of *Hellenists* supply us with a standpoint of church organisation, of ministerial officers, of doctrinal teaching and ritual, which broadly demarcate those who own it from Judaizing Christians. The accidental intercourse, *e.g.* between Caesarea and Joppa, as illustrated in the story of the Centurion, may be regarded as typical of a certain spontaneity between Gentiles of, *e.g.*, Jewish proclivities and Judaizing Christians. The sermon of St. Paul at Athens, taken in connection with portions of his epistles to Gentile converts, gives us very remarkable illustrations of what may without offence be designated as Christian opportunism. The only requisite needed to show the flexibility with which the teachings of Christianity, or in reality of a moderate Theism bordering on Christianity —a propædeutic of it, so to speak,—might be transferred to the organisation of a new Christian church is afforded us by St. Paul's sermon on the Areopagus. The connection of other Christian disciples, as, *e.g.*, Aquila and Priscilla, who came from or might be connected with places so widely apart as Alexandria, Caesarea, Antioch, Joppa, Tyre, Corinth, and Damascus suggests, as we shall presently see more fully, diversities in the environment and indigenous circumstances of the Christian communities pertaining to each locality, which demarcated each (1) from its supposed founder, (2) from its traditional parent church, (3) from those similarities of discipline, doctrine, and worship in which the surrounding churches most resembled each other. Probably the main initial causes of demarcation, of authenticity, of absolute inclusive and exclusive independence, were summed up in the names, teachings, and alleged writings of traditional founders. St. Paul's enumeration of some main leaders of ecclesiastical parties, confessedly imperfect though we know it to be, may be taken as indicating at least one source of the demarcation or delimitation of Christian sects and communities—which probably included doctrinal differences as well as some varieties of organisation. Roughly speaking, these principles of division might be distinguished under the following heads:

1. The Personal Influence of the Founder.
2. Racial and Linguistic Causes.
3. Ecclesiastical and Religious Influences.
4. Political and Commercial Influences.
5. Family Ties.

1. *Personal Influence of the Founder.*—Every one of the great Name-Teachers among the apostles may be regarded more or less as church founders, and therefore as types, more or less different, of ecclesiastical organisations. Paul, Apollos, Cephas, James, Jude stand for personal sources of probably various ministerial arrangements in communities and independent churches. The two first named are the apostles—neither of them, be it remembered, belonging to the Jewish apostolic assembly at Jerusalem

—who exercised most authority *ab extra* in the details of church-founding, though the sphere even of St. Paul himself does not seem to have been very great in co-ordinating the official orders of the churches he established. The weight and direction of the great apostle's jurisdiction were certainly more moral than official, and it is to him that we are indebted, not for any form of government or specific and unalterable order of worship, so much as for an inculcation of spiritual freedom both as respects doctrine and ritual, which was really equivalent to a regeneration of Christian thought and life. The influence of Apollos was to a still greater extent of a Gentilising kind. The eloquent Jew of Alexandria helped to introduce into the nascent Judaism of the Christian church such modifications as would be afforded by the half-Greek, half-Oriental culture of Alexandria. We can hardly be wrong in attributing to his influence what St. Paul might have regarded as an excessive stress on $\sigma o \phi i a$, such as is marked by the two epistles to the Corinthians, while the stress of those epistles on a semi-mystic definition of Christian love, or the Neo-Platonic speculation of the second epistle as to the unclothing of the Christian's present body and his being clothed upon by a new ideal body, manifest clear affinities with the teaching which had already found its home in Alexandria.

2. (A.) *Racial and Linguistic Causes.*—Less important, however, than the personal influence of the foremost leaders of thought in the Christian world, as a determinant of variety of organisation in separate communities, was the agency more than once alluded to, which might have been termed Racial prepotence. Almost in every instance the founding of a church was the planting in the midst of a more or less

alien environment of a new religion. Whether the seed-plot was Jew or Gentile, Greek or Roman, Eastern or Western, European, African, or Asiatic, or, with stronger racial demarcation, whether the aboriginal distinctions and proclivities were Celt or Teuton, Syro-Palestinian, Roman, or Hellenic, the circumstances of the *planting*, or rather, as we may say in most cases, the *intrusion* of the new seed into soil only partially prepared for its reception, must have been of a more or less similar or analogous character. The main fact in every instance where the new *depositum* of Christianity had been placed in a fresh, partly cultivated seed-plot, was to induce in the produce some modification of the seed sown. The harvested grain represented and perpetuated not only the qualities of the seed but the nature of the soil. Few phenomena are more remarkable, albeit they have until recent times been comparatively seldom heeded, than this dual fructification of the planting of Christianity. Actuated perhaps by a pious but uncritical persuasion of the overwhelming supremacy of the seed of the Gospel, Christian historians have credited it with a prepotency which history, minutely investigated, proves it never actually possessed. To take a single instance, Bishop Lightfoot [1] insists with commendable particularity on the racial qualities of the Galatians, which he shows to have been Celtic.

"The main qualities of the Gaulish character are traced with great distinctness by Roman writers. Quickness of apprehension, promptitude in action, great impressibility, an eager craving after knowledge—this is the brighter aspect of the Celtic character. . . . A late Greek rhetorician commends the Galatians as more keen and quicker of apprehension than the genuine Greeks, adding that

[1] *Epistle to Galatians*, p. 251.

the moment they catch sight of a philosopher they cling to the skirts of his cloak as the steel does to the magnet. It is chiefly, however, on the more forbidding features of their character that contemporary writers dwell. Fickleness is the term used to express their temperament. This instability of character was the great difficulty against which Caesar had to contend in his dealings with the Gaul. Nor did they show more constancy in the discharge of their religious than of their social obligations. The hearty zeal with which they embraced the apostle's teaching, followed by their rapid apostasy, is only one instance out of many of the reckless facility with which they adopted and discarded one religious system after another." [1]

This diagnosis of tendencies, religious and intellectual, is but one example out of many of similar proclivities dependent on indigenous and racial qualities which might be applied to other districts and towns in every instance of a special localisation of special tendencies. What was true of the Galatians might, *e.g.*, have been true of the inhabitants of Rome, Corinth, Ephesus, Philippi, etc. In other words, the tenor of the written advice of St. Paul or of any one of the twelve might have been determined by the qualities inborn and autochthonous of the dominating influences in a complicated commingling of various ancestral populations,—taking, *e.g.*, the churches of Asia Minor or Northern Syria, in which an aboriginal element of a Syro-Phenician, or oriental kind might have been modified by successive migrations from Persia, Parthia, or Arabic sources, the commingling of races to be still further complicated by the changes of populations incident to to the continuous victories of the Roman arms, and the settlement of the Roman legionaries in different towns and districts

[1] Lightfoot, *Galatians*, p. 15.

which they had subjugated; or the overflow of conquered peoples into neighbouring countries, as, for instance, the *Diaspora* of the Jews with reference to Palestine; the dispersal of the Hellenes from Greece; in short, the scattering of all newly conquered peoples over the provinces previously subdued. How the racial distinctions that emerged from this partially accidental commixture of various populations affected their reception of Christianity, and the modes in which they solved such problems as the question of the official organisation of the Christian communities that became established in their midst, is a large theme into which it is not needful for us to enter. What seems certain as an outcome of the general question is, that the doctrines and ritual usages of the nascent creed were profoundly modified by the beliefs and modes of worship that were already in existence. Whether it was borrowed from the Roman policy of admitting the Deities of newly conquered nations and peoples into their Pantheon, as well as tolerating all alien usages that were tolerable from the standpoint of Roman Law, or not, it is certain that the leaders of Christianity, whether belonging to the Jerusalem apostolate or possessing affinities with foreign schools of thought, as in the case of Paul, Apollos, Barnabas, Aquila, and Priscilla, introduced as few modifications into resemblances and analogies of Christianity with older modes of faith as they could possibly help. The precedent of St. Paul finding the rudiments of Christian Theism in Aratus and Menander, or his decision as to the expediency of permitting Christians to eat meat once offered to idols, may be taken as well-known cases of the modification of the belief and practice of the new Christianity by predilections and religious customs which were traceable to race and old indigenous beliefs and usages. Most of the tendencies to new so-called heretical beliefs which manifested themselves in the propagation of the nascent faith, as, *e.g.*, Gnosticism, Ebionism, Millenarianism, are explicable by racial attributes or religious predilections. The tendencies of the Galatians, just alluded to, to an ornate sensuous mode of worship; the natural affinities of the Greeks for intellectual culture and speculation; the tendencies of native Romans to lay stress on elaborate organisation; the metaphysical inclinations of certain centres of population in Asia Minor, in Alexandria, in the Jews of Lower, or among the Copts of Upper, Egypt; the capacity for subtle ratiocination or refined abstraction, which also found a source of regeneration and permanent home in the most eastern portions of Asia Minor, so as to manifest a not improbable alliance with Buddhism and other oriental faiths—all may be regarded as impresses, tendencies, re-shapings, and modifications with which the older races and religions stamped afresh the new gospel of Christianity, to the extent not only of altering its physiognomy but even of changing for good or ill its most essential spirit. Few subjects in the later development of historical Christianity are fuller of interest than the tenacity with which the older creeds or modes of thought have maintained a kind of existence wholly irrespective of Christianity, or the strange perversity with which the newly commingled and adulterated articles of faith have chosen to attest their continued existence. Any student of mediæval history, especially that of the Italian Renaissance in the thirteenth and two following centuries, is aware how much the revival of classicalism was facilitated by the survival, especially in provincial districts, of names and beliefs derived from the religious culture of Greece and Rome, as, *e.g.*, the names and attributes of the Deities of Olympus, which the spread of Christianity for so many centuries had not succeeded in annihilating. One of the most interesting features of Dr. Döllinger's latest work,[1] and that not his least useful or elaborate, is his striking investigation of examples of the retention for so many centuries of racial affinities, traditions, and usages in the sphere of religion and worship. Some of the sects in which this uncouth amalgamation of the newer faith and older predilections was most marked are the Paulicians, the Armenian Paulicians,[2] the Monarchists, the Katharists, the Oophites, etc. The degree of modification of nascent Christianity by older faiths, or aboriginal tendencies, of course depended on a great variety of causes and circumstances; but, these being allowed for, the phenomena were, in most cases, alike. Some of the indigenous tendencies were of Eastern origin, as, *e.g.*, Parseeism, Buddhism; and their prevalence may be traced from the beginning of the second to the end of the eleventh centuries. They are also distinctively marked by the fact that they favour various aspects or presentations of Christianity. To some, *e.g.*, the Messianic or Millenarian phases of Christianity recommended themselves in finding points of assimilation with earlier beliefs or superstitions derived from other sources. The Gnostic (so-called) heresies again were the more readily received by peoples of greater imaginative or speculative power. The prevalence, moreover, of Circumcision or of Ebionite tendencies implied among certain peoples a predilection in favour of those beliefs of Christianity that were more distinctively Jewish. It has even been held that certain indigenous ideas among the Druids of Old Britain and Gaul facilitated the adoption and diffusion of certain notions of Christianity. In short, throughout the

---

[1] *Beiträge zur Sittengeschichte des Mittelalters*, 2 vols. 1890.

[2] For the distinction see Döllinger, *op. cit.* chap. i.

INTRODUCTION lxxxi

whole of Christendom, or, as it might be better put, the sphere of overt Christianity, racial differences constituted an important agency of a variety, not only of belief and of ritual usage, but of organisation and ministerial arrangement. Readers were most generally included among the functionaries of a given community, in all cases in which :—

(i.) The worship or Divine service took an especially didactic turn.

(ii.) The authoritative records of a given church consisted of written documents.

(iii.) In especial cases wherein the oral teaching of the planters of Christianity had already assumed a written form, and repositories of λόγια, epistles, written narratives of various kinds, were regarded as the chief if not sole instruments of religious culture.

2. (B.) *Languages and their variety, considered in reference to the inclusion of Readers and Interpreters among the ordinary staff of the officials of a Church.* — As part of the effects of race, nationality, blood, etc., in producing variety in the ministerial organisation of Christian congregations it is impossible to omit the agency of Languages. In a Palestinian or North Syrian Church, *e.g.*, part of the functions of a Reader would be to translate either from the Hebrew or Chaldee into the Hebrew-Syriac or Greek. This, *e.g.*, would be his ordinary official duty as often as he was required to translate portions of the Old Testament into Greek, or, on the other hand, parts of the LXX. into Chaldee or Syriac. No acquirements were more useful in the early church when the rhetorical volubility befitting the ferment and enthusiasm of its earliest foundations had subsided, and

the more staid and permanent bases of written records had taken their place. Whatever may be the reasonable interpretation of the Pentecostal story of the second chapter of the Acts of the Apostles, the narrative has an incidental value of the highest importance, inasmuch as its list of tongues indicates the languages already needed as vehicles of inter-communication between Christian converts during the first century of the Christian era. In point of fact, these names mark not only nationalities but ecclesiastical communities, between every pair of which the services of a Reader or interpreter might conceivably have been required. How important languages had already become as conditions and instruments of official organisation and ministration is shown by the enumeration, already referred to, of the Spirit-directed officers whose functions are described in St. Paul's Epistle to the Ephesians. No less than two of the functions thus described pertain to languages, and are so far functions of the Reader. These separable offices are :—

(i.) Divers kinds of tongues.

(ii.) Interpretation of tongues.

Doubtless the necessity in almost every congregation for linguistic functionaries does not prove the existence of separately named and ordained ministers such as the Readers subsequently became. For we may accept it as a rule pertaining not only to ecclesiastical but to every species of organisation, that the more imperative the duties, the less need was there of any special segregation of a particular office. Thus, wherever reading or interpretation formed the most ordinary function of a religious service, the more reasonable was it to require that every minister should show some proficiency, whether in reading, interpretation, or any other office allied to them. Thus when the ecclesiastical offices commenced to segregate themselves, the duties of Reader might conceivably have been performed by the bishop or overseer, the presbyter, the elder, the apostle, the prophet, the exorcist, or by any other official, permanent or temporary, accustomed to take part in the official duties of the Church. Reverting again to the passages above adduced of 1 Cor. xiv. 26, it is evident that whatever contribution was brought to the performance of a religious service was either given in the same language or was so rendered by the aid of the interpreter. At any rate, and this is the main portion of this purpose of the argument, the linguistic conditions of the early Church, the language or languages of its birth-place and cradle, the growth of the Roman empire and its policy with reference to alien creeds, were all data which claimed to be included in the full consideration of the problem. All, or most of them, pointed to the expediency of including Readers among the officials of the Christian Church. All depend upon or are governed by the rules of similarity, the inevitable adhesion to precedents, which govern the establishment of any new religion among older creeds—a new religion promulgated and diffused by records and documents of various kinds, as well as by public and ritual acts of worship, and solemn confessions and proclamations of faith. The new Christianity entered upon the manifold religious cultus of the Roman empire with something of the appropriating tendencies that annexed the gods of Hellas and re-created them—new statues and images on newly-graved pedestals, identified by new inscriptions and glorified by new rites of worship—in her own Pantheon. As a recent writer has remarked :—

"The fall of Corinth in the year 146 B.C., the year in which

Carthage was destroyed, was a most important epoch in the religious as well as the civil history of the world. The tendency strongly felt by the Roman at this period" (and which, it might be added, went on steadily increasing) . . . "to find his own Gods again in those of the nations he subdued, and, when he had none of his own that in any way corresponded, to adopt the new, brought him, as respects religion also, into subjection to the superior mind of captive Greece. The stories, many of them grossly human, that were told of the gods of Olympus, were transferred to Jupiter, Juno, Mars, and other Latin divinities."[1]

Doubtless Greece and its subjugation, remembering that it was then and long subsequently the centre of religious and philosophic thought for the whole civilised world, affords us a peculiarly striking illustration of the effect of racial qualities in determining the form Christianity was certain to take up in its peaceful propagandist invasion of her intellectual sovereignty. Yet there were other examples hardly less noteworthy of the same truths. The influx of Oriental culture, whether it penetrated the new-founded Christendom by way of Greece, or by the more direct trading route of Alexandria and the Levant, was a powerful instance of the modifying effects which Christianity at once exercised on tendencies which were undoubtedly racial and indigenous, both in their origin and enduring power. It would be hardly too much to say that there was no case in the first missionary energies of the Church in which some phases of the beliefs and usages of the new faith were not changed, for better or for worse, by the preponderating character and tendencies of the new soil or depository in which it was placed.

3. *Ecclesiastical and Religious Causes of Variety of*

[1] Duff: *Early Church*, p. 7.

Organisation in the Early Church.—But the local environment of early Christianity, regarded as a congeries of influences tending to create and sustain a variety of organisation in its official arrangements, depended not only on distinctions of race and idiosyncrasies of blood and nationality. Other causes, themselves also dependent on varieties of race, contributed to the same end. The growth of the Roman power was not only a development of rule and political aggrandisement, but was a vehicle and impetus to interchange of thought in religion, philosophy, and, in short, on all questions of human concernment. This was largely owing to the Roman policy of tolerating all the alien religions and modes of worship whose principles and usages were not opposed to the ideas of Roman universalist dominion. Thus when Christianity began to stir itself in large centres of mixed nationalities—such as Alexandria, Corinth, Ephesus—it found itself confronted not by godless and religionless populations, but by a number, less or more, of philosophic sects, religious confraternities, esoteric communities, and semi-ecclesiastical or hierarchical persuasions. Philosophic schools were still not only in existence, but manifesting no small amount of intellectual and spiritual activity. The Stoics, Epicureans, Neo-Platonists were only a small number from the sum total of the philosophical sects which Roman culture derived from its intellectual parent, the later Greek philosophy; and we must remember that wherever a school or community of philosophers existed there was a *religious or theological side* of the philosophical teaching. Taking, *e.g.*, the Stoic philosophy, and this as exemplified, *e.g.*, in Cicero or Lucretius, the thoughtful Christian could not help finding himself face to face with questions of a theological purport which Christianity, if it did not attempt to answer, at least was not backward to suggest. When we come to the more philosophical among the Christian Fathers of the third, fourth, and subsequent centuries, such thinkers, *e.g.*, as Justin Martyr, Clemens Alexandrinus, Origen, Lactantius, and Augustine; and when the earlier relations of Christianity to the religio-philosophical phases of the highest culture of the Roman empire had become matured, yet not to such an extent that its gradual evolutionary aspects might not easily be traced, we find, and are perhaps astonished at finding, how many and how various were the points of view which the religious thought of the Roman Empire offered to the nascent and half-persuasive, half-polemical incursions of the Christian Church. To some points of this general question, especially as relating to the mutual connection of Greece and Rome, we have already called attention. There are, however, other aspects pertaining to it which deserve notice, but which would take up too much space to treat with the fulness they merit. Thus Professor Moeller, following the steps of Mommsen and Foucard, points out the precedents which the so-called *collegia* or *sodalitia* among the Romans afforded to certain rites of the Christian Church :—

"In these cultus associations, the common religious bond brought a collection of persons, who were otherwise separated from one another by differences of rank, into close and brotherly combination, with equal rights as regards the founding of laws, the admission of new members, and the exercise of discipline in the society. Hence they afforded a pattern after which those who believed in Christ might organise themselves. Among them there existed solemn acts of initiation for those who were to be admitted, with which the baptism of Christians may be compared; and there were feasts for which the common table of the love feasts afforded a parallel. But the Christian assemblies for Divine worship which stood open to the uninitiated also, and served to attract them likewise, corresponded to the procedure of these associations in their exoteric assemblies." [1]

The parallelism here adduced forms, however, only one of a certain number, all of them of greater or less significance. Here, be it remembered, we are for the time being shutting out of sight the precedents, analogies, and similarities to Christian acts of worship found in Jewish public worship, as well as in certain devotional forms and usages restricted to domestic and private use. Confining ourselves to Gentile parallels, we merely indicate for *a posteriori* purposes the possible origin, or it may be modification and remoulding, of Christian rites and forms, whether public or private. Not that the precedents to ostensibly Gentile sources altogether excluded their connection with Jewish usages wherever synagogues existed; and it would be difficult, after the complete scattering of the Diaspora, to name any part of Christendom where synagogues, or their substitutes *Proseuchae*, did not exist. "To the Jew," as Dr. Edersheim expressed it, "the synagogue formed the bond of union throughout the world." These were not so much places of worship as of religious teaching. The ministers employed therein were Readers or Translators, and the Christian communities most in touch with these meeting-places were certain to employ the ministerial functions of Readers, whether they were officially set apart for those duties or not. Probably too, the lectionary employed in the synagogues supplied a scheme of something like uniformity of Scripture, *i.e.* Old Testament, readings. Still, as we have

---

[1] Moeller : translation, published by Sonnenschein and Co., vol. i. pp. 56-61. This work may be recommended with the utmost confidence to the English reader as among the best of recent compilations on Ecclesiastical History.

already intimated, the more immediate and preponderating precedents were derived from Gentile sources. It was more natural that a poor, recently-founded and struggling sect should defer to a superior and conquering, than to a subject race, even though there were acknowledged points of union between the new-gendered community and the subject race. It would be difficult to name any custom, whether of public or private life, which could not plead some analogous usage in the Roman or Gentile environment that surrounded it. Thus the Christian usage of holding religious meetings in private houses resembled those domestic rites in which the Lares and Penates were the divinities most commonly propitiated (*sacra privata*), although they were sometimes employed as well for the worship of the superior divinities. The Public Feriae, again, were not only analogous to the Christian Sunday, but were actually abolished when Christianity became the established religion of the Roman Empire. The works permitted to be done in the Feriae by Christian bishops and consuls bore a curious and even literal similarity to those allowed in the Gospels (comp. *e.g.* Matt. xii. 11). The oracles of Fortune, again, derived as they were from the Greek oracles, supplied the precedent for the choice of an apostle instead of Judas Iscariot. The esoteric rites of the Greek mysteries, transplanted as they were, and superadded, to the Temple worship of every great town in the Roman Empire, as, *e.g.*, the rites of Aphrodite at Corinth, those of Diana at Ephesus, bore evident resemblances of derivation and analogy to Christian sacraments and Agapae. The baptisms of the Christian churches were as closely affiliated to the lustrations of Gentile rites as to the circumcision of the Jewish Church. The resemblance between the mysteries of Greek and Roman religions, and the more esoteric rites of the

Christian church extended as far even as the names, because the μύστης, or Mystagogue, was applied to Christian bishops. There were especial cases in which the new leaven of a foreign cult—Indian, *i.e.*, Hindoo or Parsee, Persian or Arabic, induced a fermentation, and produced a subsequent religious and ritual diet, a daily bread, as it might be termed, of a peculiar kind, in the varied forms of Gnosticism, which found a cradle in Alexandria, and on the eastern bounds of the Roman Empire. The manifold derivation of functions or functionaries employed in the Christian church from Greek politics has recently been made the theme of an instructive paper in the CLASSICAL REVIEW. The subject is treated at too great a length to permit more than a passing reference. Here we learn what Greek affinities are possessed by such New Testament terms as πόλις, πάροικος, ξένος, πολίτευμα, κ.τ.λ., and a number of other words of semi-political meaning. The line and object of the paper may be indicated by the following quotation. Speaking of St. Paul's employment of the term προστάτις as applied to Phœbe, Rom. xvi. 2, and its interpretation by modern commentators as the *Patronus* of a Roman Collegium, the author proceeds:—

"I prefer to think that St. Paul's use of the words was derived immediately from its common political sense. The Christians at the port of Corinth were in the position of resident aliens in the presence of Græco-Roman society, and even in respect of the Jews established there; and Phœbe may well have been a woman of some social position, and of wealth, who employed her influence (after her baptism) to protect and befriend the church of which she was a διάκονος."

4 and 5. *Commercial Causes. Family ties and minor causes of variation in Ecclesiastical Organization.* Little need be added in these brief paragraphs on what may be termed

the lesser causes of variation of organisation among the different ecclesiastical communities scattered throughout the recently formed but rapidly expanding Christendom. Even a superficial reading of the Acts of the Apostles, the Pauline Epistles, and the Apostolical Fathers, will suffice to show how powerful were the influences underlying and, so to speak, hidden beneath the political circumstances of the time. Only to mention one, to which attention has rarely been called by Christian historians, yet possessed of an energy whose potency can hardly be exaggerated : the final subjugation of the Jews and their expatriation from Palestine, forming the final scenes of the general movement styled the Diaspora, were events of the highest importance to the rapid spread of Christianity. The Diaspora was in fact an irregular kind of colonisation on a large scale. In every town or large centre of population throughout Europe, Western Asia, and Northern Africa, colonies of Jews became settled, bearing with them a greater or less amount of the Christian leaven which had become diffused throughout Palestine and adjacent countries. The native energies of these Jewish colonies, quickened into fresh activity by their new position under novel circumstances, took inevitably that form which more than any other was natural to the Jew at this period, *i.e.*, that of commercial energy. Not only was there an increased traffic among the new colonies originated by the Diaspora, but there was for some time, partly in the rear of the Roman subjugation, partly as an independent movement, a continuous outflow of Jewish settlers from Palestine, carrying with them exports not only of material products, but also of thought and belief. Doubtless the chiefest of these new exports of a religious and spiritual kind was a newly modelled and quickened belief in the speedy advent of the

INTRODUCTION

Messias; but besides that, partly by necessary inclusion, was the motley diversified Christianity which, from its origin and limits, might bear the name of Palestinian. It thus happened to early Christianity as to the earlier development of Greek philosophy—it was largely propagated and diffused by the colonies. The new religion—like the speculations of the Eleatics—followed the course of traffic. The teachings of Christ to a certain extent became an article of export, so to speak, first from Palestine to the Jewish settlements without, and then from one colony to another. If it were needed to give some idea of the extent of this half-commercial, half-religious activity, we might, perhaps, draw a line round the area included within the Missionary Journeys of St. Paul. It is certain that there was no town which formed a part or stage of the Pauline Itinerary in which a colony of more or less christianised Jews might not be found. The interchange of religious commodities within the limits of this circumscription was of course not only or even chiefly oral. Messianic beliefs and hopes forming the varied material of different Apocalypses, letters to and from leading Apostles on different questions relating to Christianity, such as, *e.g.* were the Pauline Letters, or those addressed to the seven Churches of Asia Minor—letters addressed to private persons who were so far persons of eminence as to make communications addressed to them authoritative. Different collections of the written records belonging to Christian Churches, as, *e.g.*, parts of the LXX. version of the O. T. Scriptures, all formed part of an active interchange of spiritual exports and imports, as it might be called. The existence of such a traffic implied necessarily the duties of such ministers as Readers, Interpreters, Teachers of languages, and generally officials concerned with linguistic studies and didactic instruction. The circumstances of each particular Church, especially its environment in respect of linguistic custom and proficiency, would be a primary factor in determining the character of its ministerial organisation. Obviously, the greater the need of the Reader or Interpreter, the more important became his office. . These were functions, be it remembered, wholly unlike the performance of any ritual act, which could not be discharged in virtue of any special consecration. The Bishop or Presbyter—as the same general overseer was wont to be called—might be an acknowledged Reader in virtue of linguistic talent or study, but the Reader needed not any other aid or intervention besides that of the function which gave him his name. So far as the instruction of the young newly founded Churches was concerned, and we need hardly be reminded that this was their especial requirement, the Reader was of *more importance than any other official*. Indeed, the fact that the office of the Reader soon became merged in, or was considered as equivalent to, that of Preacher or Evangelist, is itself a proof of its importance and dignity. It was the office which, become conjoined with or merged in other ministerial functions, imparted to them whatever superiority they were entitled to claim.

THE APOSTOLIC FATHERS AND THE DIDACHÉ.

The group of writings known as the Apostolic Fathers is charged with unusual importance for the history of the Church. Not that they have much value as a literature, or even as a trustworthy record of historical events. Their chief, but still undeniable interest arises from other causes.

They stand as the vestibule or entrance porch to an enormous but still irregular building or temple in which we can trace vaguely and dimly the style of the architect. They are not accredited and demonstrable history, but *mémoires pour servir*. Like the preliminary studies to an enormous picture they enable the close observer or accurate student to trace the rudimentary lines, forms, shades and colourings which subsequently, by various laws and spontaneous processes of self-evolution, coalesce and blend into a grand historical picture of world import in its duration, its human interests, and general significance. It is partly the recognition of their varied importance that has since the beginning of Church history made them the centre, 1st, of a foolish and superstitious reverence; 2nd, of an uncritical estimate in the interests of ecclesiasticism; 3rd, of a fair, sane, and enlightened judgment, which, determining their actual value and resisting all temptation to exaggeration of a tendential kind, has finally succeeded in equalising their position with that of all other ecclesiastical writings from the commencement of Christianity until our own time.

One inevitable effect of the place occupied by these writings at the commencement of Church history is their importance for the light they throw on the schematology of the Christian Church. Taking, *e.g.*, the question of our present concernment, it would be impossible to ignore or deny the importance of the Apostolic Fathers in the consideration of the official organisation of the Early Church. Under any circumstances this would be a duty of the most imperative kind; it is, however, rendered of far more importance by the truth—now undenied and undeniable—that the testimony of these writings, in times as unscrupulous as they were uncritical, was warped and perverted in the cause of hierarchical aggrandisement. Turning to their now purer and impartial judgment, we have to note and to discriminate two main facts.

(1) We have to take cognisance of the general tone of the writings on all questions bearing on Church government.

(2) We have to note, to discriminate, and to consider in a separate paragraph, the sudden and unexpected incursion of a new thought so inconsistent with the general tenor of all prior thought on the subject, so clearly animated by ecclesiastical motives, that we have no choice but to regard it not as pertaining to Apostolic times but as being an audacious forgery of probably several centuries afterwards.

Now the first consideration that emerges from the former of these critical points is that the Apostolic Fathers, in some respects like the canonical books of the New Testament, are dispersed abroad in time as in place. Roughly they may be said to occupy, so far as the best critical guesswork can grapple with the question, the period from A.D. 57 to A.D. 160. We may take the former as the best approximate date of the Pauline Epistles, while the latter we may accept as at least nearing the date of the *Didaché*—a recently discovered writing to which we must presently call attention. Here then we have these landmarks, each of them dealing with the official organisation of the Early Church.

The tone of the Pauline Epistles we have already had occasion to notice. We have seen that nothing can be more informal, indeterminate, freer from solidarity, organisation or systematisation. Nothing can be more opposed, not only to an identity, but even to a similarity between the official arrangements of different religious communities. It will be quite easy to prove that this tone pervades to an equally marked extent the *Didaché* at the middle of the second century and the Apostolic Fathers irregularly filling up the period between that date and that of the Pauline Epistles. In order, however, to appreciate the strength of the argument, it might be well to juxta-posit the utterances :—

(i.) Of the Pauline Epistles, about 57 A.D.
(ii.) The *Didaché*, about 160 A.D.
(iii.) The Apostolic Fathers, filling up vaguely the intermediate space.

Thus we have in the history contemporaneous with the earlier Pauline Letters the following :—

Acts xiii. 1, 2.—" Now there were in the church that was at Antioch certain *Prophets* and *Teachers* ; as Barnabas, and Simeon that was called Niger, and Lucius of Cyrene, and Manaen, which had been brought up with Herod the tetrarch, and Saul," etc., etc.

Romans xii. 6, 7, 8.—"Having then gifts differing according to the grace that is given to us, whether *prophecy*, let us prophesy according to the proportion of faith ; or *ministry*, let us wait on our ministering ; or he that *teacheth*, on teaching ; or he that exhorteth, on exhortation."

1 Cor. xii. 7-12.—" But the manifestation of the Spirit is given to every man to profit withal. For to one is given by the Spirit the word of wisdom ; to another the word of knowledge by the same Spirit ; to another faith by the same Spirit ; to another the gifts of healing by the same Spirit ; to another the working of miracles ; to another prophecy ; to another discerning of spirits ; to another divers kinds of tongues ; to another the interpretation of tongues."

1 Cor. xii. 28.—" And God hath set some in the church, first apostles, secondarily prophets, thirdly teachers, after that miracles, then gifts of healings, helps, governments, diversities of tongues."

1 Cor. xiv. 26.—" How is it then, brethren ? when ye come together, every one of you hath a psalm, hath a doctrine, hath a

tongue, hath a revelation, hath an interpretation. Let all things be done unto edifying."

Eph. iv. 11.—" And he gave some, apostles; and some, prophets; and some, evangelists; and some, pastors and teachers; for the perfecting of the saints, for the work of the ministry, for the edifying of the body of Christ."

The aggregate exegesis of these well-known texts cannot possibly be mistaken by any impartial critic. Indeed, the only marvel is that the traditionally ecclesiastical opinions as to the threefold order of the Christian ministry or the figment of an Apostolical succession could ever have been maintained in the teeth of such antagonistic testimony. The outcome of the New Testament evidence on the subject is so well put by Bishop Lightfoot in his famous dissertation *On The Christian Ministry*, that I must be pardoned for making a few quotations from the last edition of it, which he published just before his death;[1] especially as he has been thought, nor indeed without reason, to have drawn back somewhat from the freer and more unecclesiastical position he had adopted in earlier editions.

"So it was also with the Christian priesthood. For communicating instruction and for preserving public order, for conducting religious worship and for dispensing social charities, it became necessary to appoint special officers. But the priestly functions and privileges of the Christian people are never regarded as transferred or even delegated to these officers. They are called stewards or messengers of God, servants or ministers of the church and the like, but the sacerdotal title is never once conferred upon them.

"As individuals, all Christians are priests alike. As members of a corporation, they have their several and distinct offices. The similitude of the human body, where each limb or organ performs its own functions, and the health and vigour of the whole frame

---

[1] *Commentary on the Epistle to the Philippians* (edition 1891), p. 185.

INTRODUCTION xcvii

are promoted by the harmonious but separate working of every part, was chosen by St. Paul to represent the progress and operation of the Church. In two passages written at two different stages in his Apostolic career, he briefly sums up the offices in the Church with reference to this image. In the earlier he enumerates 'first apostles, secondly prophets, thirdly teachers, then powers, then gifts of healing, helps, governments, kinds of tongues.' In the second passage the list is briefer: 'Some, apostles; and some, prophets; and some, pastors and teachers.' The earlier enumeration differs chiefly from the latter in specifying distinctly certain miraculous powers, this being required by the Apostle's argument, which is directed against an exaggerated estimate and abuse of such gifts. Neither list can have been intended to be exhaustive. In both alike the work of converting unbelievers and founding congregations holds the foremost place, while the *permanent government* and instruction of the several churches is kept in the background. . . . But the *permanent ministry*, though lightly touched upon, is not forgotten, for under the designation of teachers, helps, governments, in the one passage, of pastors and teachers in the other, these officers *must be intended.*" ! ! ! [1]

Passing on to the *Didaché*, and recognising the patent truth that we are still in the same region of Church government— the temperate zone, as we may term it, of Ecclesiastical History —as that whereinto the Pauline Letters introduced us, we need not stop to investigate the historical antecedents or value of this famous document. Certainly of no writing that has come to light since the commencement of the Christian era has the exploration been more remarkable, more exhaustive, or more

---

[1] The tendential tone of the *must be intended*, uncorroborated as it is by any decisive passage or argument in its support, is obvious. Though a prelate of enormous learning, especially in the lore of Church History and Antiquities, Bishop Lightfoot is not free from the predilections which render our English Church History so untrustworthy.

satisfactory. With the implication of TEACHING contained in the name we find that the Instruction, both in content and value, which it imparts to our nineteenth century is immeasurable—so great and diversiform is its recognised importance that it has become already a nucleus for a complete literature of its own. Not the least among the varied streams of light it has shed forth, in so many directions, is its illuminating *vis viva* with regard to early church government. As I have already remarked, the position it lays down in church government, as in discipline and doctrine, is that of the Pauline Letters. This may readily be confirmed by a few extracts from its Part III. Chap. 11.

Apostles and Prophets.

1. Whosoever shall come and teach you all these things we have above mentioned, receive him.

2. But if the teacher turn and teach another doctrine to destroy what we have said, hear him not. But if he teach with a view to add righteousness and knowledge of the Lord, receive him as the Lord.

3. As to the Apostles and Prophets according to the oracle of the Gospel, do this:

4. Let every Apostle who comes to you be received as though he were the Lord.

5. He shall remain one day, and if there be need, another day also; but if he stay three days, he is a false prophet.

And when the Apostle cometh forth, let him not receive anything except bread until he go to rest; if he beg for money he is a false prophet.

Not every one that speaketh in the spirit[1] is a prophet, but only if he have the character of the Lord.

. . . . . .

Every true prophet who is willing to settle among you is worthy of his maintenance.

So also a true teacher is worthy, even as the labourer, of his maintenance.

Therefore all the first fruits of the winepress and the threshing floor, etc., etc., thou shalt take and give to the Prophets. . .

Chapter xv.—Appoint to yourselves Bishops and Deacons worthy of the Lord, meek men and without covetousness, true and approved, for they also minister to you the holy service of the Prophets and Teachers.

Do not therefore despise them, for they are those who are honoured among you *with the Prophets and Teachers.*[2]

There are few features in the history of the Church for the first two centuries, or up to A.D. 250, for which eager appeal has not been made to the *Didaché*, as the latest and most unbiassed witness on the subject. It has been invoked to bear its testimony to the mode of worship in general use—so far as such a

---

[1] This clearly includes every office, *e.g.*, Prophesying, the Gift of Tongues, Interpretation of Tongues, of which the immediate impulse was held to be spontaneous, intuitional, and direct, and to be independent of all teaching and suggestion of a merely human kind. The passage is interesting as confirmatory of more than one similar passage in St. Paul's Epistle to the Corinthians, and proving the need of caution and watchfulness on the parts of the rulers of the church in repressing the wilder utterances of the more enthusiastic among their Christian converts, notwithstanding, or may we say—on account of—their claim to INSPIRATION.

[2] Dr. Harnack points out that the series of church officials here mentioned corresponds with marvellous exactitude to that contained in 1 Cor. xii. 28— ἀπόστολοι, προφῆται, διδάσκαλοι, ἐπίσκοποι, διάκονοι.—*Lehre der Zwölf Apostel*, i. p. 38.

mode of worship could be said to exist,—on the manner of administering the Eucharist, on the usages of early Christians in respect of Agapae and other occasions for "the assembling of themselves together"; and almost more than on any other feature or fact of early Church History, appeal was made to the *Didaché* as to (1) the general organisation of the Primitive Church; (2) whether there was any established official order or whether as a special question the threefold stages of ministers existed in any one church, or in any one selection—on local grounds or circumstances as, *e.g.*, Palestinian or Asia Minor— of assorted churches or communities.[1]

i. A careful reading of the *Didaché* allows certain inferences to be made bearing closely on the organisation, or we should say the want of organisation, in the early church. Thus we find evidence that the churches, especially those which might be locally designated as Palestinian, or those of the Diaspora—those, in other words, in which the traditional usages, etc., reverted to the Temple Service, or the customary routine of the Synagogues— such, for instance, was the distinction in point of age between the elders and the younger members of the community, though here, as in all other distinctions, there is no trace of a hard and fast line being laid down,—the question of fitness, or men endowed with "gifts," χαρίσματα, being allowed the final privilege of choice in all Christian offices.

[1] Mr. Cruttwell in his valuable *Literary History of Early Christianity* writes thus, i. p. 88 :—The improbability of a developed Episcopal Government at so early a date thus becomes greatly lessened if we adopt Lightfoot's view that this development was *local, not universal*; originating at or near Ephesus, where the last of the Apostles had probably filled the office himself, and spreading rapidly from its striking adaptability to the needs of the time; but not for some time transcending the limits of Western Asia, the European churches being either governed like Philippi by a Council of Presbyters or by a Bishop acting jointly with such a council, but without separate prerogative." Mr. Cruttwell adds very sensibly: " *Where all is so uncertain we can at best estimate probabilities.*"

ii. The practical independence (αὐτάρκεια) of the churches commencing with the Palestinian or the communities of the Diaspora is another inference from the *Didaché*. That these communities might in some cases have been a superimposing of a superficial Christianity, *e.g.* an informal acknowledgment of Christ not as the *expected Messias*, so much as a later prophet or forerunner of the Messias, is a suggestion that seems warranted by certain passages of the *Didaché*. We must remember that a common policy of organisation was precluded by the wide-spread belief in an immediate *Parousia*. Like all other features and requirements of the new faith, all aims at a permanency in respect of form of worship or of doctrine could have had no place in a religious society where the continual cries and aspirations were " The night is far spent, the day is at hand." " The end of all things is at hand." All the rules of Christian worship or whatever else might have taken the form of a routine were based on a rule of living, so to speak, from hand to mouth. The exigencies of the moment were the only requirements listened to, if we except the difference in point of number between the communities which probably brought the smaller churches into a kind of submission to those of greater numerical strength. Indeed the requirement, or let us say the prevailing usage, that the smaller churches should borrow from the larger a number of qualified persons who could help them in the selection of a bishop, supplies both a proof and an illustration of this practical independence which pertained inherently to each church without distinction or difference.

iii. The feature of spontaneousness, or of enthusiasm, of the early churches is also an inference from the *Didaché*. The effect of this spontaneousness, or a deduction from it, was the exaltation of the prophet among the officials of the church. These being men especially GIFTED, that is endowed with the supernatural graces, χαρίσματα, might officiate in any way they chose without any special appointment or ordination. St. Paul, we have seen, is an interesting example of this special divine call, although he is so convinced of the mischief that might arise from the subjective claim to such a call apart from any rules or laws imposed on them by the community, that he is inclined to deprecate both the office and the function pertaining to it. These men, as Mr. Bartlet remarks in a paper contributed to the (Oxford) SOCIETY OF HISTORICAL THEOLOGY, *Proceedings* 1892-3,—

"received their call with their gift direct from God. Churches could but recognise or reject. They could not appoint. A prophet was sometimes though not always itinerant. But in any case the highest functions in worship fell to him when present, *i.e.*, to an *unordained man* (*Didaché* xi., comp. 1 Cor. xii. etc.). When such were absent these functions devolved on the administrative officers of the community, who were elected simply on the bases of fitness for discipline and faithful use of the public funds (*Didaché* xv.). The spontaneous rise of a local ministry is seen in the early Pauline Epistles (εἰς διακονίαν τοῖς ἁγίοις ἔταξαν ἑαυτούς, 1 Cor. xv. 15. So 1 Thess. v. 12; cf. Rom. xii. 6), and the brethren are called on to recognise (εἰδέναι) them in virtue of their good work, the outcome of divine χαρίσματα."

The inferences thus derivable from the *Didaché* as to the organisation of the early church, clearly show that there was at the end of the second century nothing like homogeneousness or similarity in respect of the different churches, but that in their accidental government from time to time they were dominated by such factors as the size of the community or their ancestral environment, as, *e.g.*, whether it

INTRODUCTION ciii

was Jewish or Pagan, are further confirmed by other documents more or less resembling the *Didaché*. Thus in Dr. Harnack's notes in the following translation references are frequently made to the Epistle of Clement; but Mr. Bartlet in the paper above referred to gives a more summary comparison between the two which seems to merit quotation. He says:—

"Here (*i.e.* in the *Apostolische Kirchenordnung* 16-21 and 22-28, pp. 7-27 of the Translation) we get a parallel to the ἐλλόγιμοι ἄνδρες, who in Clement (xliv. 3) institute bishops in their office with the consent of the whole Church—in the three ἐκλέκτοι ἄνδρες, summoned from the adjacent churches by a very small church (*e.g.* 12), to conduct their δοκιμασία for a bishop (c. 16). Is this the germ of the later three ordaining bishops? Deacons as well as the bishop have the care of morals (c. 19), and as such are on the fair way to the ποιμενικὸν τύπον (c. 21). Conversely the presbyters appear not only as those to whom the ministering widow should report cases of need (c. 20), but also as συμμύσται τοῦ ἐπισκόπου (c. 17) . . . In the *Didaché* (c. 15) the bishops had as a college been the church's ἀρχιερεῖς, *i.e.* received and in prayer offered the people's gifts or thank-offerings. Thus Polycarp calls widows θυσιαστήριον θεοῦ for such gifts. *Rotation* seems then to have been the rule," etc., etc.

That is, the functions of almsgiving, as of all the offices of the church, were determined by the accidents of the occasion. The picture is in short that which is furnished by the Pauline Epistles as well as by the most authentic of the Apostolic Fathers. Moreover, it is the representation which we must regard as the more probable outcome of the half-directions, half-suggestions on the point, which we find attributed to Christ in the Gospels. As yet, *i.e.* up to the second century, church government was in a crude inchoate condition.

Those who had been with Jesus; those who could claim to remember His teachings; those who were spiritually gifted or inspired; those who claimed to have been instructed by St. Paul—such were the men who naturally came to the front as leaders, founders, or teachers of the different Christian communities in the earlier days of the Church, dating, one might say, from the fall of Jerusalem to the end of the second century. The general atmosphere in which these primitive Christians lived was on the whole one of spiritual freedom. Their beliefs were for the most part undogmatic and practical. The one preponderating article of faith—their conviction of the immediate return of Christ for His millennial reign on earth—was itself of such an engrossing kind that it rendered all speculative beliefs almost wholly superfluous; all the while it intensified and enhanced both the worth and importance of practical Christianity. The oral traditions which found their home or centre of circulation in the different and scattered churches of Palestine and Asia Minor—to take in their order the two first centres of Christian activity—consisted largely of short narratives or parables, *i.e.* didactic lessons, or, in the case of semi-Judaic communities, of Old Testament prophecies. The nature of some of these is well suggested by *the Two Ways* of the *Didaché*. Gradually, too, the function of the Reader came to the front in the same proportion that the extempore improvising gift of the Prophet began to cease; but as yet the officials of the Church were more of an instructing than a sacerdotal kind, nor was there any order of men as such that in the case of all and every ministration claimed to exercise a despotic irresponsible power over the Church. I am far from assuming that such a state of general disorganisation was likely to last. It is obvious that among the teachers of the Church there were some who claimed authority over the rest, or to whom such power was willingly conceded by their brethren, because they had been better taught, *e.g.*, by some of the twelve; or they possessed larger knowledge of the Old Testament, or for some other reason of decided fitness for the office to which they were appointed. But the main point to be noted in these early days, vaguely covered by or embodied in the *Didaché*, is the general sense of freedom in all departments of ecclesiastical activity. There was a plasticity in the choice and arrangement of officials, in the modes of worship adopted by individual churches, and to a certain extent, *i.e.*, within the limits of Christian instruction as laid down by Christ and His apostles—within the scope of simple ethical duties, which, while not unknown in the heathen world, had received a profounder, a diviner, and an infinite sanction by means of their spiritualisation through Christ. The new life of Christianity was, in a word, a life of freedom. On every side it was an emancipation, a deliverance based on the highest human privileges and duties, a life of which the motto and principle might well have been: "Stand fast therefore in the liberty wherein Christ hath made you free, and be not again entangled in the yoke of bondage."

The Ignatian Letters.

Assuming the date of the *Didaché* to be towards the end of the second century, the document next in chronological sequence, bearing directly on the question of ecclesiastical organisation, is one of striking abruptness in its claim of sacerdotal authority. I mean the Ignatian Letters. With the consideration of these we arrive at the chief corner-stone of the traditional hypothesis—(1) of the threefold order of the

Christian ministry; (2) of the supreme autocratic power of the bishop. If the authenticity of these letters could be demonstrated, the question so far as Patristic authority is concerned is set at rest; on the other hand, if the authority is disputable, still more if the foundation on which it is attempted to base it can be shown to be absolutely worthless, the question is settled in an equally definitive manner, though in a opposite direction.

We have no space to recapitulate in however brief a form, and confine ourselves wholly to its more prominent features, the Ignatian controversy. It is not that we are treading on the embers of an extinct fire; taking as our guide the general consensus of Patristic scholars, the flames are still in a more or less fitful blaze. It is true, as we shall presently see, the question is finally and absolutely closed for a few scholars of more penetrative insight than their brethren, among whom there was at one time reason to hope that our scholarly Bishop Lightfoot would allow himself to be enrolled; but the tide of discussion which seemed until recently to have reached its ebb has again began to flow, and with the notable exception of Lipsius, most scholars, both English and continental, have found a residuum of ground for holding to a minimum of belief in the authenticity of at least a small portion of the Ignatian documents. Most readers who are acquainted with the outline of ecclesiastical history are aware of the different recensions of the Ignatian letters, *e.g.* the longer recension of the seven Latin letters; the shorter recension of the seven Greek letters; the Syriac recension, edited by Cureton, which has held its ground longer than the rest. These are the documents between which the issue lies. The present position of the controversy is well summarised by Professor Moeller in his admirable *History of the Christian Church* (vol. i. p. 113):

'The attempt to fall back on the three Syriac epistles as the genuine kernel is now universally given up as impossible. Even Lipsius has given the matter up (*ueber den Ursprung und ältesten Gebrauch des Christenthums* ; Jena, 1873); and so, on the one hand, a return has been made to Baur's hypothesis of the spuriousness of the Ignatian letters in general (Merx, *Meletemata Ignatiana*, Halle, 1861 ; cf. Ewald, Gött., G. A., 1862 ; Hilgenfeld); on the other, to a decided defence of the genuineness of the seven epistles already mentioned by Eusebius, which is also maintained by Uhlhorn, etc. etc. . . . The most important contribution to this opinion is that offered by Th. Zahn in his most valuable monograph (Gotha, 1873), and in his edition of the Apostolic Fathers; of Harnack, Gebhardt, and Zahn, vol. ii. Comp. also Funk, *Die Echtheit der Ignat. Briefe*, Tübingen, 1883, and in his edition of the Apostolic Fathers; and more recently, especially Lightfoot, *The Apostolic Fathers*, ii. 1 and 2, 1886.'

English scholars, with a few notable exceptions, seem inclined just now to follow the lead of Bishop Lightfoot, who has, however, varied somewhat in his critical estimate of the controversy ; and Mr. Cruttwell in his important contribution to ecclesiastical history has summarised very accurately the grounds on which Lightfoot's latest opinion has been founded. These grounds are open, as I venture to think, to the fatal objection that they include what may be called the circumstantial evidence of the issue ; and they wholly ignore the overwhelming change in the tone and spirit of the Ignatian Letters compared with the other incontrovertible witnesses approximating to their date. The ordinary student of ecclesiastical history, who is only partially conversant with the growth of that history, parting company with the *Didaché* and its undeniable tone of equality among the officials of the Church, and freedom among her members, is overpowered with astonishment in finding in the Ignatian Letters a sacerdotalism and a claim of Episcopal supremacy which is scarcely rivalled by the claims and policy of a Hildebrand in the darkest period of the Middle Ages. His wonderment is as profound and justifiable as if he were asked to believe in a physical science,—evolution without any intervenient stages from the lower grades of invertebrate to the highest of vertebrate animals. Even if the local circumstances of a few Christian communities were of such an anomalous kind as to justify on the part of their rulers such an extravagant claim of lordship and autocratic power, it is evident, on the most rudimentary reasoning, that bishops claiming to possess such unlimited power would be very few, and the churches governed by them would have a fair claim to have resigned once and for all the simplest obligations of a Christian's life and duty. Here, *e.g.*, are a few of the extraordinary claims made for bishops by the Ignatian Letters. I quote a few sentences from Mr. Cruttwell's rendering, after comparing them with the original:—

'Ye are attached to your bishop as closely as the church is to Christ, and as Christ is to God the Father. . . .

I advise you, be zealous to do all things in godly concord, the bishop presiding after the likeness of God; and the presbyters after the likeness of the council of the apostles with the deacons also, who are most dear to me. . . .

Be subject to your bishop and to one another as Jesus Christ to the Father, and the apostles to Christ and the Father.

It is needful that ye should do nothing without the bishop; but be ye obedient also to the presbytery as to the apostles of Jesus Christ.

It is not lawful without the bishop to baptize or hold a love-feast.

It is well to know God and the bishop. He that honoureth

the bishop is honoured of God. He that doeth ought without the knowledge of the bishop serveth the devil.

As many as are God's and Jesus Christ's, these are on the side of the bishop. Be not deceived. If any follow a maker of schism, he doth not inherit the kingdom of God.'

It would be easy to add to these striking passages others of a not less extravagant animus. But these are sufficient to indicate the extreme claims of sacerdotalism and episcopal rule even at so early a date as the end of the second century. As we have already suggested, the difficulty of conceding the genuineness of letters making such a claim is lessened if we assume, as Bishop Lightfoot did finally, that this abrupt development was wholly local. As a bare possibility, and under conditions of a peculiar kind, we may thus allow that a claim to sacerdotal rule may have obtained in one or two churches of Asia Minor; but, regarding the Ignatian epistles, as most ecclesiastical historians have done, as indicating a general stage of thought and feeling common to the church as a whole, we can only arrive at one opinion concerning them, and that is, that they are wholly spurious and untrustworthy. They represent a stage of thought and feeling equally perverted and extravagant; and they are wholly at variance with all the Christian writings of any value which have treated the question of the official organisation of the early Church. This is the ground taken up by an English scholar who has approached the question without bias, and considered it thoughtfully, and from every point of view. Hence, for impartial English scholars, the Ignatian controversy may, in my opinion, be considered as finally settled for the future by the two letters (published as pamphlets) which Canon Jenkins addressed three years ago to the Dean of Peterborough. They are called *Ignatian Difficulties and Historic Doubts*, and in addition to their entering fully into the merits of the controversy, they have the greater authority, because the position they take up is also that of Professor Lipsius, the greatest continental authority on the question, exceeding even that of our own Bishop Lightfoot. The general conclusion thus arrived at may be stated in a quotation from a letter which the Professor addressed to Canon Jenkins, and which the last-named writer has put deservedly in the forefront of his pamphlets (pp. 3 and 4). I give the quotation in full, because I fear that the very able summaries of Canon Jenkins are almost wholly unknown to English students :—

'I am still fully convinced that the form of these letters (*which embraces the seven*) cannot possibly be derived from Ignatius. The learned and acute [scharfsinnige] performance of the much-lamented Bishop Lightfoot has not altered my judgment in this respect. I agree with you fully in the view that the representation of the power of the bishops is incompatible with a writing of the second century.'

'We have here,' continues Canon Jenkins, 'the matured judgment of a divine as far removed from the teaching of the Tübingen School as the Bishop himself, and whose study of the writings of the Apostolic Fathers began still earlier than his, and has probably been more continuous.' The remainder of the Canon's argument may be thus summarised—to myself, I confess, it is as conclusive as we can reasonably expect.

I. The two earliest notices of the Ignatian Letters are, in the Eastern Church, that of Origen ; and in the Western, that of Irenæus. But the incidental manner of these notices shows 'that his sayings had been traditionally handed down to his followers, and first assumed a written form at their hands.'

Equally doubtful, for other reasons, are the allusions in Athanasius, Theodoret, and Chrysostom. The last-named, for example, records the sayings and doings of Ignatius on his journey, but says *not a word of the letter.*

'After these fifth-century writers,' says Canon Jenkins, 'a long and profound silence appears to have fallen on the Church in regard to the Ignatian Letters. Had they been produced at Nice, the Arians would have been confounded by the constant and emphatic assertions they make of the *Homoousios*. Had they been produced at Ephesus, the high Episcopal doctrine they contain would have proved the independence of the church of Cyprus, and obviated the necessity of its appeal to the Council,' etc. etc. . . . 'Not a single controversy which arose during the Middle Ages could have failed to receive illustration or solution from the body of doctrine they contain. . . . Like the "Seven Sleepers," the seven Ignatian Letters had fallen into a state of inanition until the critical energies of Usher and Pearson called them back to life.'

II. Not less forcible is the next argument adduced by the author, viz., the silence of the defenders of episcopacy *when it first became a subject of controversy*. Epiphanius, *e.g.*, must have employed it when he was opposing the Arian doctrine. Jerome again must have been ignorant of the Ignatian claim of hyperepiscopal authority when he penned that wise advice to bishops and presbyters : 'Sicut presbyteri sciunt se *ex ecclesiæ consuetudine* ei qui sibi præpositus fuerit esse subjectos—ita episcopi noverint se *magis consuetudine quam dispositionis Dominicæ veritate* presbyteris esse majores.'

III. Another argument arises from the comparison between the first epistle of Clement and those of Ignatius. There are only twenty years between the probable dates of those writings, yet the former proves that there were then only the two orders in the church—of the bishop (or presbyter) and the deacon.

Such are the three first links in a strong chain of argument which proves clearly that the Ignatian Letters must be given up by every ingenuous and learned man who without prejudice has thoroughly sifted the question of their genuineness. Canon Jenkins concludes his treatise by two arguments which, as containing the general grounds on which Lipsius bases his rejection of the Letters, seem to me worthy of particular notice. These are vii. and viii.

vii. The greatest difficulty in accepting the Letters arises out of the conflict of doctrine which runs through every page. Two conflicting elements meet us everywhere, which may be thus described.

(a) The Episcopal, or rather Pontifical, elements, which, merging the individual in the community, the Christian disciple in the Church, delivers him into the hands of the bishop to be raised and moulded by him—(in the language of another Ignatius)—as though he were a lifeless object—a corpse, *tanquam si cadaver esset*. The autocracy of the bishop is to extend even to the thoughts and opinions of those under him. Nothing is to be done without him. They are to know him as they know God. In this teaching the doctrines of Grace can have no place. The right of private judgment is extinguished. We recognise, as though born out of due season, the theory of the papacy and the *voluntas Pontificis pro lege*, of which the great and good Cardinal Contarini exclaimed:—*Facessat, deum immortalem precor, a Christianis liminibus hæc impia doctrina.*

(b) In opposition to this element in the letters is the doctrine, which we may term the evangelical one, which asserts the presence of Christ in every believer. Consistently with this view, but very inconsistently with the episcopal theory, he bids us to hear Christ, to obey Christ, not to listen *to any one save Jesus Christ.*

viii. Finally, we affirm that the pictures given us by the early Fathers, as Justin Martyr, Irenæus, Tertullian, Clement of Alexandria, and Origen (to which we must now add the *Didaché*), are incapable of being brought into the most distant reconciliation with that which the supposed Ignatian Letters place before us. There is not a single figure in them which recalls the image of Christianity as its early apologists have represented it. This contrast must appear most conspicuously to all who remember their beautiful and simple description of the earliest Christian assemblies and the primitive Christian teachers. All these we should have to surrender if we could accept the strange theory that a hierarchy closely resembling that of the Jewish Church had suddenly sprung up to supersede it, and that the Christian worship instead of ' growing up out of the synagogue had sprung from the Temple.'

The collapse of the evidence derived from the Ignatian Letters, occurring so nearly contemporaneously with, and in part occasioned by, the discovery of the *Didaché*, may be said to conclude the general question of the organisation of the early Church. Hereafter it can hardly be alleged :

(*a*) That three orders of ministers existed in the early Church.

(*b*) That, taking the Church as a whole, there was any difference up till the end of the second century between the bishop and the presbyter.

(c) That there was in any part of the *Christendom* of that time, in districts, *e.g.*, centralised over by great towns, such as Rome, Antioch, Jerusalem, any ecclesiastical official to which the churches of less important towns professed to yield obedience or deference of any kind; that uniformity in organisation, in ritual usage, or, except vaguely, in doctrinal teaching, had in reality no existence.

(d) That there could have been a succession of bishops from the time of the apostles, created and sustained by them, and claiming their sanction and appointment as the basis of their own authority; in other words, that the dogma known as the 'apostolical succession' had any existence in the Church of the first two centuries; that the principle on which the different Christian communities was based was the congregational, or in districts wherein the Jewish Diaspora formed the nucleus of the Christian Congregation, as *e.g.* in the Palestinian Churches, the Synagogical, so to speak.

It is this conception as a rule of freedom and independence which is common to all the Ante-Nicene Fathers, with the sole exception of Ignatius; so that, as Canon Jenkins sums up his plea :—

'We affirm that the pictures of the Primitive Church given us by Justin Martyr, Tertullian, Irenæus, Clement of Alexandria, Origin. and (though last, not least) the recently discovered *Didaché*, are incapable of being brought into the most distant reconciliation with that which the Ignatian Epistles place before us. There is not a single figure in them which recals the image of Christianity as its early apologists have represented it.'—Pp. 21, 22.

This is the maturely formed opinion of a capable and impartial student of the whole question. It is one which, as I venture to think, is bound to grow with whatever reconsideration of the question the future is likely to give. Such a judgment will harmonise with the development of Church History on that specific point during the last half-century. More and more has the current of well-informed opinion taken the direction of the comparatively slow progress of the early Church as well in ecclesiastical organisation as in ecclesiastical thought and systematized doctrine. However natural and seemly an Ignatian bishop, with his ideas of autocratic rule, would have seemed to our uninquiring forefathers of two centuries ago, to enlightened and impartial inquirers of our time a bishop of that type would be an anachronism. Not the least singular feature of the whole controversy, when regarded from its ecclesiastical standpoint, is that this amazing growth of absolute power on the part of the traditional rulers of the Church should be removed by scarcely more than a century from the time of St. Paul, when the officials of the Church maintained a status of more or less equality, and when the members were exhorted to 'stand firm in the liberty in which Christ had made them free.'

The Oracles of Papias: the λόγια, ἄρχαια, βίβλια, εὐαγγέλιον κατά, etc., which constituted the Didactic Matter employed by the Readers.

We have already noticed, drawing our inferences (1) from the antecedent probabilities of the case, (2) from the phenomena presented by the Synoptic Gospels, that the early Christian communities soon after the fall of Jerusalem and the consequent diaspora, especially as the latter event induced the dispersal of the apostles and the other living witnesses of the life and words of Christ, began gradually to make a hoard of authoritative documents of various kinds. By degrees each

Church began to distinguish itself by the quality or quantity of such documentary treasures. It became the custom of one community to lend or borrow the documents or books of the other. Oftentimes they were copied or translated from one language to another, as indeed we find traces in several passages and allusions in the Synoptic Gospels. Employment was thus given to scribes and interpreters of tongues, as they are called in St. Paul's enumerations, and in all cases they postulated in the earliest days a function which demanded in time an official who was specifically designated as a Reader. It is plain that the collection of documents pertaining to any one especial community was determined by the race, religion, etc., of the environment wherein it was founded, or the apostle by whom the first converts were made. Probably the names, *e.g.* of Paul, of Peter, of James and John suggest derivative affinities which extended not only to modes of worship, sacramental usages, formulas and creeds, but comprehended especially the authoritative documents which the Readers were used to read aloud on Sabbath days as on other occasions. Probably all the earliest leaders of the Christian Church, disciples as well as apostles, took part in the authorship of these documents, nay, those who had however casually and occasionally been with Jesus, who could recall words and acts which they had seen and heard, were requisitioned, if not for complete narratives and discourses, at least for portions of them. The verbal resemblances and dissimilarities in the same narratives which we find in the Synoptics furnish us with useful suggestions not only for the origin of these documents but also for their authors. The variety in the names, positions, and opportunities of the authors, suffices to give us the reason of their different names, such as λόγια, λόγοι, εὐαγγέλιον.

While the enumeration of the ministers of the Church given by St. Paul and by the earliest Scriptural writings indicates more than one function related directly or indirectly with them, there is, however, among early Christian writers one name especially identified with this class of literature,—one who has come down to our times as a writer, or, as it may be, a compiler or collector of oracles or sacred extracts—viz. Papias. He is not a writer of great importance; indeed, Papias is a name to which in the historical memory of any scholar a stigma attaches. He is indeed a striking illustration of the effect of a depreciatory epithet, especially when it is short and pithy, so that probably few students of Eusebius ever hear mentioned the name of Papias without mentally adding the Eusebian characteristic, σφόδρα σμικρὸς τὸν νοῦν. But however intellectually puny Papias may have been, his name has so far a suggestive use that it brings before us one of the most important pictures of early Church history; in other words, it introduces us to the most important of the features of early Christian literature, viz., the constituent elements of the Synoptic Gospels in the term λόγια.

The signification of this word has given rise to much controversy. All agree that it is connected derivatively with λόγος. Regarded from the standpoint of oracle, word, utterance, etc., we may, I think, take it to mean any collocation of words which is marked by point, or brevity. Any narrative, story, parable, discourse, etc., that is marked by point or allusiveness might be termed a λόγιον; or, again, any quotation, chapter, extract that is determined by inclusiveness, finality, explanatory appropriateness, etc., might, in like manner, be entitled a λόγιον. Hence a concatenation or string of λόγια united together would naturally present a piecemeal appearance, such as, *e.g.*, is presented by an average chapter in the Synoptics, where parable, discourse, quotation, etc., etc., are joined together by a minimum of connecting narrative.

Now, on casting our eyes over those materials in the early church which would naturally take the form of λόγια, we are struck by their variety in respect of origin and matter. Thus, in the churches within or adjacent to Palestine, in which the religious element of Judaism was largely predominant, the chief λόγια or authoritative scriptures would be :—

I.   I. Messianic prophecies and quotations.
        II. Millennial prophecies.
        III. Allusions to the Mosaic Law as still possessing authority.
        IV. Descriptions of Synagogue or Temple worship.
        V. Quotations from liturgical forms and prayers employed in the synagogues.

II. In Christian communities where the influence of Mosaism and millennial Judaism was less, the λόγια would partake more of the character of quotations, etc., from the reported words of Christ. Thus we have a work, which is no longer extant, but fragments of which have been preserved by Irenæus, Eusebius and others. This work had the suggestive name of λογίων κυριακῶν ἐξηγήσεις—quotations of, or comments on, our Lord's sayings. This work was doubtless one of a class, and that not a small one, the materials of which were incorporated partly into our canonical Gospels, partly into the non-canonical Gospels, as *e.g.*, the Gospel of the Nativity, the Gospels of St. Thomas, Nicodemus, etc., etc. It would not be impossible to divide these apocryphal Gospels according to the classification of their chief λόγια or quoted extracts. Thus we have a class in which the incarnation or the miraculous birth of Christ is made the preponderating feature, while another class may be distinguished by its millennial prophecies and expectations, while a third class may be regarded from the standpoint of Jewish prophecy, regarded from their retrospective signification. Indeed, a complete survey of the λόγια materials in the first two centuries of Christian history would comprehend almost all of those books classified as apocryphal. Such a survey would include also those sayings ascribed to Christ in the first century after His death, but not recorded in the Synoptics.

III. Another class of λόγια, which may bear the title of Neo-Platonic or Alexandrian, or possibly Apollonian (from Apollos), would comprehend all the writings known as Johannine. The metaphysical discourses of St. John's Gospel, and of St. John's and the other general epistles, have, indeed, quite a character of their own. They represent a phase of Christianity altogether foreign to Jewish thought, and have the greater value as an illustration equally of the plasticity and comprehensiveness of the New Faith.

IV. A fourth class of λόγια of a somewhat diversified character, which might possibly be entitled Judæo-Græco, may be found in the extracts, arguments, etc., contained in the Pauline epistles. Sometimes their origin is clearly Judaic, or Judæo-Rabbinic, while at other times they have clearly a Hellenic origin. Indeed, we might find λόγια of every class in some one or other of Paul's epistles, and this might incidentally be taken as a proof of the breadth of culture of him who is fittingly designated the apostle of the Gentiles.

Turning now to the λόγια which have been connected with Papias, a recent writer has attempted, in a lengthy and carefully written monograph,[1] to ascertain the general meaning of

[1] *The Oracles ascribed to Matthew by Papias of Hierapolis.* Lond., 1894.

the word as employed, *e.g.*, by Philo, Josephus, Clement, and Justin Martyr. He finds that it is employed generally for quotations, extracts, referable passages of all kinds, mostly, however, for extracts and prophecies from the Old Testament. Thus it is used for—

I. Books of the Old Testament.
II. Chapters from the Old Testament.
III. Brief passages, maxims, rules, laws, etc., as, *e.g.*, the ten commandments.

But Papias's use of the term λόγια seems to have been of the broadest description; at least he applies it to all kinds of traditional stories, etc., recorded of Christ. Thus Eusebius says that 'he reported as having come from unwritten traditions certain strange parables of the Saviour and teaching of His, and other things rather fabulous.' Eusebius continues[1]:—

'To these belong his statement that there will be a period of some 1000 years after the resurrection of the dead, and that the kingdom of Christ will be set up in material form on this very earth. . . . Papias gives also in his own work (the above-named ἐξηγήσεις κ.τ.λ.) other accounts of the words of the Lord on the authority of Aristion, who was mentioned above, and traditions as handed down by the Presbyter John, to which we refer those who are fond of learning.'

This passage is noteworthy for the reason that Papias refers to two authorities who give accounts of the words of the Lord different from those contained in the canonical Gospels. The authorities here mentioned, Aristion and Presbyter John, occur together in the well-known preceding passage, in which Papias avows his preference for oral to written tradition, viz.:—

[1] See by all means the valuable edition of Eusebius, vol. i. of the SELECT LIBRARY OF NICENE AND POST-NICENE FATHERS, p. 172, notes 1-24.

"If then any one came who had been a follower of the elders, I questioned him in regard to the words of the elders—what Andrew or what Peter said, or what was said by Philip, or by Thomas, or by James, or by John, or by Matthew, or by any other of the disciples of the Lord, and what things Aristion said and the Presbyter John, the disciples of the Lord, saying that I did not think that what was to be gotten from the books would profit me as much as what came from the living and abiding voice.'

This passage is suggestive as enlarging the horizon of those sources from whence the canonical Gospels were compiled, and assuming that these sources, collected from all quarters, and incorporated, without much heed to order and arrangement, in the Synoptic Gospels, were known generally, or at least frequently, as λόγια, formed the material of the reader, partly in his function of arranger of reading matter, partly in his office of instructor of the congregation. The former was the office which Mark discharged in reference to Peter when he compiled the Gospel called after his own name by that apostle's instructions, probably oral and written, and is for that reason styled by Eusebius ὁ ἑρμηνευτής Πέτρου.[1] Indeed, we may even infer from the fact of the Reader and Interpreter being related and interchangeable offices, that the authors, or rather compilers, of the Gospels, whether canonical or uncanonical, were Readers; that is, to take an instance, the official named the reader was in the time of Tertullian, as we shall see presently, also styled evangelist, so that *Mark the evangelist* was also known in the church as *Mark the reader*.

[1] See Eusebius, *ut supra*, p. 171.

CHURCH ORGANISATION AFTER THE TIME OF IGNATIUS TO THE
DATE OF THE *Sources of the Apostolic Canons* (edited by
Harnack); THE EVOLUTION OF THE OFFICE OF THE READER.

Since the discovery of evolution as a law embracing every department of human and scientific progress, few illustrations of the parallelisms and aptitudes of which it is found capable have aroused greater interest than the parallelism between the organic growth of society and that which obtains in some branches of physical science. Thus we find a similar differentiation between the commencement of a political society and that of some animal organisation. In early stages of the growth of a society or of some body politic, the ruler is often the high priest, or he combines with one or both of those functions the duties of the legislator or the commander of an army—just as a Roman general was qualified to act as an haruspex if it were needed. Similarly, in some stages of animal development, the functions of digestion and alimentation were discharged by the nervous organs which sustained life. So also in the early life of a church, wherein the various functions of ruling, instruction, etc., were afterwards performed each by its own ministers, these special offices were first of all discharged by one minister. The function of ruler or overseer was joined in the same person to the teacher, or, as in the Christian Church, the same official was or might be bishop or presbyter, interpreter (or one gifted with tongues), translator, exorcist, reader, etc., etc. This, in point of fact, was the condition of the church when Paul wrote the Epistles to the Corinthians. As Dean Stanley remarks in his Commentary on that Epistle :—' The Christian assemblies of the first period of the apostolic age, unlike those of later times, appear not to have been necessarily controlled by any fixed order of presiding ministers.'[1] Nothing indeed could better portray the absence of anything like definitive organisation than (1) the juxtaposition of officials whose duties and faculties are interblended so confusedly, and (2) the commixture of ecclesiastical persons and powers, without any classification or distinction. So we have (I use Stanley's translation): 'God set some in the church, first apostles, secondly prophets, thirdly teachers, after that miracles, after that gifts of healings, helps, insights [a better rendering of κυβερνήσεις would perhaps be *ruling principles*], divers kinds of tongues. In this unclassed classification it is evident that Readers would come under the term Prophets or Teachers—in the first case, as interpreters, *e.g.*, of Hebrew into Aramaic, or of either into Greek, or *vice versa*. If we want to see these persons and faculties in actual use in public worship, we have only to turn to the passage we have above referred to (1 Cor. xiv. 26): ' *What is it then, my brethren, when ye be come together, each of you hath a psalm, hath a doctrine, hath a tongue,*' *i.e.*, a chapter or lesson in the *charisma* of tongues; De Wette renders *einen Vortrag in Zungen* (this would form part of the Reader's functions), *hath a revelation, hath an interpretation* (this again would form a part of the Reader's duties). The service thus arranged, and described, is one conducted by *charismatic* men, most of the acts of worship and instruction being spontaneous and extempore; yet even here the functions of most importance are evidently those of the Reader and Interpreter. Moreover, it does not seem that the order in which the materials of worship are here placed indicates the order in which they

[1] Stanley's *Commentary*, etc., p. 290.

must invariably occur, nor that each contribution to the religious service requires a separate minister or official to make it. Of the five gifts enumerated, all of them pertain, or may pertain, to every separate member of the congregation. Nothing can give us a more distinct notion of the absolute freedom of the order of public worship in relation to the persons conducting it than the fact that both gifts and persons, functions and officials, are *indefinitely interchangeable*. The minister prepared with a psalm is also prepared with a doctrine, a tongue or a revelation—and apparently might be invited to confer or minister one or more, perhaps all the enumerated gifts, to their fellow-worshippers in turn. The only stipulation was that all was to be done for edification.

The parallel passage of Eph. iv. 11, with its enumeration so closely akin to that we have just considered, viz., apostles, prophets, evangelists, pastors and teachers, need detain us no longer than to observe that two out of the five contain a distinct implication of the function of reader, viz., the evangelists and teachers. In all probability λόγια of some kind were used in any religious community requiring the ministration of the Interpreter or the Reader for purposes of translation or instruction. Thus the Messianic or millennial λόγια or extracts from Old Testament prophets had to be translated from Hebrew to Aramaic or from both into Greek, or in Northern Palestine and Syria the needed translation might be Greek into Aramaic. We must remember that in proportion with the decline of officials especially endowed with χαρίσματα was the rise of others whose chief mode of worship and teaching resolved itself into reading λόγια and other readable material. Long before the end of the first century the charismatically conducted services in the different Christian communities were coming to an end, though, of course, as long as millenarianism held its own there was always room for religious improvisation. A few passages in Irenæus about the qualities of the millennium—too well known to bear quotation—suggest to us the wild rhapsodical manner and matter which was common to the millennial prophets.

There was hence from the commencement of the second century a decided growth in all these ministerial functions which belonged directly or indirectly to the Reader, and the manner of public worship gradually assumed for that reason a decided change. The nature of this depended largely—

(1) On the self-evolution of the Church, and the growth of its distinctively Christian literature.

(2) On the environment which formed the local conditions, etc., of separate churches.

(1) It is evident that this largely favoured the differentiation of the Reader from other officials, with whose functions it was at one time closely connected. The completion, *e.g.*, of the Old Testament Canon, the translation of the LXX., the extension of the Church to centres in which its literature would naturally excite an abiding interest, as, *e.g.*, Alexandria in the East, and Rome and Athens in the West, the different and many tentative efforts to form Gospels of different kinds by the concatenation of λόγια themselves also of manifold origin were all causes which contributed to the increase of Readers as well as to the multiplication of materials on which their vocation was founded. Thereupon gradually sprang into being a number of Gospels, most of which have been lost, but at the same time not a few have been preserved. Thence came first the Apocryphal Gospels, or the non-canonical writings of which the Apostolic Fathers and the *Didaché* may be taken as

examples, until, in the fulness or maturity of time, when the sense of literary finish and of spiritual and moral beauty became sufficiently developed, the matchless synoptics, though *critically* anonymous productions, came into being—to be followed by the literary development of the Alexandrian or Neo-Platonic phase of Christian thought—called after, perhaps written by, the aged Ephesian Bishop, St. John.

This stage in the evolution of Christianity—the formation of the New Testament Canon—forms the culminating point in the history of Christianity. But the process by means of which it was attained was the function of Interpreter or Reader. He it was who collected and arranged the λόγια of the different churches, adopting, as a general principle, the preponderating thought and doctrine of different parts of the Diaspora. Hence it is not surprising to find that the Reader, in the earliest distinct mention of that official, is put on the same plane as the Evangelist, since it is he who is responsible for those separate collections of λόγια and ἐξηγήσεις as the work of Papias was termed, which are known as the Synoptic Gospels. Roughly speaking, and the subject does not admit of dogmatic statement, we might classify the four canonical Gospels, in reference to the Readers, Interpreters, who brought them into being, in the manner following :—

I. Matthew, the Interpreter of the Hebrew Matthew, ...
Matthew, the Interpreter of the Greek Matthew, ...
} The churches of Palestine—Messianic and Millennial.

II. Mark, the Interpreter of the Gospel of Peter, ...
} Representing a modified Judæo-Christian standpoint.

III. Luke, the Interpreter of the Gospel of Paul, ... $\begin{cases} \text{The Gospel of} \\ \text{the Gentiles—} \\ \text{Asia Minor, etc.} \end{cases}$

IV. John, the Interpreter of the Alexandrian Gospel of Apollos, . . . $\begin{cases} \text{Neo-Platonic} \\ \text{Metaphysics—} \\ \text{Asia Minor and} \\ \text{the East.} \end{cases}$

It is thus seen that the scope of the canonical Gospels practically includes all the main lines of thought that distinguished the chief portions of the Diaspora, and that the specific functions in the organisation of the Early Church, to which we are indebted for them, are those pertaining to the office of Reader, Interpreter, or Expounder.

At this point, however, we are met by the interesting question: When and where have we the earliest mention of the Reader, as a completely differentiated function among the other offices of the Christian Church? That we have no specific mention of the official until the middle of the second century need not excite our surprise, for the two following reasons:—

1st. The preponderance in the public worship of the different churches of gifts and activities which were charismatic; *i.e.*, the prayer, the psalm, the doctrine, the teaching, were the outcomes of extempore and impassioned feeling; the men who gave utterance to them were prompted or moved by strong spiritual impulse, which only finds partial record in the writings of Early Christian authors.

2nd. The function of Reader was one which might have been discharged by any official in the church. Indeed there were obviously occasions when the Bishop, the Presbyter, the Prophet, the Exorcist, or any other member of the official staff of any given church filled the office of Reader, and both selected the λόγια, or the Apostolic Epistle, or any other materials selected for reading, and also expounded such chosen passages. It is therefore quite in harmony with the nature of the case that we have no distinct mention of Reader until we come to the times and works of Tertullian. In the *De Præscrip.* (41) we read: 'Eo die diaconus qui cras lector'; where the language shows, says Bishop Lightfoot, 'that this was already a firmly established order in the church.' The statement is made, as is often the case with the learned Bishop, in a too unqualified and dogmatic manner. If his meaning be that the function had long existed in the church, we must needs accept it as harmonising with all the necessities of the case. When the culture of the church consisted not in formal lengthy treatises, but in brief sententious λόγια, extracts, chapters, parables, discourses, etc., the anecdotical literature of oral tradition run into a verbal mould of greater or less excellence, and beauty of expression, and a greater or less sharpness of definition, it was clear that the duties of Interpreter or Reader must have existed from the very beginning; but, if his meaning be that in the earliest times and in the smallest communities, notwithstanding the need of translation from one language to another, there was always a Reader formally separated from other ecclesiastical functionaries, the statement is more liable to question. In point of fact, as we have repeatedly insisted, no absolute statement can be made on early church organisation where the internal conditions and external environment of almost every congregation differed from those of all the rest. Nor must we forget the immeasurable influence of those circumstances and relations which were strictly local, and how the qualifications and position of Readers would be affected by the fact that five or six languages were in use in those different portions of the church in which that office came gradually into use. Thus the λόγια of the Palestinian and Jewish congregations were often in Hebrew, and needed to be translated into the Aramaic of Syria and Northern Palestine, or into the Greek of Asia Minor, of Alexandria and Upper Egypt, or the Latin of Rome and adjacent churches, or into the Arabic and Coptic of Lower Egypt or North Africa. Nor was a less variety of Reader attainments demanded by the difference in form and matter of the materials required by the churches. Such scholastic attainments, especially when the charismatically endowed officials were beginning to lose their power, came inevitably into the forefront among the regular ministers of the different communities. This fact had an indisputable effect in raising the status of the Reader to a level of the Diaconate or the Evangelists. We are told, indeed, that the Reader was appointed by the Deacons, where the meaning of the statement seems to me to be that the Deacons *selected* the man best qualified *from among themselves*, though, here again, peculiarities of local custom and usage must be allowed for. Dr. Harnack has treated in the following fragments the question of the position of the Reader at due length (see below, pp. 54, etc.). The outcome of such investigations seems to be that with the progress of the church, its increased employment of sacred writings of various kinds —not the least important of these being the letters of Apostles and Apostolic men—its advance, in other words, in literary culture, the status of the Reader evinced a tendency to become higher. At the same time it was exposed, as the purely cultural officialism of the church has always been exposed, to the rivalry and repressive efforts of its priestly and sacerdotal functionaries. Some idea of the status of Reader may be gathered from the enumeration of officials and other persons connected with the church, contained, *e.g.* in Eusebius and the Apostolical Constitutions. Thus we find in the former the church officers at Rome given by Cornelius—*e.g.*, Presbyters, Deacons, Sub-deacons, Acolytes, Exorcists, Readers, Gate-keepers, and Widows. So we have in the Apostolical Constitutions the following enumerations, viz. III. 11 :—Among the other *Clerici* . . . Readers, *Singers*, Gate-keepers, Servants, ὑπηρέταις; and VIII. 12: Patriarchs, Prophets, Deacons, Apostles, Martyrs, Confessors, Bishops, Presbyters, Deacons, Sub-deacons, Readers, Singers, Virgins, Widows, Laics; where the enumeration of martyrs and confessors among the regular officials of the church conveys a curious notion of the circumstances of the Christianity of the time, and the standpoint from which martyrs and confessors were considered, viz. not as incidental and casual officials of the church, but as those who had regular membership or *vocations*. If we may assume that the date of the Fragments here given by Dr. Harnack is later than that of the Apostolical Constitutions, the description therein given would seem to indicate that the Reader had attained a still higher status among the officials of the church. We need not follow the evolution of the Reader further, nor would it be seemly to anticipate what we learn from the following *Services of the Apostolic Canons* (see below, p. 15, etc.) the chief point in the requirements there given of the Reader. Διηγητικός, εἰδὼς ὅτι εὐαγγελιστοῦ τόπον ἐργάζεται, ὁ γὰρ ἐμπιπλῶν ὦτα μὴ νοοῦντος ἔγγραφος λογισθήσεται παρὰ τῷ θεῷ seems, however, worthy of especial attention; it emphasises the fact that the Reader's function was one of information and enlightenment. His duties included not only the reading but the expounding or explanation of the passages read. We learn, further, from Du Cange that the Lector, whom he styles *Secundus gradus Ordinis Ecclesiastici*, was not merely nominated to the office by his ecclesiastical superiors but was duly ordained. He quotes to this effect Marcellinus, the friend of Chrysostom, who writes of a certain John of Antioch : *Lector Ecclesiæ ordinatus per singulos officii Gradus ascendit*; adding, *Lectorum munus erat Lectiones pronuntiare, et ea, quæ Prophetæ vaticinarunt, populis prædicare.* Further evidence as to the functions of the Reader, when the office had become established in the church, is found in the *Acta Passionis, SS. Martyrum Cibalitanorum*, n. 2, where the colloquy of Probus, the Judge or President, and a Christian, Pullio, is thus related :—

'The President said, What office dost thou bear? Pullio answered, The chief of the Readers (*Primicerius Lectorum*).

'Probus, the President, said, Of what Readers? Pullio answered, Those who are accustomed to read Divine eloquence to the people.'

Apparently the Greek equivalent for the above Primicerius was ἀρχιαναγνώστης, the function of which officer Du Cange thus defines : *Non tamen Evangelium et Epistolam in ipsa Sacræ Missæ Liturgia legebant, quod velle videntur viri docti*, etc. Whence it would seem that the material of the Reader was not confined to what we should term the Scripture. Indeed, we know that later on in the middle ages, when the Reader was in some cases a duly appointed officer, and in others a function which the inmates of the monastery took in turns, all kinds of legends, sometimes stories, not wholly free from superstition and other still more unworthy qualities, formed the material of the Reader's function by which the ears of their brethren were tickled at meal-times and on other occasions; the *Gesta Romanorum* being one of the most frequently used collections, whose humorous, and sometimes not over cleanly, stories used to keep the mediæval Refectory in a roar of laughter.

PAST, PRESENT, AND FUTURE OF CHRISTIANITY IN REFERENCE TO THE RIVALRY OF THE SACERDOTAL AND DIDACTIC FUNCTIONS. PRIEST *versus* READER.

The Past of Christianity to the Time of the Reformation.

A comprehensive glance over the history of Christianity up to the sixteenth century serves to show that the general direction and tendency of the Church has been in favour of the Sacerdotal moiety of her functions, not of the didactic and critical moiety; that it is the Priest, not the Reader, whose influence has been most marked in her development. Her office as the instructor, the intellectual enlightener, of mankind has been virtually abrogated, and her self-arrogated function of spiritual despotism, placing herself and her claims in the room of God Himself, has been asserted with extreme and mischievous emphasis in its stead. Hence in place of the enlightenment which comes from the didactic and inquiring methods of the Reader, she has fettered the human mind and forbidden the exercise of man's intellectual power by insisting on the blind acceptance of dogmas, doctrines and creeds, most of them in greater or less antagonism to the primary teachings of the Gospel. We can thus readily understand why the Priest, the Bishop, the Pope, the highest sacerdotal functionaries, have claimed for themselves the amplest room and consideration in the history of the Church up to the time of the Reformation, while the functions pertaining to and allied with the Reader have fallen into the background of desuetude and oblivion. In the darkness of the middle ages nothing is more remarkable than the inversion of the due and proper relations of—taking the functions *for principles* of—Reader and Priest. Whatever was calculated to inform the human mind, to impart and diffuse intellectual enlightenment, was regarded not only with coldness but with virulent hatred and cruel persecution. It was a part of this anti-Christian policy that what should have been the lessons of the Reader, especially the inculcation of those λόγια or Christ-oracles in the utterance of which Christianity had its first foundation, fell into disuse as an integral part of Religion, and what was substituted in its place was the ministrations of the Priest—the Sacraments and other religious rites being carried into a mischievous excess, and superstition, the invariable ally of sacerdotalism, became diffused through the length and breadth of Christendom. The net or at least chief result of this gradual deterioration of the vital germ of Christianity was a reversion to that precise state of things which the mission and words of Christ were intended to subvert and destroy, viz.: the substitution of the function and lessons of the ethical and general Teacher for the principles of sacerdotalism then arrogated by the Pharisees, Scribes —the sacerdotal aristocracy of the Jews. To what great excess the hatred of the didactic function, of the ethical, *i.e.*, humane, teaching, the scientific illumination, the general enlightenment of mankind, has manifested itself on the part of sacerdotalism, when its power for centuries was absolute, we learn from the capture and sack of Constantinople, the massacres that disgraced more than one of the Crusades, especially the taking of Jerusalem by the savage soldiery of Godfrey of Bouillon, the diabolical massacre of the Albigenses, the expulsion of the Moors from Spain, the martyrdom of Giordano Bruno and Vanini, and divers other black pages and ruthlessly cruel incidents in the records of history. Indeed, the darkness of the dark ages has been owing to no other cause than the unscrupulous triumph of sacerdotalism, than the tyrannical sway of those very orders in the Church which were ostensibly devised as a readier means of access to God, as a source of spiritual enlightenment transcending anything which earth, or earth-born mortals had in their power to offer.

With the Renaissance and the Reformation, intending by the former the name of the general and partly secular enlightening, and by the latter that of the religious and spiritual moiety of the same movement, came in the reign, metaphorically speaking, of the Reader—the Rule of Books and writings— his tools and materials ; the rapid spread of the Printing Press ; while contemporaneously with the new sovereignty in Christendom was the commencement of the decay of sacerdotalism—two complementary processes which are still in operation. Slowly and deliberately, but with no symptoms of a decided halt or stoppage, the movement of the Reader, the function of Christian organisation which postulates the Teacher, the Enlightener, the ethical starting-point of Christianity, the meaning and method of Christian Revelation which makes it consist in λόγια or reading matter, may be said to characterise the Christendom of modern days. During the last three centuries this is the movement within the Church which has most vitality. In every direction we seem able to mark its activity. No longer is Christianity, on the broad ethical foundation laid down by Christ, thought to be incompatible with secular enlightenment, with the training of the human reason, with the advance in knowledge of the human intellect.

The reign of Sacerdotalism, of absolute dogma, of doctrines unoriginated by and unconnected with the λόγια of Christ, —the New Testament oracles which formed the starting-point of Christianity,—manifests on the other hand, if not symptoms of decay, at least unequivocal signs of a diminished sovereignty and a less universal sway over the hearts and consciences of the Christian world. By this is not meant, as we shall see a little further on, that Sacerdotalism is in its essential and least tyrannical form doomed to destruction. For that matter, the innermost germ of Sacerdotalism—the worship of the Eternal by a ministerial and ritual organisation not incompatible with human reason and with the modestly defined injunctions and example of Christ himself—may be said to have a perennial basis in humanity itself; but it is not the Sacerdotal but the Reader function to which thoughtful men will allot the supremacy in the dual division of Christian Church organisation.

THE PRESENT, AND ITS RELATION TO THE RIVALRY JUST SPOKEN OF, OF PRIEST *versus* READER.

The tendency just spoken of as commencing with the Reformation of the reassertion by the Reader of his legitimate authority as against the pretensions of Sacerdotalism may claim a result, a wholesome movement and tendency, which seems apparent in the chief conflict of thought of our own time; and that is, it seems to invite and prepare the way for a return to the primary λόγια, the original oracles, the ethic and didactic teachings of Christ Himself. Christianity, like Antæus, seems bent in the present day to acquire new strength by actual contact with its mother Earth—in other words—with its first origin; or, using another illustration: whereas in the first century of the planting of Christianity the maxims and moral teachings of Christ were like the veins of gold becoming embedded in a soluble and plastic matrix of quartz, now in the fulness of time the reverse operation is taking place; now, the miners with improved methods and mining tools are again extracting the pure gold from the quartz and other alluvial sedimentary deposits in which the precious metal has been embedded, and it is made to show its purity and its consequent lustre and beauty as never before.

The Future of Christianity in relation to Priest *versus* Reader.

> "Let KNOWLEDGE grow from more to more,
> But more of REVERENCE in us dwell,
> That mind and soul according well
> May make one music as before,
> But VASTER."

The poet's well-known aspiration may be taken as conveying a probable forecast of the rivalry we are here considering —between the priest on the one hand and the didactic and ethical teacher on the other—in the future of Christianity. The materials for forming an estimate on the subject are neither few nor unimportant. Taking first of all the contrasted functions :—The scope of knowledge must immensely exceed that of reverence or awe. Knowledge or science, though falling far short of omniscience, possesses yet a conceivable extension almost boundless. Taking as the basis of our estimate the enormous strides physical science has made since the commencement of the present century are almost incredible. Astronomy, geology, chemistry—all the other branches of what is known as physical science have advanced not by ordinary strides but by leaps and bounds. Nor has the progress of what may be distinguished as the application of science to the needs and requirements of men been less marked. This practical science must needs increase indefinitely in the future, and the more it ministers to the especially imperious among the wants of men, so much the more will it aid the cause of civilisation, and thereby also of religion. Of course, however, it is theoretical science—the knowledge that necessarily transcends human experience, and deals with the infinites of space and time and number—the speculative parts, *e.g.*, of astronomy, of geology, of anthropology, etc. These more vague and hazy extensions of a science that encircle like a divine halo the demonstrable and experimental nucleus have a necessary effect in theologising a science and bringing it into a category of adoration and worship in which it can be measured and compared with ritual and sacramental acts. This is the standpoint of science—science at any rate capable of metaphysical and mystical extensions—where the refined and cultivated student meets the priest or devout worshipper. If, as the poet said,

' An undevout astronomer is mad,'

it is an aberration of reason that may be extended indefinitely not only to sciences which are in their germ metaphysical but to others that are in their essence physical, but are capable of being extended in one or other directions beyond the narrow limits of terrene conditions. These are aspects of knowledge that are, in my judgment, bound to increase in the future. They form compensations of a certain kind by means of which the didactic researches and lessons of the future will make up for, *e.g.*, superstitions and unreasonably anthropomorphic forms of theology. Such metaphysical extensions of physical sciences may conceivably find almost indefinite extensions in the future. Whenever men of science are gifted with a tender impressionable side to an unusually strong and vigorous intellect, or whenever the force and reach of a strong mind is supplemented and qualified—as it was in the case of Tyndall—with a tender, graceful, and poetic imagination, the evolution of a theology and a worship from the driest and most materialistic details of a physical science is merely the gratification of the most natural instincts. Already we seem to be on the verge of a period in which the Religion or Christianity of the future has already begun to assume that semi-physical form we are now endeavouring to describe. What functions the Christian priest will then discharge, or in what way existing sacraments or any other forms of prayer and modes of worship will be made reconcilable with larger interpretations of creation and with the laws and processes of the universe, it would be as yet premature to guess. It is at any rate one excellence of Christianity as expounded by its Founder, that we can hardly conceive any form of future faith into which its most essential requisitions cannot enter—a faith, *e.g.*, in which conclusions of physical science may not find a place in combination with which every possible use and interpretation— of the Lord's Prayer, for instance—is wholly unimaginable—or again, any similar faith of the future into which the two sacraments of the Christian Church may not find some mode of reasonable introduction, albeit in attempting it Christians may well remember the sublime indifference to all external form and rite that their Teacher enjoined. I am far from supposing that these rational and physical science forms of Christian sacerdotalism are the only ones the future may have in store for us

But they are some to which, estimating from the auguries and forecasts of the present, the future may by its own self-development be leading us. We may, however, easily conceive forms of sacerdotalism, in which for persons of peculiar temperament and training the power of the priest may be the exercise of a wholesome function. We can at all events conceive that the spiritual and ethical influence of a Christ over, *e.g.*, such a disciple as Simon Peter, or 'the woman who was a sinner,' would be both priestly and wholesome in the highest possible sense.

Another point of view in which the Christianity of the future will necessarily become assimilated to that of the past will be in its use of the same credentials. As we saw already in noting the phenomena of the present, the λόγια or *oracles of Christ* will receive greater accentuation as they are more marked in the broader New Testament researches, which, I take leave to guess, will be one distinctive characteristic of the future of Christianity. The part which those λόγια played in the first century of the Christian era will be better understood and appreciated on a fuller investigation : then also, the freedom of communities governed by these λόγια, their ethical purity and profundity, will be more clearly recognised, while their simplicity and human sympathy will, finally, receive the deference that is rightly their due.

May we not possibly find in this recuscitation of Christ and Christian oracles, of Christ and Christian knowledge, of Christ and Christian love and charity, a higher, truer, and altogether better interpretation of the Son of Man's return to earth than any other to which tradition has lent a great but wholly unlikely significance. This would be an extension of Christianity, virtual as well as nominal, infinitely greater as well as more probable than any other we can think of; it would be a fulfilment of every well-worn prediction of the indefinite spread of Christianity such as 'the knowledge of the Lord shall cover the earth as the waters cover the sea'; it would be a realisation of the last and grandest scene of the world-drama of Christianity. Even so, come, Lord Jesus! Amen.

SOURCES OF THE APOSTOLIC CANONS.

In my edition of the Διδαχή I have already treated (pp. 193-241) of the so-called Apostolic Canons, that piece of writing of canonical law at once so important and yet until now so enigmatical, on which a bright light has fallen by the discovery of the Διδαχή. After a survey of the history of the starting into life and criticism of the Apostolic Canons, I have there investigated the composition of the book[1], and have shown that the editor had before him five documents of the time of the early church, viz. :—1. The Epistle of Barnabas; 2. the Διδαχή; 3. an old and very peculiar list of the Apostles; and 4. and 5. two pre-catholic compositions of canonical law, which I have named, in order to distinguish them, κατάστασις τοῦ κλήρου and κατάστασις τῆς ἐκκλησίας[2]. Much has since been written on the relation of the Apostolic Canons to the Διδαχή, and the correct conclusion of the latest investigations appears to be that the editor had not in his possession the whole Διδαχή, but only an abridgment of it[3]. I shall not return in the following pages to this point, as the decisions, whatever they may be, are irrelevant to the understanding of the Apostolic Canons; I intend, however, after a survey of the work of the editor on the book, to examine those two anonymous treatises of Canon Law of which he has made use, and which, in fact, he has incorporated in his work. It will be shown that from more than one point of view they claim the highest interest, and bring before us the most precious information on the legal arrangements of the church from the most ancient time. In this investigation I shall not repeat what I have already examined and proved in my former work. Those labours[4], with this new study, together with the investigations on 'the two ways,' will contain a complete treatise on this hitherto neglected law-book.

[1] Διδαχή, pp. 193-209. [2] *Ibid.* pp. 209-222.
[3] See especially the article of Holtzmann, 'Die Didache und die Nebenformen' in the *Jahrb. f. Protest. Theologie*, 1885, pp. 154 and foll., besides the treatises of Bratke, Warfield, Taylor, and others.
[4] The text of the Apostolic Canons is printed in the edition of the *Didache*, pp. 225 to 237.

CHAPTER I.

THE WORK OF THE EDITOR.

THE work of the editor on this law-book, measured quantitatively, has been exceedingly small. He has, apart from the introduction, arranged his sources very unskilfully, and contented himself with little additions and cancellings. Thus is it explained how it was possible that experts have referred the whole book in its present form to the second century. To the editor belong—1. paragraphs 1-3 complete; 2. the assignment of single groups of sentences to the several apostles; 3. unimportant additions in paragraphs 4-15. For this the Διδαχή and the Epistle of Barnabas form the foundation; what the author has added, with the exception of the longer portion of paragraph 8 and the thorough working up of paragraph 12, is extremely unimportant. 4. Small but important cancellings and an addition in paragraphs 16-23. The cancellings relate to the figures; for instance, the original document contains the regulation to appoint two presbyters, one reader, three deacons, and three widows. The editor, to whom these figures seemed too small, has placed three presbyters instead, and struck out the numbers for the reader and deacons, but left the number three for the widows [1]. The addition is reduced to the parenthesis in paragraph 20, taken from The Proverbs, ὀργὴ γὰρ ἀπόλλυσιν ἄνδρα φρόνιμον. This passage does not suit the character of the original; it however agrees completely with the additions of the editor in paragraphs 4-15. Apart from these alterations, which have had the result of the interpolation of a few short sentences, in that part which refers to the presbyter, there is in the section consisting of paragraphs 16-23

[1] See the proof for the alteration of or striking out of the figures against the presbyters and deacons on p. 212, note 36. It may, however, be concluded with great probability that in the original the figure *one* stood against the reader.

nothing which with any probability can be attributed to the editor. 5. As surely as a distinction can be perceived up to paragraph 23, so is the settlement of the work of the editor in the concluding paragraphs 24-30 uncertain. On one side the words (paragraph 25) περὶ τῆς προσφορᾶς τοῦ σώματος καὶ τοῦ αἵματος ἀκριβῶς μηνύσωμεν show plainly that we have to do with a writer at the earliest of the time of Cyprian, or at any rate of the time of Eusebius [1]; on the other hand, paragraph 26 contains what is extremely ancient, and the passage concerning the women agrees excellently with that concerning the laity, thus suiting the original, which has been here followed. But we cannot restore the text literally with certainty, for the style of the editor is to be recognised in the whole section. It will be perceived of what use the paragraphs 29 and 30 are.

Though, measured outwardly, the work of the editor has been little, he has completely altered the sense and the meaning of the sources he has made use of; for while the editor has written his compilation as an ordinance of the twelve apostles, and has placed in the mouth of the individual apostles the several regulations, while further he has designated this apostolic law-giving as brought about by a direct special command of Christ, he has given to the whole as well as to the single parts quite a new sense. The introduction, after placing in advance the names of the twelve apostles [2], thus runs :—

Κατὰ κέλευσιν τοῦ Κυρίου ἡμῶν Ἰησοῦ Χριστοῦ τοῦ Σωτῆρος συναθροισθέντων ἡμῶν, καθὼς διέταξεν πρὸ τοῦ [3]. Μέλλετε κληροῦσθαι τὰς ἐπαρχίας, καταλογίσασθαι τόπων ἀριθμούς, ἐπισκόπων ἀξίας, πρεσβυτέρων ἕδρας, διακόνων παρεδρείας, ἀναγνωστῶν νουνεχίας, χηρῶν ἀνεγκλησίας καὶ ὅσα δέοι πρὸς θεμελίωσιν ἐκκλησίας, ἵνα τύπον τῶν ἐπουρανίων εἰδότες φυλάσσωνται ἀπὸ παντὸς ἀστοχήματος, εἰδότες ὅτι λόγον

---

[1] See my *Dogmengeschichte*, vol. i. pp. 354 and 696.

[2] See for the list of the apostles p. 217 of the Διδαχή, and Lipsius, *Apokr. Apostelgesch.* i. p. 21 and following.

[3] Instead of πρὸ τοῦ we should perhaps read προλέγων or πρότερον. (The Aethiopic gives us 'praecepit nobis et dixit.') Lagarde has made the following restoration according to the Coptic text, which is itself a corrupted one (in Bunsen's *Analecta Antenic.* ii. p. 451): συναθροισθέντων ἡμῶν διέταξεν ἡμῖν λέγων πρὸ τοῦ κληροῦσθαι ἡμᾶς τὰς χώρας, ὅτι πρὸ τοῦ μέλλειν κληροῦσθαι τὰς χώρας καταλογίσασθε τόπων ἀριθμούς κ.τ.λ. However, in the *Reliquiae Jur. eccl.* the text stands as printed above.

ὑφέξουσιν ἐν τῇ μεγάλῃ ἡμέρᾳ τῆς κρίσεως περὶ ὧν ἀκούσαντες οὐκ ἐφύλαξαν—καὶ ἐκέλευσεν ἡμᾶς ἐκπέμψασθαι τοὺς λόγους εἰς ὅλην τὴν οἰκουμένην· ἔδοξεν οὖν ἡμῖν πρὸς ὑπόμνησιν τῆς ἀδελφότητος καὶ νουθεσίαν ἑκάστῳ ὡς ὁ κύριος ἀπεκάλυψε κατὰ τὸ θέλημα τοῦ θεοῦ διὰ πνεύματος ἁγίου μνησθεῖσι λόγου ἐντείλασθαι ὑμῖν.

The premiss in this badly composed paragraph is given in the συναθροισθέντων ἡμῶν, the conclusion begins with the ἔδοξεν οὖν ἡμῖν [1]; the καθὼς διέταξεν, and the καὶ ἐκέλευσεν following later, are as exegeses to κατὰ κέλευσιν. The author has here thus discovered a special command of Christ to the apostles. They were to settle the *constitutio ecclesiae* even to the smallest detail in a general session, and to make known this settlement to the whole world. The apostles obeyed this command—when is not said [2]—while each in a solemn session promulgated what had been revealed to him by the Lord, and together they published these revelations to the whole world [3]. As to single passages, the following is worthy of consideration.

The expression ἐπαρχία is not met with in ecclesiastical language in the sense of 'church province' before the time of Eusebius. However, in the sense of 'province' it is much older, and thus occurs also in ecclesiastical writers [4]. In this passage there is no necessity that we should think of church provinces, consequently it is of no value for fixing the date of the editor [5]. Κληροῦσθαι = 'to divide by lot.' The apostles

---

[1] See Acts xv. 25; Luke i. 3.

[2] See Praedic. Petri in Hilgenfeld's Nov. Test. extra can. recept. Fasc. 4 ed. ii. p. 56, 15, where the command to the apostles runs : μετὰ δώδεκα ἔτη ἐξέλθετε εἰς τὸν κόσμον : compare Apollonius in Eusebius, Hist. Eccl. v. 18. 14, ὡς ἐκ παραδόσεως τὸν σωτῆρά φησι προστεταχέναι τοῖς αὐτοῦ ἀποστόλοις ἐπὶ δώδεκα ἔτεσι μὴ χωρισθῆναι τῆς Ἰερουσαλήμ.

[3] The single sentences are referred back to special revelations of the Lord. See Muratori, Fragment Z, 9 and follg. : [Johannes] cohortantibus condiscipulis et episcopis suis dixit : conieiunate mihi hodie triduo, et quid cuique fuerit revelatum, alterutrum nobis enarremus, etc. Such representations go back thus to the second century.

[4] See Marquardt, *Röm. Staatsverwaltung*, vol. i. (1873) p. 340, n. 6. In the Martyrium Carpi et Papyli et Agathonices (see Aubé, *L'église et l'état dans la seconde moitié du III*[e] *siècle*, p. 503), we read, ἐν πάσῃ ἐπαρχίᾳ καὶ πόλει εἰσὶν μου τέκνα κατὰ θεόν. Also when used by Eusebius, Hist. Eccl. vii. 30, 1, provinces of the Empire are probably meant : ἐπιστολὴν διαπέμπονται ἐπὶ πάσας τὰς ἐπαρχίας.

[5] In opposition to my remark on p. 218 of the work mentioned.

were thus to dispose of the provinces among themselves, and they were besides to make a catalogue of the number of the τόποι. Τόπος may mean here a degree of rank just as well as a place (town); and it is indeed to be taken in its first meaning, as the following appears as an exegesis of τόποι. The author [1] reckons as steps of rank : bishops, presbyters, deacons, readers, and widows. He has, in agreement with the general rule, placed the readers after the deacons [2], but, except the widows, has closed the list with them. It would, however, be premature to conclude from this that at his time there were no subdeacons. Rather, as to the date of the editor, the following points should be considered:

1. The division of the individual regulations among the several apostles.
2. The proof that the clerical degrees even down to the widows and readers are formed according to the τύπος τῶν ἐπουρανίων.
3. The pre-supposition that the bishop alone appoints the presbyters after his own examination. (See the sentence interpolated by the editor at paragraph 17 : 'Ιωάννης εἶπεν· ὁ κατασταθεὶς ἐπίσκοπος, εἰδὼς τὸ προσεχὲς καὶ φιλόθεον τῶν σὺν αὐτῷ, καταστήσει οὓς ἂν δοκιμάσῃ πρεσβυτέρους.)
4. The expression ἡ προσφορὰ τοῦ σώματος καὶ τοῦ αἵματος.
5. The omission of the whole second half of the Διδαχὴ τῶν ἀποστόλων as useless—that the editor was acquainted with it is evident from paragraph 12—as well as the use made of Διδαχή iv. 1. 2 in paragraph 12.

On the ground of these observations it may be considered rash to place the time of the editing earlier than the third century. We may not, however, put it later than the middle of the fourth century, as from this time uniform church ordinances were fixed. In fact the whole undertaking is more easily

---

[1] The designations ἀξίας, ἕδρας, παρεδρείας, νουνεχίας, and ἀνεγκλησίας should be observed. The three first are easily to be understood and characteristic. However, the two last are striking—'discretion' and 'irreproachableness.' The latter is a ἅπαξ λεγόμ. (Bickell's ἀνεκκλησίας = 'separating the widows from ecclesiastical arrangements' is monstrous.) The former is dark in its special relation to the 'readers.'

[2] In the source which he has used the reversed order was observed. See paragraphs 19, 20.

understood if we date it in the second half of the third century, say about the year 300, rather than later. With regard to the place where the editing was done, the history of the book points to Egypt. At any rate these canons are no monument of the Imperial church; they could hardly have arisen from one of the chief churches, but rather from a provincial one, as the admission of chapters 16-21, including the corrections, proves. The compilation is by no means clear. What value or what acceptance such church regulations could have had about the year 300 is not at all clear to us. The document is not, however, in its way singular. There are several church ordinances and even dogmatic compilations which, particularly in the time in which they arose, are quite inconceivable to us. The materials were probably forced upon their authors, who by re-editing them tried to make them to a certain extent innocuous. Even in the present time we might be able to produce parallel cases.

CHAPTER II.

THE ORIGINAL SOURCES AT THE BASIS OF CHAPTERS 16-28 OF THE APOSTOLIC CANONS.

THAT there were *two* original documents forming the basis of chapters 16-28 I have already shown in my edition of the Διδαχή, pp. 212-216. The duplicate (to chapter 20) chapter 22 teaches us that the author has for this chapter gone to a new original document. The connection of chapters 22-28 is, however, evident by other observations: thus in chapters 22 and 26 Christ is called ὁ διδάσκαλος, while this designation is wanting in chapters 16-21. The first Epistle of Clement is made use of in chapter 22 as well as in chapter 23, while it is considered of no value in chapters 16-21.

The editor has used, just as out of the Διδαχή, only fragments of the two original documents which were at his disposal. We can have no conception as to what form they had as a whole. But what he has taken from his sources is without difficulty recognised. In what follows the two large fragments are separated and commented on:—

A.—(APOSTOLIC CANONS, Chapters 16-21.)

1. Ἐὰν ὀλιγανδρία ὑπάρχῃ καὶ μήπου πλῆθος τυγχάνῃ τῶν δυναμένων ψηφίσασθαι περὶ ἐπι-

1. If there are few men and not twelve persons who are competent to vote at the election of

1. 1. ὀλιγανδρία. A similar definition is found nowhere else, yet we may compare it with Const. App. II. 1. p. 14, 11 (ed. Lagarde): εἰ δὲ καὶ ἐν παροικίᾳ μικρᾷ ὑπαρχούσῃ που προβεβηκὼς τῷ χρόνῳ μὴ εὑρίσκηται μεμαρτυρημένος καὶ σοφὸς εἰς ἐπισκοπὴν κατασταθῆναι, νέος δὲ ᾖ ἐκεῖ . . . δοκιμασθεὶς . . . καθιστάσθω ἐν εἰρήνῃ. It is to be remarked that in the whole division there is no question of the election, still less of the consecration, but of the preparation for the election and the qualities of the person to be chosen.

2. πλῆθος. The author is not thinking of the clergy, but of the laity: that is, of the members of the congregation; he has in view small congregations in which there may not be even twelve persons qualified to vote. The congregation selects. See Διδαχή 15. 1 : Χειροτονήσατε οὖν ἑαυτοῖς ἐπισκόπους.

8 SOURCES OF THE APOSTOLIC CANONS

σκόπου εντός δεκαδύο ανδρών, εις a bishop, the neighbouring
5 τὰς πλησίον εκκλησίας, όπου churches should be written to,
τυγχάνει πεπηγυῖα, γραφέτωσαν, where any of them is a settled
όπως εκείθεν εκλεκτοὶ τρείς άνδρες one, in order that three selected
παραγενόμενοι δοκιμῇ δοκιμάσαν- men may come thence and ex-
τες τὸν ἄξιον ὄντα, εἴ τις φήμην amine carefully if he is worthy,
10 καλὴν ἔχει ἀπὸ τῶν 'εθνών, εἰ that is, if he has a good report
αναμάρτητος ὑπάρχει, εἰ φιλό- among the heathen, if he is fault-
πτωχος εἰ, σώφρων, μὴ μέθυ- less, if a friend of the poor, if

5. ἐκκλησίας. What follows shows that this plural is not to be so understood as if several neighbouring churches were to be written to, but rather a
firmly established congregation is to be invited to assist.
6. πεπηγυῖα. 'Fixedness,' 'having a standing,' in this connection, consequently, having a larger number of members. Churches which have not
even twelve members qualified to vote are in danger of disappearing.
γραφέτωσαν, that is, the congregation, not the clergy of the congregation.
7. ἐκλεκτοὶ τρεῖς ἄνδρες. These need not be clergymen. In general we may
compare 1 Clem. 63, 3, as well as the Epistle of Polycarp. (See also Lucian,
Peregr. Proteus 13 ; Ignat. ad Smyrn. 11 ; and ad Polyc. 7.) In these cases
there is no question of the election of a bishop. See Zahn, *Weltverkehr und
Kirche*, and my treatise, 'Die Sorge f. arme u. gefährdete Gemeinde u.s.w.' in
the *Monatschrift f. Diakonie*, etc., Dec. 1879—Jan. 1880.
8. δοκιμῇ δοκιμάσαντες. See § 3, 4 ; 2 Cor. viii. 22 : συνεπέμψαμεν δὲ αὐτοῖς
τὸν ἀδελφὸν ἡμῶν ὃν ἐδοκιμάσαμεν. 1 Tim. iii. 10: οἱ διάκονοι δοκιμαζέσθωσαν
πρῶτον, εἶτα διακονείτωσαν. 1 Clem. 42, 4 : καθίστανον τὰς ἀπαρχὰς αὐτῶν
δοκιμάσαντες τῷ πνεύματι εἰς ἐπισκόπους καὶ διακόνους. 44, 2 : οἱ ἀπόστολοι
ἐπινομὴν ἔδωκαν ὅπως ἐὰν κοιμηθῶσιν, διαδέξωνται ἕτεροι δεδοκιμασμένοι ἄνδρες τὴν
λειτουργίαν αὐτῶν. 47, 4. Διδαχή 11, 11 ; 12, 1 ; 15, 1 : χειροτονήσατε . . .
ἐπισκόπους . . . ἄνδρας δεδοκιμασμένους. The three invited men have only to
examine the candidate placed before the congregation ; they have not to join
in the election.
9. ἄξιον. See Διδ. 15, 1 : ἀξίους τοῦ κυρίου—εἴ τις κ.τ.λ. From here to
ὅμοια the necessary qualifications are enumerated ; then follow those which
are desirable.
φήμην κ.τ.λ. See 1 Tim. iii. 7 : δεῖ δὲ τὸν ἐπίσκοπον καὶ μαρτυρίαν καλὴν
ἔχειν ἀπὸ τῶν ἔξωθεν. Const. App. II. 6 : ἔστω δὲ ὁ ἐπίσκοπος μὴ αἰσχροκερδὴς
καὶ μάλιστα ἐπὶ τῶν ἐθνῶν βλαπτόμενος μᾶλλον ἢ βλάπτων.
11. ἀναμάρτητος. This word, which is not a common one, is found also
in Test. XII. Patr. Benjam. 3 ; Celsus in Origen c. Cels. III. 65 ; Hom.
Clem. II. 6, p. 23, 8, ed. Lagarde, Const. App. II. 13, p. 23, 22 ; p. 24,
14 ; II. 18, p. 33, 2, 13, 24 ; II. 14, p. 26, 6 ; VIII. 6, p. 240, 18. It
can hardly be taken here in its strict sense, but as in Const. App. II. 1,
p. 13, 22 : τὸν ἐπίσκοπον δεῖ ὑπάρχειν ἀνέγκλητον, ἀνεπίληπτον, ἀνέπαφον πάσης
ἀδικίας ἀνθρώπων. See 1 Tim. iii. 2 : δεῖ τὸν ἐπίσκοπον ἀνεπίλημπτον εἶναι ;
Tit. i. 7.
φιλόπτωχος. See Const. App. II. 6, p. 17, 17, where it is said of the
bishop, μὴ φιλοπλούσιος, μὴ μισόπτωχός.
12. σώφρων. See 1 Tim. iii. 2 : ἐπίσκοπον σώφρονα. Tit. i. 8 : μὴ μέθυσος—

SOURCES OF THE APOSTOLIC CANONS 9

σος, μὴ πόρνος, μὴ πλεονέκ- honourable—no drunkard, no
της ἢ λοίδορος ἢ προσωπολήπτης, adulterer, not covetous or a
καὶ τὰ τούτοις ὅμοια. καλὸν μὲν slanderer, or partial, or such like.
εἶναι ἀγύναιος, εἰ δὲ μή, ἀπὸ It is good if he is unmarried; if
μιᾶς γυναικός· παιδείας μέτοχος, not, then a man of one wife; edu-
δυνάμενος τὰς γραφὰς ἑρμηνεύειν· cated, in a position to expound

see paragraph 3; 1 Tim. iii. 2, μὴ πάροινον; Tit. i. 7. The following enumeration comes from 1 Cor. v. 11 : πόρνος ἢ πλεονέκτης . . . ἢ λοίδορος ἢ μέθυσος—μὴ πόρνος. This definition is not expressly used in the Pastoral Epistles.
13. μὴ πλεονέκτης. Const. App. II. 6, p. 17, 16 : μὴ πλεονέκτης. 1 Tim. iii. 3; Διδ. 15, 1 : ἀφιλάργυρον. Tit. i. 8 : μὴ αἰσχροκερδῆ. Hippolyt. (Philos. IX. 7) on Zephyrin : ἀνὴρ ἰδιώτης καὶ αἰσχροκερδής. Polyc. ad Philipp. 6, 1 : μακρὰν ὄντες πάσης φιλαργυρίας (of the presbyters and bishops); 5, 2 ; ἀφιλάργυροι (of the deacons). Herm., Sim. IX. 27, 2.
14. προσωπολήπτης. See § 2 (bis). 4. 6 ; Polyc. ad Philipp. 6, 1 : ἀπεχόμενοι προσωποληψίας. Const. App. II. 5 p. 16, 16 : ἔστω ὁ ἐπίσκοπος ἀπροσωπόληπτος, II. 9 p. 21, 9 : εἶναι χρὴ τὸν ἐπίσκοπον ἀπροσωπόληπτον. Act. x. 34 : προσωπολήπτης. Tit. i. 8 : δίκαιον (of the bishop).—καὶ τὰ τούτοις ὅμοια. See Gal. v. 21 : . . . φθόνοι, μέθαι, κῶμοι, καὶ τὰ ὅμοια τούτοις.
15. καλὸν μὲν εἶναι ἀγύναιος, κ.τ.λ. As to the form see 1 Cor. vii. 1 : καλὸν ἀνθρώπῳ γυναικὸς μὴ ἅπτεσθαι. The author goes in his desire a step further than the author of the First Epistle to Timothy (see iii. 2 : μιᾶς γυναικὸς ἄνδρα), and Const. App. II. 2 p. 15, 9 : μιᾶς γυναικὸς ἄνδρα γεγενημένον, μονόγαμον. It was not rare to find married bishops in the third century. See Hippolyt. Philos. IX. 12, p. 460 : ' Ἐπὶ Καλλίστου ἤρξαντο ἐπίσκοποι καὶ πρεσβύτεροι καὶ διάκονοι δίγαμοι καὶ τρίγαμοι καθίστασθαι εἰς κλήρους· εἰ δὲ καί τις ἐν κλήρῳ ὢν γαμοίη, μένειν τὸν τοιοῦτον ἐν τῷ κλήρῳ ὡς μὴ ἡμαρτηκότα. The explanation of Pitra to our passage, 'oportere episcopum esse aut caelibem aut omnis uxoris viduum,' is written with an object.
17. παιδείας μέτοχος, κ.τ.λ. Even this is only a desirable qualification. See 1 Tim. iii. 2 : διδακτικόν. Tit. i. 9 : ἀντεχόμενον τοῦ κατὰ τὴν διδαχὴν πιστοῦ λόγου, ἵνα δυνατὸς ᾖ καὶ παρακαλεῖν ἐν τῇ διδασκαλίᾳ ὑγιαινούσῃ καὶ τοὺς ἀντιλέγοντας ἐλέγχειν. In this passage the capacity to teach is founded on the rules of faith, while in the above it is on the holy scriptures. See Const. App. II. 1, p. 14, 9 : ἔστω οὖν ὁ ἐπίσκοπος, εἰ δυνατόν, πεπαιδευμένος· εἰ δὲ καὶ ἀγράμματος, ἀλλ' οὖν ἔμπειρος τῶν λόγων, καθήκων τῇ ἡλικίᾳ. II. 5 p. 16, 25 : πολυδίδακτος, μελετῶν καὶ σπουδάζων ἐν ταῖς κυριακαῖς βίβλοις, πολὺς ἐν ἀναγνώσμασιν, ἵνα τὰς γραφὰς ἐπιμελῶς ἑρμηνεύῃ (s. Ignat. ad Philad. 6, 1). The consideration that παιδεία is mentioned before ability to explain the scriptures, while there is no mention of rules of faith, makes it probable that our fragment was not edited in the West nor in the oldest time. In Const. App. I. 6 p. 17, 10, we find ἐπιμελοῦ οὖν τοῦ λόγου, ἐπίσκοπε, ἵνα, εἰ δυνατόν σοι, πάντα κατὰ λέξιν ἑρμηνεύσῃς. It is left doubtful what 'scriptures' are meant. See Const. App. V. 12 (Text): εὐλογίας καὶ ψαλμοὺς καὶ κυριακὰς καὶ θείας γραφάς ; V. 19 (Text): ἐπὶ τὸ αὐτὸ ἐν τῇ ἐκκλησίᾳ συναθροιζόμενοι γρηγορεῖτε . . . ἀναγινώσκοντες τὸν νόμον, τοὺς προφήτας, τοὺς ψαλμούς, τὸ εὐαγγέλιον ; I. 5 : ἀναγίνωσκε τὸν νόμον, τὰς βασιλείους, τοὺς προφήτας, τὸ εὐαγγέλιον· τὸ τούτων συμπλήρωμα ; II. 5 : ὁμοστοίχως τοῖς προφήταις καὶ τῷ νόμῳ τὸ εὐαγγέλιον ἑρμηνεύων.

10   SOURCES OF THE APOSTOLIC CANONS

εἰ δὲ ἀγράμματος, πραῢς ὑπάρχων,   the Scriptures; but if he is un-
καὶ τῇ ἀγάπῃ εἰς πάντας περισ-   learned, then he must be gentle
σευέτω, μή ποτε περί τινος ἐλεγχ-   and filled with love to all, so that
θεὶς ἐπίσκοπος ἀπὸ τῶν πολλῶν   a bishop should never be as one
γενηθείη.   accused of anything by the
multitude.

2. . . . (πρεσβύτεροι δύο)·   **2.** . . . (Two Presbyters): for
εἴκοσι γὰρ καὶ τέσσαρές εἰσι   there are 24 Presbyters, 12 at the

19. ἀγράμματος. See the above quoted passage from Const. App. II. 1 p. 14, 9. Hippolytus says of the Roman bishop Zephyrinus in Philos. IX. 11: ἰδιώτης καὶ ἀγράμματος. Cornelii Rom. ep. apud Euseb. Hist. Eccl. vi. 43, 8: ἐπισκόπους τρεῖς, ἀνθρώπους ἀγροίκους καὶ ἁπλουστάτους. Kopt. Heiligen-Kalender (edited by Wüstenfeld) I. p. 66: 'Demetrius was an unlearned countryman who did not know the scripture; he was married to one wife and lived with her until he became patriarch' (at the time of Clemens Alexandrinus). On uneducated bishops see Hatch, *Organization of the Early Christian Churches*, 3d ed., p. 163.

πραΰς. Gentleness and love must make up for the missing knowledge. See Διδαχή 15, 1: ἐπισκόπους . . . πραεῖς. 1 Tim. iii. 3: ἐπίσκοπον . . . ἐπιεικῆ, ἄμαχον. 1 Clem. 44, 3. Polycarp. ad Philipp. 6. 1: τῇ ἀγάπῃ . . . κ.τ.λ. See 1 Thess. iii. 12: ὑμᾶς δὲ ὁ κύριος . . . περισσεύσαι τῇ ἀγάπῃ . . . εἰς πάντας.

21. μή ποτε, κ.τ.λ. See Tit. i. 9.

22. τῶν πολλῶν—that is, ἀπὸ τοῦ πλήθους, see 1 Cor. x. 33. It is to be observed that there is no rule as to the necessary age of the bishop (otherwise 1 Tim. iii. 6, Const. App. II. 1 p. 14, 1 and follg.), and that it is not required that the bishop should be chosen from among the clergy.

2. The beginning of this section cannot now be reconstructed. Hence we do not know whether it is (as in paragraphs 1, 3, 4) a question of a δοκιμασία and κατάστασις of the presbyter or not.

1. δύο. This is at any rate the original number. The author has founded it on a reference to the Apocalypse. To him the force lies in the ἐκ δεξιῶν and ἐξ εὐωνύμων, which is indeed only a conclusion from the Apocalypse (see Const. App. II. 57 p. 84, 22: κείσθω μέσος ὁ τοῦ ἐπισκόπου θρόνος, παρ' ἑκάτερα δὲ αὐτοῦ καθεζέσθω τὸ πρεσβυτέριον). He did not of course wish to exclude a plurality of presbyters (see the remark to note 21, τῶν ἐπισκόπων), he only demanded that the number should be always an even one. Apoc. iv. 4; v. 8 (κυκλόθεν τοῦ θρόνου θρόνοι εἴκοσι τέσσαρες, καὶ ἐπὶ τοὺς θρόνους εἴκοσι τέσσαρας πρεσβυτέρους καθημένους . . . εἴκοσι τέσσαρες πρεσβύτεροι . . . ἔχοντες ἕκαστος . . . φιάλας χρυσᾶς γεμούσας θυμιαμάτων, αἴ εἰσιν αἱ προσευχαὶ τῶν ἁγίων) is at the foundation for it; but the introduction of the archangels is a pure addition, and the whole description has no support in the text of the Apocalypse. The author has transferred the functions of the earthly presbyters as he determined them (see below) to the heavenly presbyters. It is important to observe that in Apoc. iv. 5 the original picture of the Christian worship on earth is recognised, and the account adapted accordingly (see Hatch, *Organization of the Early Christian Churches*, 3d ed. p. 128). See the saying of Clemens, *Strom.* IV. 8: εἰκὼν δὲ τῆς οὐρανίου ἐκκλησίας ἡ ἐπίγειος. The δεσπότης is of course the bishop, the πλῆθος τῶν ἀγγέλων the multitude of believing laymen.

SOURCES OF THE APOSTOLIC CANONS 11

πρεσβύτεροι, δώδεκα ἐκ δεξιῶν καὶ δώδεκα ἐξ εὐωνύμων· οἱ μὲν
5 γὰρ ἐκ δεξιῶν δεχόμενοι ἀπό τῶν ἀρχαγγέλων τὰς φιάλας προσφέρουσι τῷ δεσπότῃ, οἱ δὲ ἐξ ἀριστερῶν ἐπέχουσι τῷ πλήθει τῶν ἀγγέλων. δεῖ οὖν εἶναι τοὺς πρεσ-
0 βυτέρους ἤδη κεχρονικότας ἐπὶ τῷ κόσμῳ, τρόπῳ τινὶ ἀπεχομένους τῆς πρὸς γυναῖκας συνελεύσεως, εὐμεταδότους εἰς τὴν ἀδελφότητα, πρόσωπον ἀνθρώπου μὴ λαμβάνον-
5 τας, συμμύστας τοῦ ἐπισκόπου καὶ

right and 12 at the left ; for those at the right receive from the archangels the cups and present them to the master, but those on the left hand (them) to the multitude of the angels. Hence the presbyters must be already advanced in years (in the world), abstaining as is fit from communication with women, willingly sharing with the brotherhood, not having regard to the person, companions in consecration with the bishop,

ἐπέχουσι can hardly, with Bickell, be translated by 'to have the superintendence,' it is simply 'to hand.' This passage offers the oldest example of the application of the Apocalypse to church order.

9. δεῖ οὖν εἶναι τοὺς πρεσβυτέρους. Here begins the enumeration of the qualities of the presbyters. This section is unique in the literature of the canon law before Constantine, for Tit. i. and Polyc. ad Philipp. p. 6 treat of presbyter-bishops. The Apostolic Constitutions even contain nothing which belongs here.

10. κεχρονικότας. Thus a fixed number of years is not demanded, but only an advanced age in general. The App. Const. (II. 1 p. 14, 1) demand that, as a rule, no one shall be consecrated a bishop before his fiftieth year. According to the eleventh canon of Neocaesarea (Routh, *Reliquiae S.* iv. p. 181) a presbyter must be at least thirty years old. ἐπὶ τῷ κόσμῳ is pleonastic.

11. τρόπῳ τινὶ ἀπεχομένους, κ.τ.λ. This regulation too is unique. Bishops and deacons may be married ; presbyters, however, have to abstain from sexual relations. For τρόπῳ τινὶ (Bickell has erroneously joined it to κεχρονικότας) see Const. App. II. 1 p. 14, 2 : ὅτι τρόπῳ τινὶ τὰς νεωτερικὰς ἐπιθυμίας ἐκπεφευγὼς ὑπάρχει. The author does not, we may believe, mean that the presbyter has to abstain from sexual connection 'quodammodo.' But what then does τρόπῳ τινὶ mean ? The above quoted passage out of the Apostolic Constitutions and a second (III. 1 p. 96, 10 : χήρας καθιστᾶτε μὴ ἔλαττον ἐτῶν ἑξήκοντα, ἵνα τρόπῳ τινὶ τὸ τῆς διγαμίας αὐτῶν ἀνύποπτον βέβαιον ὑμῖν διὰ τῆς ἡλικίας αὐτῶν ὑπάρχῃ) leave no other meaning than = κατὰ τρόπον ('correspondingly,' 'naturally,' 'becomingly') for the translation 'in any manner' which might be in necessity defended in this passage is excluded by the passages from the Apostolic Constitutions. Further vouchers indeed that τρόπῳ τινὶ is equal to κατὰ τρόπον I am not able to give.

13. εὐμεταδότους. See par. 4 and App. Const. II. 3 p. 15, 26. Ἀδελφότητα: this is the usual name for the Christian fellowship. See my note to 1 Clem. 2, 4.

14. πρόσωπον, κ.τ.λ. See par. 1, 4, 6 ; the presbyters have the right to speak.

15. συμμύστας τοῦ ἐπισκόπου. The word (a companion in consecration) arises from the language of the mysteries (see the old proverb : θαρρεῖτε, μύσται, τοῦ θεοῦ σεσωσμένοι, ἔσται γὰρ ἡμῖν ἐκ πόνων σωτηρία). In the first half of the second century many conceptions are already taken up in the church language out of that language (especially amongst the Gnostics ; see Koffmane, *Die Gnosis*, 1881. Even in Justin mystagogic conceptions are not wanting).

12 SOURCES OF THE APOSTOLIC CANONS

συνεπιμάχους, συναθροίζοντας τὸ   and fighting on his side, collecting
πλῆθος,   προθυμουμένους   τὸν   together the congregation, ready
ποιμένα. οἱ ἐκ δεξιῶν πρεσβύτεροι to help the pastors. The pres-
προνοήσονται τῶν ἐπισκόπων πρὸς   byters on the right should

The word συμμύστης first occurs in Ignatius. He called the Ephesians (Ep. ad Eph. 12) : συμμύστας Παύλου. See further Hippol. in Daniel. p. 174 (ed. Lagarde) : ὡς συμμύσται καὶ θεοσεβεῖς ἄνδρες. Origen in Jes. Nav. Hom. 7 (Opp. II. p. 413, ed. Delarue) : 'Paulus est symmystes Christi.' Constantine ap. Theodoret., Hist. Ev. I. 19 : ὁ τῆς τυραννικῆς ὠμότητος συμμύστης. Photius, Biblioth. p. 97, 20. Much more frequently is μύστης to be found. See e.g. Hippol. Philos. Praef. p. 4, 49. Epiph. h. 55, c. 8 : οὗ ἡμεῖς ἐσμεν μύσται, ὅπως τύχωμεν παρ' αὐτοῦ τῆς εὐλογίας. It is possible that Marcion named his followers συμμισούμενοι in opposition to the designation συμμύσται, for he was an enemy to all mysteries. In this passage we need not apply the expression to the worship alone ; still it is probable (from the following θυσιαστήριον) that the author was thinking especially of worship.

16. συνεπιμάχους. I have only met with this word here ; yet in App. Const. II. 17 p. 31, 15 is οὐ δυνήσονται οἱ ὑπὸ τὸν ἐπίσκοπον συνεπιμαχεῖν τῷ ἐπισκόπῳ.

συναθροίζοντας τὸ πλῆθος. We do not, unfortunately, learn how the presbyter is to carry out this duty ; συνάθροισμα is, since the time of Clemens Alexandrinus, a technical term for the church as well as for the heretical assembly. App. Const. II. 57 p. 84, 15 speaks of the bishop : ὅταν συναθροίζῃς τὴν τοῦ θεοῦ ἐκκλησίαν. See 1 Clem. 6, 1. It is, however, not improbable that the σύν in συναθροίζειν does not here signify a strengthening of the conception, but is to be explained by the preceding συμμύστας and συνεπιμάχους.

17. προθυμουμένους τὸν \ποιμένα. This word (' to be inclined,' ' to be willing ') is found but seldom with the acc. of the person. The shepherd is of course the bishop (see par. 6 fin. : ὁ ποιμενικὸς τόπος) ; so also Ephes. iv. 11 ; (Act. xx. 28) ; 1 Pet. ii. 25 : ὁ ποιμὴν καὶ ἐπίσκοπος τῶν ψυχῶν ὑμῶν. Herm., Sim. IX, 31, by ' pastores ' bishops are to be understood. In the first Ep. of Clement the congregation is four times (16, 1 ; 44, 3 ; 54, 2 ; 57, 2) called τὸ ποίμνιον τοῦ θεοῦ. Const. App. II, 1 (Text) : τὸν ποιμένα τὸν καθιστάμενον ἐπίσκοπον. For other passages see Hatch, Organization, etc.

19. προνοήσονται. See l. 23. ' They shall bear the cares, exert themselves ' (with the genitive of the person, see Xenophon, Cyr. 8. 1. 1 ; 7. 15 : προνοεῖσθαι τῶν παίδων. The phrase ὁ θεὸς προνοεῖται τῶν ὅλων is common). In the New Testament see Rom. xii. 17 : προνοούμενοι καλὰ ἐνώπιον πάντων ἀνθρώπων ; 2 Cor. viii. 21 ; 1 Tim. v. 8 : εἰ δέ τις τῶν ἰδίων οὐ προνοεῖ. Also Polyc. ad Philipp. 6, 1, where he speaks of the presbyters προνοοῦντες ἀεὶ τοῦ καλοῦ ἐνώπιον θεοῦ καὶ ἀνθρώπων ; Διδ. 12, 4 (of the congregation) : προνοήσατε, πῶς μὴ ἀργὸς μεθ' ὑμῶν ζήσεται χριστιανός ; Const. App. VIII. 15 p. 262, 3.

τῶν ἐπισκόπων. This plural is the plural of the category, for it follows from paragraph 1, as well as plainer from the singulars ' τοῦ ἐπισκόπου,' ' τὸν ποιμένα ' (see the lines 15 and 18), that the author only knows of one bishop in the congregation. Also in par. 1 l. 6 the plural ἐκκλησίας is thus to be understood, that in each single case only one church is to be considered.

πρὸς τὸ θυσιαστήριον, ' with reference to the altar ' ; that is, they should look after the bishop officiating at the altar. We have here one of the oldest, if not the very oldest, passage for the presence of an altar in the church, for the New Testament passages are all to be understood metaphorically, and similarly perhaps are the five passages in which the word occurs in Ignatius

τὸ θυσιαστήριον, ὅπως τιμήσωσι assist the bishops at the altar,
καὶ ἐντιμηθῶσιν, εἰς ὃ ἂν δέῃ· in order that they may distri-
οἱ ἐξ ἀριστερῶν πρεσβύτεροι bute the gifts of honour, and

(Eph. 5, Magn. 7, Trall. 7, Rom. 2, Philad. 4; see also Polyc. ad Philipp. 4 *fin.*, and Lightfoot on this passage). Tertullian in several places presupposes church altars; but from 1 Clement 44, 4 (προσφέρειν τὰ δῶρα) it does not follow that there was an altar in the strict sense of the word, and even in the second century the heathen relate that the Christians had neither temples nor altars. θυσιαστήριον is besides (in contradistinction to βωμός) not only the altar table, but also the altar space, as is plainly seen from Apoc. xi. 1 (μέτρησον τὸ θυσιαστήριον καὶ τοὺς προσκυνοῦντας ἐν αὐτῷ), and the passages in Ignatius (Eph. 5 : ἐὰν μή τις ᾖ ἐντὸς τοῦ θυσιαστηρίου, ὑστερεῖται τοῦ ἄρτου. Trall. 7 : ὁ ἐντὸς θυσιαστηρίου ὢν καθαρός ἐστιν, ὁ δὲ ἐκτὸς θυσιαστηρίου ὢν οὐ καθαρός ἐστιν).

20. ὅπως τιμήσωσι καὶ ἐντιμηθῶσιν, εἰς ὃ ἂν δέῃ. Subject of τιμήσωσι, κ.τ.λ., can only be the bishops, as in the following parallel sentence ὅπως εὐστα-ταθήσῃ, κ.τ.λ., the subject is τὸ πλῆθος ; besides, εἰς ὅ ἄν δέῃ can only be related to τιμήσωσι, κ.τ.λ., and not to προνοήσονται. But then it is impossible that τιμᾶν and ἐντιμᾶσθαι can be translated 'honour,' and 'thereby be honoured' (see par. 4, and Διδαχή 15, 2, where it is said of the bishops and deacons : αὐτοί εἰσιν οἱ τετιμημένοι ὑμῶν, and my remark at that passage) ; for the sentence, 'The presbyters shall bear the cares for the bishops at the altar, in order that the bishops should honour and be honoured in regard to what is always necessary,' is simply senseless. Τιμᾶν is thus to be taken here in its original meaning = 'to pay,' 'to value,' ' to estimate,' hence also ' to repay.' Only the last, in fact a synonymous, word can be considered here, as the following ἐντιμηθῶσιν proves, (τιμᾶσθαι stands in the sense of 'being valued' ; Matt. xxvii. 9 : τὴν τιμὴν τοῦ τετιμημένου ὃν ἐτιμήσαντο ; τιμή as equivalent to price is frequent in the N. T.—see Matt. xxvii. 6 ; Acts iv. 34, v. 2, 3, vii. 16, xix. 19 ; 1 Cor. vi. 20, vii. 23 ; 1 Tim. v. 17). This extraordinarily rare word is used (according to the kind communications of my colleague Dr. Philippi) by the Attic writers in the signification, 'under something to be reckoned as payment on account,' or ' to put a thing as part of a sum of money at the place of payment' : Mid. ' to account for oneself'—technically, for example, as part of dowry òf a wife paid usually in money—and this sense was still understood in the time of the Empire, as one passage in Dio Cassius proves. In the passage above it stands, however, in the passive, and hence nothing remains (as the bishops are the subject), but to consider ἐντιμᾶσθαι as meaning ' to be paid off at the paying ' (value). That it refers to gifts of honour is evident from the context, as shown by the preceding word θυσιασ-τήριον, the place where the gifts were laid. Thus may it be paraphrased : 'The presbyters are to provide for the bishop at the table of gifts, in order that they may distribute the gifts (to the various persons needing them and entitled to them), and themselves receive the necessary contributions (that is, as far as it is necessary).' It is consequently a question of a kind of control by the presbyters over the management of the gifts by the bishop, in order that everything may be done orderly. Included in this control is also what the bishop is justified in taking for himself. As thus the presbyters are answerable for order in the πλῆθος, so are they also officials charged with the superintendence of the financial action of the bishop, both within the service of God. This is the only possible exposition of this passage ; the position in which the presbyters here appear is in the highest degree worthy

14 SOURCES OF THE APOSTOLIC CANONS

προνοήσονται τοῦ πλήθους ὅπως   receive the same as far as is
εὐσταθήσῃ καὶ ἀθόρυβον ᾖ, πρῶτον   necessary. The presbyters on
25 μεμαθηκὼς ἐν πάσῃ ὑποταγῇ. εἰ   the left shall provide for the con-
δέ τις νουθετούμενος αὐθάδως ἀπο-   gregation, in order that it may
κριθῇ, τὸ ἓν ποιήσαντες οἱ ἐπὶ τῷ   be at rest and without disturb-

of note. There is in early Christian literature no other document which defines this function of the presbyters (see Par. 5, where what is said of the presbyters is also very worthy of attention). Our passage is partly explained by the following definitions: 1 Tim. v. 17 : οἱ καλῶς προεστῶτες πρεσβύτεροι διπλῆς τιμῆς ἀξιούσθωσαν (τιμή here is equivalent to gift of honour, honorarium; see Holtzmann, *Pastoralbriefe*, pp. 213, 352), Const. Apostol. II. 22 (Text): ἀφοριζέσθω δὲ ἐν τῇ δοχῇ τὸ τῷ ποιμένι ἐθίμιον, κἂν μὴ παραδέχηται, εἰς τιμὴν θεοῦ, τοῦ τὴν ἱερατείαν αὐτῷ ἐγχειρίσαντος. ὅσον δὲ ἑκάστῃ τῶν χηρῶν δίδοται, διπλοῦν διδόσθω τοῖς διακόνοις εἰς γέρας Χριστοῦ. εἰ δέ τις θέλοι καὶ τοὺς πρεσβυτέρους τιμᾶν, διπλοῦν διδότω αὐτοῖς ὡς καὶ τοῖς διακόνοις. τιμᾶσθαι γὰρ ὀφείλουσιν ὡς ἀπόστολοι . . . ἑκάστῳ οὖν ἀξιώματι οἱ λαϊκοὶ τὴν προσήκουσαν τιμὴν νεμέτωσαν ἐν τοῖς δόμασι. III., 1 [Text] : οἱ γὰρ τὰ δόματα διδόντες οὐκ αὐτοσχεδίως αὐτὰ διδόασι ταῖς χήραις, ἀλλά σοι συνεισφέρουσιν, ὅπως σὺ ὁ ἐπιστάμενος. τοὺς θλιβομένους ἀκριβῶς ὡς ἀγαθὸς οἰκονόμος [the bishop is meant] μερίζῃς αὐτοῖς ἐκ τοῦ δόματος. What a difficult and critical business this was is shown especially in the Const. Apostol. III. ; very instructive is also II. 25 (Text). : τὰ εἰσφερόμενα οἰκονομεῖτε ὀρφανοῖς καὶ χήραις καὶ θλιβομένοις καὶ ξένοις, ὡς ἔχοντες θεὸν λογιστευτὴν τούτων τὸν ἐγχειρίσαντα αὐτοῖς ταύτην τὴν οἰκονομίαν, πᾶσι δὲ τοῖς δεομένοις ἐπιμερίζοντες καὶ ὑμεῖς αὐτοὶ χρώμενοι ἐκ τῶν κυριακῶν, ἀλλὰ μὴ κατεσθίοντες αὐτὰ μόνοι. III. 35 : σὲ μὲν γὰρ διδόναι προσήκει, οἰκονομεῖν δὲ ἐκεῖνον. οὐ μέντοι λογιστεύσεις σου τὸν ἐπίσκοπον οὐδὲ παρατηρήσεις τὴν οἰκονομίαν αὐτοῦ, πῶς ἐπιτελεῖ ἢ πότε ἢ τίσιν ἢ ποῦ ἢ εἰ καλῶς ἢ φαύλως ἢ δεόντως. ἔχει γὰρ λογιστὴν κύριον τὸν θεόν. That it is not a question of fixed salaries is shown by the passage εἰς ὃ ἂν δέῃ.

23. προνοήσονται (see above). πλῆθους is the technical term for the congregation in opposition to the clergy; see, for example, 1 Clem. 54, 2 : ποιῶ τὰ προστασσόμενα ὑπὸ τοῦ πλήθους; Hermas, Mand. xi. ; Iren. in Eusebius, Hist. Eccl. v. 20, 6, etc.

24. εὐσταθήσῃ, κ.τ.λ. The congregation should behave quietly and noiselessly in divine service. According to the App. Const. II. 57, the deacons have to preserve order during divine service, see p. 85, 4: προνοίᾳ τῶν διακόνων εἰς τὸ ἕτερον μέρος οἱ λαϊκοὶ καθεζέσθωσαν μετὰ πάσης εὐταξίας καὶ ἡσυχίας. p. 86, 23 : ὁμοίως ὁ διάκονος ἐπισκοπείτω τὸν λαόν, ὅπως μή τις ψιθυρίσῃ ἢ νυστάξῃ ἢ γελάσῃ ἢ νεύσῃ). On εὐσταθήσῃ see 1 Clem. 61, 1 ; 65, 1 : εὐστάθεια.

πρῶτον μεμαθηκώς, κ.τ.λ. See 1 Tim. ii. 11 : Γυνὴ ἐν ἡσυχίᾳ μανθανέτω ἐν πάσῃ ὑποταγῇ.

25. εἰ δέ τις, κ.τ.λ. A special regulation for the case when one who has been admonished by a single presbyter is contumacious ; that is, that all the presbyters (those on the right with those on the left) shall come together, and as a body decree a disciplinary punishment.

26. νουθετούμενος. See 1 Thess. v. 12 : Ἐρωτῶμεν ὑμᾶς, ἀδελφοί, εἰδέναι τοὺς κοπιῶντας ἐν ὑμῖν καὶ προϊσταμένους ὑμῶν ἐν κυρίῳ καὶ νουθετοῦντας ὑμᾶς. v. 14 : νουθετεῖτε τοὺς ἀτάκτους. Tit. iii. 10 : αἱρετικὸν ἄνθρωπον μετὰ μίαν καὶ δευτέραν νουθεσίαν παραιτοῦ. αὐθάδως, see Tit. i. 7.

27. τὸ ἓν ποιήσαντες οἱ ἐπὶ τῷ θυσιαστηρίῳ. The οἱ ἐπὶ τῷ θυσιαστηρίῳ are of course the presbyters, that is, the presbyters on the right ; these shall

SOURCES OF THE APOSTOLIC CANONS

θυσιαστηρίῳ τὸν τοιοῦτον μετὰ ἴσης βουλῆς, ὃ ἂν ᾖ ἄξιον, δικασά-
30 τωσαν, ἵνα καὶ οἱ λοιποὶ φόβον ἔχωσι, μήποτε ἑνὸς πρόσωπον λά-
βωσι, καὶ ἐπὶ πλεῖον νεμηθῇ ὡς γάγγραινα, καὶ αἰχμαλωτισθῶσιν
οἱ πάντες.

ance, after it has first been proved in all submission. But if one who is admonished should answer rudely, those at the altar should unite (that is, with the presbyters on the left) and condemn such a one by a general resolution to the punishment deserved, so that the others may also be in awe, in order that they (the presbyters) look not at the person of any one, and that it may not spread as a cancer and be taken up by every one.

3. Ἀναγνώστης καθιστανέσθω (εἷς), πρῶτον δοκιμῇ δεδοκιμασμένος, μὴ γλωσσοκόπος,
μὴ μέθυσος μήτε γελωτολόγος,

3. For reader, one should be appointed, after he has been carefully proved; no babbler, nor drunkard, nor jester; of good

come together—with whom, the context says—with the presbyters on the left, and with them form a judicial assembly.

28. μετὰ ἴσης βουλῆς, 'with a universal unanimous resolution.' See ψῆφαι ἴσαι = equality of votes.

29. ὃ ἂν ᾖ ἄξιον, the apportioned punishment.

δικασάτωσαν. The presbyters are thus the judges. δικάζειν is here construed with the double accusative, for which elsewhere examples are not known to me. According to the Apostolic Constitutions II. 47 (text) the jurisdiction shall consist of the bishop, the presbyters, and the deacons.

30. ἵνα καί, κ.τ.λ. See 1 Tim. v. 20 : τοὺς ἁμαρτάνοντας ἐνώπιον πάντων ἔλεγχε, ἵνα καὶ οἱ λοιποὶ φόβον ἔχωσι.

31. μήποτε, κ.τ.λ. This sentence is not subordinated to the preceding (ἵνα, κ.τ.λ.), but co-ordinated. The juridical procedings commanded are, 1st, to impress fear on the others by its severity ; 2d, to render, by its manner of procedure, partiality impossible to the presbyters (see Διδαχή 4, 3 : κρινεῖς δικαίως, οὐ λήψῃ πρόσωπον ἐλέγξαι ἐπὶ παραπτώμασιν).

32. ἐπὶ πλεῖον νεμηθῇ, κ.τ.λ. See 2 Tim. ii. 17 : καὶ ὁ λόγος αὐτῶν ὡς γάγγραινα νομὴν ἕξει. Const. App. II. 41, p. 69, 7 : ἀλλ' ἐπεκτείνεται ἡ νομὴ καὶ προλαμβάνει πᾶσαν ἴασιν, ὡς ἡ γάγγραινα πᾶν μέλος σήπουσα.

33. αἰχμαλωτισθῶσιν. See 2 Tim. iii. 6 Ignat. ad Philad. 2, 2.

3. 1. ἀναγνώστης... εἷς. The reader is named before the deacons (see on this the excursus). That the editor has struck out an original εἷς is made probable by par. 1 n. 5.

2. δοκιμῇ δεδοκιμ. See par. 1, 4. The following list of the qualifications of the reader is unparalleled in old church literature.

3. γλωσσοκόπος is an ἀπ. λεγ.

4. μέθυσος. See par. 1.

γελωτολόγος is an ἀπ. λεγ. The connection in which these demands stand with the office of reader is to be observed.

5 εὔτροπος, εὐπειθής, εὐγνώμων, ἐν ταῖς κυριακαῖς συνόδοις πρῶτος σύνδρομος, εὐήκοος, διηγητικός, εἰδὼς ὅτι εὐαγγελιστοῦ τόπον ἐργάζεται, ὁ γὰρ ἐμπιπλῶν ὦτα μὴ

morals, submissive, of benevolent intentions, first in the assembly at the meetings on the Lord's day, of a plain utterance, and capable of clearly expounding,

5. εὐπειθής, εὐγνώμων refers probably to his behaviour to the bishop. See par. 2, l. 19 : προθυμουμένους.
6. ἐν ταῖς κυριακαῖς συνόδοις. The synods are the divine services. See App. Const. II. 57 p. 84, 17, where the bishop is thus addressed : μετ᾽ ἐπιστήμης πάσης κέλευε ποιεῖσθαι τὰς συνόδους. The expression αἱ κυριακαὶ σύνοδοι does not occur in the older literature ; compare κυριακὸν δεῖπνον (1 Cor. xi. 20), κυριακὴ ἡμέρα (Apoc. i. 10, etc.), κυριακὴ τοῦ κυρίου (Διδ. 14, 1), κυριακαὶ γραφαί (Dionys. of Corinth in Eusebius IV. 23, Clem. Alex., Tertull., App. Const. I.-VI. etc.), κυριακαὶ παιδεῖαι (Const. App. II. 6 (text). All these passages are, however, so far different that in this passage the κυριακός is to be translated probably not simply as 'belonging to the Lord,' but 'belonging to the Lord's day.' Similarly in the Const. App. II. 25, where τὰ κυριακά signify the gifts offered to the Lord.

πρῶτος σύνδρομος. He should be at his place first ; see Canon Hippol. 37 (Haneberg, p. 94) : 'Etiam Anagnostae habeant festiva indumenta et stent in ambone . . . donec totus populus congregetur.' Acts xxi. 30 : συνδρομή. Ignat. ad Philad. 2. 2 (ad. Polyc. 7. 2) : θεοδρόμος. (In the Mithras worship there were ἡλιοδρόμοι.) On his place in the church see App. Const. II. 57, p. 85, 7 : μέσος δὲ ὁ ἀναγνώστης ἐφ᾽ ὑψηλοῦ τινος ἑστὼς ἀναγινωσκέτω, and Canon Hippol. l. c.

7. εὐήκοος is here to be understood in the passive sense (see Passow s. h. v.) = 'he who is heard well'; in the other case it would have been identical with εὐπειθής (see above).

διηγητικός, 'skilful in relating (explaining).' Of the bishop it was said above δυνάμενος τὰς γραφὰς ἑρμηνεύειν. That is hardly anything else than διηγητικός. The reader should in the first place have a plain, loud delivery (εὐήκοος), and in the second place must be in a position to explain what has been read (διηγητικός).

8. εἰδὼς ὅτι εὐαγγελιστοῦ τόπον ἐργάζεται. ἐργάζεσθαι does not here probably mean 'working' or 'superintending,' but 'acquiring;' (see par. 6, τόπον ἑαυτοῖς περιποιοῦνται τὸν ποιμενικὸν). The reader gains for himself the rank of an evangelist. Still the εἰδὼς speaks more for the former signification. Εὐαγγελιστής (see my Prolegomena to the Διδαχή, p. 114) does not often occur in the literature of the ancient church. See Eph. iv. 11 : Χριστὸς ἔδωκεν τοὺς μὲν ἀποστόλους, τοὺς δὲ προφήτας, τοὺς δὲ εὐαγγελιστάς, τοὺς δὲ ποιμένας καὶ διδασκάλους, Acts xxi. 8 : Φίλιππος ὁ εὐαγγελιστής, 2 Tim. iv. 5 : ἔργον ποίησον εὐαγγελιστοῦ, Tertull., de Praescr. 4, Orig. c. Cels. III. 9, Euseb., H.E. iii. 37 ; V. 10, 2. The reader's office is very highly valued, when it is advanced to the office of an evangelist.

9. ἐμπιπλῶν. See Romans xv. 24 : ἐὰν ὑμῶν πρῶτον ἀπὸ μέρους ἐμπλησθῶ, Acts xiv. 17.

μὴ νοοῦντος. See 1 Tim. i. 7. The whole sentence shows that the reader has in some circumstances also to explain what has been spoken, which follows from the διηγητικός : for this cannot mean only good delivery in reading.

SOURCES OF THE APOSTOLIC CANONS 17

νοοῦντος ἔγγραφος λογισθήσεται παρὰ τῷ θεῷ.

mindful that he rules in the place of an evangelist: for whoever fills the ear of the ignorant will be accounted as having his name written with God.

4. Διάκονοι καθιστανέσθωσαν (τρεῖς), γέγραπται (γάρ)· ἐπὶ τριῶν σταθήσεται πᾶν ῥῆμα. ἔστωσαν δεδοκιμασμένοι πάσῃ διακονίᾳ, μεμαρτυρημένοι παρὰ τοῦ πλήθους,

4. There shall be three deacons appointed, for it stands written, 'By three shall every matter be established.' They shall be approved in every service, with a

11. ἔγγραφος, κ.τ.λ. See 1 Clem. 45, 8 : ἔγγραφοι ἐγένοντο ἀπὸ τοῦ θεοῦ ἐν τῷ μνημοσύνῳ αὐτοῦ : Herm., Sim. v. 3 ; Clem. Alex., de div. serv. 21. The oriental versions (see Lagarde in Bunsen's Analecta Antenic. II. p. 458) give ὁ γὰρ ἐμπιπλῶν ὦτα ἑτέρων, μᾶλλον προσήκει αὐτῷ εἶναι ἐργάτην πιστὸν παρὰ τῷ θεῷ.

4. 2. τρεῖς. See the Prolegomena. Lagarde (also in other places) has completed the sense of καθιστανέσθωσαν by τριῶν μαρτυρούντων τῷ βίῳ αὐτῶν. But a number is expected, as in par. 2, 3, 5. In Const. App. III. 19 (Text) it is simply demanded that the number of the deacons shall be in proportion to the size of the congregation. However, in the 14th Canon of the Synod of Neo-Caesarea (Routh l. c. IV. p. 185) we read : Διάκονοι ἑπτὰ ὀφείλουσιν εἶναι κατὰ τὸν κανόνα, κἂν πάνυ μεγάλη ἡ πόλις· πεισθήσῃ δὲ ἀπὸ τῆς βίβλου τῶν πράξεων. According to Sozom. VII. 19, it is a special peculiarity of the Roman church that in it there are always only seven deacons.

2. γέγραπται, κ.τ.λ. The passage Deut. xix. 15 runs : ἐπὶ στόματος δύο μαρτύρων καὶ ἐπὶ στόματος τριῶν μαρτύρων στήσεται πᾶν ῥῆμα. Matt. xviii. 16 : ἐπὶ στόματος δύο μαρτύρων ἢ τριῶν σταθῇ πᾶν ῥῆμα. 2 Cor. xiii. 1 : ἐπὶ στόματος δύο μαρτύρων καὶ τριῶν σταθήσεται πᾶν ῥῆμα. Thus the κυρίου which the manuscript has after ῥῆμα, though the oriental versions do not have it, is found nowhere else ; the σταθήσεται only in St. Paul. Still we have no right to assume that the author in using γέγραπται was thinking of St. Paul's epistle, for he certainly had in his mind Deut. xix. 15. The deacons have to act as inquiry officers ; on that account they should be three, in order to be able to lay before the disciplinary judgment of the presbyters a valid witness. Here, therefore, ῥῆμα is to be taken in the sense of 'affair,' 'dealing.' Hence the κυρίου which the Greek manuscript offers us is indefensible. According to 1 Tim. v. 19 two or three witnesses are necessary to raise an accusation against a presbyter. But of this there is no question here.

4. δεδοκιμασμένοι, κ.τ.λ. See par. 1, 3 ; 1 Tim. iii. 10 : δοκιμαζέσθωσαν πρῶτον εἶτα διακονείτωσαν. In this passage, however, it is expressly commanded that they must be experienced in every service before they are appointed.

5. μεμαρτυρημένοι, κ.τ.λ. The deacon does not require, like the bishop, a good witness ἀπὸ τῶν ἔξω, but only from the congregation. 3 John 12 : Δημητρίῳ μεμαρτύρηται ὑπὸ πάντων. 1 Clem. 44, 3 : (ἐπισκόπους καὶ διακόνους) μεμαρτυρημένοι πολλοῖς χρόνοις ὑπὸ πάντων : 47, 4. Const. App. II. 1 p. 14, 12. Tertull. Apolog. 39 : 'Seniores... honorem non pretio, sed testimonio adepti.'

πλήθους. See par. 2.

B

μονόγαμοι, τεκνοτρόφοι, σώφρονες, good testimony from the congre-
έπιεικεῖς, ἥσυχοι, μὴ γόγγυσοι, gation, husband of one wife, edu-
μὴ δίγλωσσοι, μὴ ὀργίλοι, μὴ cating their children, honourable,
πρόσωπον πλουσίου λαμβάνοντες, gentle, quiet, not murmuring, not
10 μηδὴ πένητα καταδυναστεύοντες, double-tongued, not quickly an-
μηδὲ οἴνῳ πολλῷ χρώμενοι, εὔ- gry, not looking on the person of
σκυλτοι, τῶν κρυφίων ἔργων καλοὶ the rich, also not oppressing the
προτρεπτικοί, ἐπαναγκάζοντες τοὺς poor, also not given to much wine,
ἔχοντας τῶν ἀδελφῶν ἁπλοῦν τὰς intelligent, encouraging well to
15 χεῖρας, καὶ αὐτοὶ εὐμετάδοτοι, secret works (viz., alms-giving),

6. μονόγαμοι. See par. 1 ; 1 Tim. iii. 12 : διάκονοι ἔστωσαν μιᾶς γυναικὸς ἄνδρες. Const. App. II. 2 p. 15, 10 : μονόγαμος, of the bishop (the word is also in Methodius, Conviv.). According to our author the presbyters must completely abstain from women ; the bishop *is permitted* once to be married, but it is considered desirable that he should be without a wife ; the deacons should (at most) be married once.

τεκνοτρόφοι. See 1 Tim. iii. 12 : τέκνων καλῶς προϊστάμενοι.
σώφρονες. See par. 1. It is to be observed that on the whole the qualities especially required for the deacons are much more nearly related to those which are required for bishops, than they are to presbyters' qualities.

7. ἐπιεικεῖς. See 1 Tim. iii. 3, of the bishop.
μὴ γόγγυσοι. See my note to the Διδαχή 3, 6.

8. μὴ δίγλωσσοι. See Διδ. 2, 4 (Barn. 19, 7).
μὴ ὀργίλοι. See Tit. i. 7 (of the bishop). The following words in the text of the Apostolic Church Order, ὀργὴ γὰρ ἀπόλλυσιν ἄνδρα φρόνιμον (see Prov. xv. 1), I have omitted. See Prolegomena.

μὴ πρόσωπον, κ.τ.λ. See § 1. 6. 2 ; Const. App. II. 5 p. 16, 16 : ἔστω ὁ ἐπίσκοπος ἀπροσωπόληπτος, μήτε πλούσιον ἐντρεπόμενος . . . μήτε πένητα παρορῶν ἢ καταδυναστεύων. James ii. 1 follg. Διδ. 5, 2 : ἀποστρεφόμενοι τὸν ἐνδεόμενον, καταπονοῦντες τὸν θλιβόμενον, πλουσίων παράκλητοι, πενήτων ἄνομοι κριταί.

10. καταδυναστεύοντες. See James ii. 6 : οἱ πλούσιοι καταδυναστεύουσιν ὑμῶν ; Const. App. *l. c.*

11. μηδὲ οἴνῳ, κ.τ.λ. See par. 5 ; 1 Tim. iii. 8 : μὴ οἴνῳ πολλῷ προσέχοντας (of the deacons); in connection with our passage the words are strange.

εὔσκυλτοι. See Const. App. II. 3 p. 15, 27 : εὐδιάκονος, εὔσκυλτος. Const. App. III. 15, p. 110, 3 : διακόνους . . . εἰς τὰς τῆς διακονίας χρείας εὐσκύλτους. III. 19 p. 111, 20 : διάκονοι . . . εὐσκυλτότεροι τοῦ ἐπισκόπου ; 113, 15. The word is extremely rare ; it might be translated by 'intelligent,' 'polished.'

12. τῶν κρυφίων, κ.τ.λ. Alms are meant. See Matt. vi. 3, 4. Still here such kinds of assistance may be more particularly intended as in a special manner must remain secret. See Canon. Hippol. arab. 5 : 'In like manner shall they be at the service of those other men, who *secretly* languish in penury.'

13. τοὺς ἔχοντας. ἔχοντας here as in James iv. 2.

14. ἁπλοῦν, 'to open'—thus used in the later Greek.

15. εὐμετάδοτοι. See par. 2. They should not only encourage gifts but give themselves. 1 Tim. vi. 18 : εὐμεταδότους εἶναι, κοινωνικούς.

SOURCES OF THE APOSTOLIC CANONS 19

κοινωνικοί, πάσῃ τιμῇ καὶ ἐντροπῇ καὶ φόβῳ τιμώμενοι ἀπὸ τοῦ πλήθους, ἐπιμελῶς προσέχοντες τοῖς ἀτάκτως περιπατοῦσιν, οὓς
20 μὲν νουθετοῦντες, οὓς δὲ παρακαλοῦντες, οὓς δὲ ἐπιτιμῶντες, τοὺς δὲ καταφρονοῦντας τελέως παραπεμπόμενοι, εἰδότες ὅτι οἱ ἀντίλογοι καὶ καταφρονηταὶ καὶ
25 λοίδοροι Χριστῷ ἀντετάξαντο.

while they compel those among the brethren who have much to open their hands, also themselves generous, communicative, honoured with all honour and esteem and fear by the congregation, carefully giving heed to those who walk disorderly, warning the one, exhorting the other, threatening the third, but leaving the scoffers completely to themselves; mindful of this: that the gainsayers, and scoffers and defamers have resisted Christ.

5. Χῆραι καθιστανέσθωσαν τρεῖς, αἱ δύο προσμένουσαι τῇ προσευχῇ περὶ πάντων τῶν ἐν

5. Three widows shall be appointed, two to persevere in prayer for all those who are

16. τιμῇ ... τιμώμενοι. See Acts xxviii. 10 : πολλαῖς τιμαῖς ἐτίμησαν ἡμᾶς.
17. τιμώμενοι. See Διδ. 15, 2. The bishops and deacons are shown as the τετιμημένοι of the congregation.
19. ἀτάκτως, κ.τ.λ. See 2 Thess. iii. 6 : ἀδελφοῦ ἀτάκτως περιπατοῦντος ; iii. 11. 1 Thess. v. 14 : νουθετεῖτε τοὺς ἀτάκτους.—οὓς μὲν, κ.τ.λ. See 1 Thess. l. c. ; 2 Tim. iv. 2 : ἔλεγξον, ἐπιτίμησον, παρακάλεσον (Διδ. 2, 7). Const. App. III. 7 p. 104, 17 : ἐπιτιμάσθω ὡς προπετής.
22. τελέως παραπεμπόμενοι. See par. 6. There is of course no question here of excommunication on the part of the deacons. They are to leave the scoffers completely to themselves ; what further is to be done with them is not said. Yet the duties of the deacons, as appointed here, are comprehensive to a degree not found in a later period. In App. Const. II. 44 it is said : πάντα μὲν ὁ διάκονος τῷ ἐπισκόπῳ ἀναφερέτω ὡς ὁ Χριστὸς τῷ πατρί, ἀλλ' ὅσα δύναται εὐθυνέτω δι' ἑαυτοῦ, τὰ δὲ ἄλλα ὁ ἐπίσκοπος κρινέτω.
24. καταφρονηταί. See Acts xiii. 14.
25. λοίδοροι. See par. 1.
ἀντετάξαντο is opposed to the συντάσσειν, which takes place at baptism.

5. 1. Χῆραι. See 1 Tim. v. 3-16, and the commentary of Holtzmann upon it. Ignat. ad Smyrn. 13 : ἀσπάζομαι τὰς παρθένους τὰς λεγομένας χήρας, and the commentaries thereon by Zahn and Lightfoot, as well as Zahn's *Ignatius von Antioch*, p 334 f., 580 f. ; Clem. Strom. VII. 12, p. 875 ; Orig. Hom. 17 in Luc. Opp. III. p. 953 ; Tertullian de Pud. 13 ; de Virg. Vel. 9 ; de Praescript. 3 ; Dieckhoff, *Die Diakonissen d. alten Kirche* (Monatsch. f. Diakonie), I. 1877, pp. 289 and fol., 348 and fol., 394 and fol.
2. τρεῖς. Thus as many widows as deacons.
προσμένουσαι. See 1 Tim. v. 5 : χήρα προσμένει ταῖς δεήσεσιν καὶ ταῖς προσευχαῖς : Polyc. Ep. 4, 3.
3. περὶ πάντων τῶν ἐν πείρᾳ. They have thus to take to their heart all

20   SOURCES OF THE APOSTOLIC CANONS

πείρᾳ καὶ πρὸς τὰς ἀποκαλύψεις in temptation, and for the re-
5 περὶ οὗ ἂν δέῃ, μία δὲ παρεδρεύ- ception of revelations where such
ουσα ταῖς ἐν ταῖς νόσοις πει- are necessary, but one to assist
ραζομέναις εὐδιάκονος ᾖ, νηπ- the women visited with sick-
τική,τὰ δέοντα ἀπαγγέλλουσα τοῖς nesses, she must be ready for
πρεσβυτέροις, μὴ αἰσχροκερδής, service, discreet, communicating

suffering members of the congregation and bring their necessity in prayer before God. Const. App. III. 5: μηδὲν ἕτερον τῇ χήρᾳ μελέτω εἰ μὴ τὸ προσεύχεσθαι ὑπὲρ τῶν διδόντων καὶ ὑπὲρ ὅλης τῆς ἐκκλησίας. The widow as the intercessor for the congregation appears also in III. 7. In the Canones Hippolyti (§ 9) it says : 'Viduis propter copiosas precationes, infirmorum curam et frequens ieiunium praecipuus honor tribuatur' (Haneberg's edition, Munich, 1870, p. 69).

4. ἀποκαλύψεις. These can refer neither to the actual unveiling of women (say at baptism) nor to the 'confidential communications of helpless women' (Bickell), but purely to 'revelations from God.' It was expected of these widows that they would receive at their constant prayers special communications in relation to the necessities of the members of the congregation. Prayer (especially with fasting) and revelation belong closely together ; for example Acts xiii. 2 : λειτουργούντων δὲ αὐτῶν τῷ κυρίῳ καὶ νηστευόντων εἶπεν τὸ πνεῦμα τὸ ἅγιον (see Murat. Fragm. sub ev. Joh., but especially Tertullian de ieiun. 12, Passio Perpet. iv. 7). But a *charisma* of the widows is of course presupposed. On the power of prayer see James v. 13-18. In the App. Const. there is nothing to be found in relation to widows that is comparable to this passage ; even the double division is absent.

5. περὶ οὗ ἂν δέῃ. See par. 2. οὗ is perhaps not to be taken as neuter here.

μία δέ, κ.τ.λ. Thus only one of the three widows is deaconess of the congregation in the strict sense of the word, and even then only for the female members of the congregation. To this one alone do the following requirements relate.

7. εὐδιάκονος. See Const. App. II. 3, p. 15, 27.

νηπτική. See the description in 1 Tim. v. 3 and follg.

8. τὰ δέοντα, κ.τ.λ. It is not a question of the bishop, but of the presbyters, notwithstanding that the existence of a bishop in the congregations is presumed. The presbyters appear as the προεστῶτες. They are the highest court ; to them therefore are the necessary communications to be made. This is of the utmost importance for the relations of the constituent parts (see par. 3). Polyc. ad Philipp. 6, 1 is, perhaps, to be compared : οἱ πρεσβύτεροι . . . ἐπισκεπτόμενοι πάντας ἀσθενεῖς, and James v. 14: ἀσθενεῖ τις ἐν ὑμῖν ; προσκαλεσάσθω τοὺς πρεσβυτέρους τῆς ἐκκλησίας, and the Shepherd s. v. πρεσβύτεροι. It is very instructive that in the Syriac text of the Apostolic Constitutions III. 7 we have σεμνὰς δεῖ εἶναι τὰς χήρας, πειθομένας τοῖς ἐπισκόποις καὶ διακόνοις, but in the re-editing (l. c. p. 104, 11), πειθομένας τοῖς ἐπισκόποις, τοῖς πρεσβυτέροις καὶ τοῖς διακόνοις, ἔτι μὴν καὶ ταῖς διακόναις. III. 19, p. 113, 13 : περὶ τῶν θλιβομένων ἀναγγέλλετε τῷ ἐπισκόπῳ ὑμῶν. Canon Hippol. arab. 5 : 'The deacon shall inform the bishop about the sick among the people whom nobody assists.'

9. αἰσχροκερδής. See 1 Tim. iii. 8. Thus the widow also, as well as the deacons, stood by reason of her office in danger of falling into avarice.

SOURCES OF THE APOSTOLIC CANONS 21

10 μὴ οἴνῳ πολλῷ προσέχουσα, ἵνα
δύνηται νήφειν πρὸς τὰς νυκτερινὰς ὑπηρεσίας καὶ εἴ τις ἕτερα
βούλοιτο ἐργαγαθεῖν. καὶ γὰρ
ταῦτα πρῶτα κυρίου θησαυρίσματά
15 εἰσιν ἀγαθά.

what is necessary to the presbyters, not avaricious, not given to much love of wine, so that she may be sober and capable of performing the night services, and other loving service if she will ; for these are the chief good treasures of the Lord.

B.—(APOSTOLIC CHURCH ORDER, Chapters 22-28.)

6. . . . Διάκονοι ἐργάται τῶν
καλῶν ἔργων, νυχθήμερον ἐπιλεύσσοντες πανταχοῦ, μήτε πένητα
ὑπεροπτεύοντες μήτε πλούσιον

6. . . . The deacons, doers of good works, searching about everywhere day and night, neither despising the poor nor re-

10. μὴ οἴνῳ, κ.τ.λ. See par. 4, 1 Tim. iii. 8 ; Tit. ii. 4.
ἵνα, κ.τ.λ. Too much love of wine would hinder the widows while watching by night by the side of the sick, and hinder them from any energetic activity. For the form of the sentence, see Const. App. II. 5, p. 16, 22, regarding the bishop : ἵνα δυνηθῇ νήφειν πρὸς τὸ νουθετεῖν.
12. ἕτερα βούλοιτο ἐργαγαθεῖν. See 1 Tim. v. 10 : χήρα καταλεγέσθω . . . εἰ παντὶ ἔργῳ ἀγαθῷ ἐπηκολούθησεν. 1 Tim. vi. 18 : ἀγαθοεργεῖν. The word ἐργαγαθεῖν is, I believe, very rare.
14. ταῦτα, that is, such helpful services.
πρῶτα, that is, the foremost.
θησαυρίσματα. The passage in Matthew vi. 19, 20 probably occurred to the author.

6. 1. Here begins a new piece. Par. 6 is partly identical with par. 4, although from another pen, as the different form also shows.
ἐργάται. See 2 Cor. xi. 13 : ἐργάται δόλιοι ; 2 Tim. ii. 15 : σπούδασον σεαυτὸν δόκιμον παραστῆσαι τῷ θεῷ, ἐργάτην ἀνεπαίσχυντον. Const. Apost. III. 19, p. 113, 7 : ἐργάται ἀληθείας. In the Gospel of the Egyptians (see 2 Clem. ad Cor. 4, 2) : ἐργάται ἀνομίας (see Justin. Apol. i. 16). Luke xiii. 27 : ἐργάται ἀδικίας.
τῶν καλῶν ἔργων. See 1. 9 : ἔργα ἀγαθά. The expression ἔργα καλά (ἀγαθά) is found fourteen times in the Pastoral Epistles.
2. νυχθήμερον. See 2 Cor. xi. 25.
ἐπιλεύσσοντες. The manuscript gives ἐπελεύσοντες ; but this is no word at all ; hence M. Schmidt has also conjectured ἐπιλεύσοντες ; still better would be the present ἐπιλεύσσοντες = ' looking forward '; still the conjecture is by no means certain, for ἐπιλεύσσειν is solely found in Homer. Besides, νυχθήμερον is a very rare word. The sense of the corrupt passage is not doubtful in general ; the deacons should make themselves personally acquainted with the circumstances of the congregation ; see Hom. Clem. iii. 67.
3. μήτε πένητα, κ.τ.λ. See the parallel case in par. 4.
4. ὑπεροπτεύοντες. Comp. Acts vi. 1, παραθεωρεῖν.

5 προσωπολημπτοῦντες ἐπιγνώσονται   garding the person of the rich,
τὸν θλιβόμενον καὶ ἐκ τῆς λογίας   shall acknowledge the oppressed,
οὐ παραπέμψονται, ἐπαναγκάσουσι   and not exclude him from a share
δὲ τοὺς δυναμένους ἀποθησαυ-   in the collections of the congrega-
ρίζειν εἰς ἔργα ἀγαθά, προορῶντας   tion, but compel those having
10 τοὺς λόγους τοῦ διδασκάλου ἡμῶν·   possessions to lay up for good

5. προσωπολημπτοῦντες. See par. 1, 2, 4; James ii. 9 : εἰ δὲ προσωπολημπτεῖτε. ἐπιγνώσονται. The word is used as in 1 Cor. xvi. 18.
6. θλιβόμενον. 1 Tim. v. 10 : εἰ θλιβομένοις ἐπήρκεσεν. Ignat. ad Smyrn. 6, 2 : οὐ μέλει αὐτοῖς, οὐ περὶ χήρας, οὐ περὶ ὀρφανοῦ, οὐ περὶ θλιβομένου. Const. App. III. 4, p. 98, 18, and elsewhere.
ἐκ τῆς λογίας. See 1 Cor. xvi. 1 : περὶ τῆς λογίας τῆς εἰς τοὺς ἁγίους : v. 2 : μὴ ὅταν ἔλθω, τότε λογίαι γίνωνται. See Heinrici on this passage: 'Phavorinus: λογία· ἡ συλλογὴ παρὰ τῷ ἀποστόλῳ καὶ τὸ ἐκ πολλῶν συνεισφερόμενον· λέγει δὲ τὴν ἐλεημοσύνην. The word is unknown in classical Greek in this meaning, and also in the Septuagint.' The deacons are to exclude no needy sufferer from the distribution (the collection of the congregation). On these λογία, see Tertull. Apolog. 39 : 'Etiam si quod arcae genus est, non de honoraria summa quasi redemptae religionis congregatur. Modicam unusquisque stipem menstrua die, vel cum velit, et si modo velit, et si modo possit, apponit; nam nemo compellitur, sed sponte confert. Haec quasi deposita pietatis sunt. Nam inde non epulis nec potaculis nec ingratiis voratrinis dispensatur, sed egenis alendis humandisque. etc.'; de ieiun. 13 : 'non dico de industria stipium conferendarum.'—Münter, Primordia eccl. Afric. p. 63 sq. Our passage belongs to the very few in which (that is, in documents of the first three centuries) there is a question of a congregational collection. It appears here as if the deacons had, in the division of the relief, been able to act with a certain independence.
7. ἐπαναγκάσουσι, κ.τ.λ. See par. 4 : ἐπαναγκάζοντες τοὺς ἔχοντας, κ.τ.λ.
8. δυναμένους = 'those who have possessions,' ἀποθησαυρίζειν. See 1 Tim. vi. 17 f. : τοῖς πλουσίοις . . . παράγγελλε . . . ἀγαθοεργεῖν, πλουτεῖν ἐν ἔργοις καλοῖς . . . ἀποθησαυρίζοντας ἑαυτοῖς θεμέλιον καλόν.
9. προορῶντας. The author has chosen this word, because he was dealing with a word of our Lord which would have its fulfilment at the last judgment. The word of the Lord is thus introduced, as in 1 Clem. 13, 1 : μάλιστα μεμνημένοι τῶν λόγων τοῦ κυρίου Ἰησοῦ, οὓς ἐλάλησεν διδάσκων ἐπιεικείαν καὶ μακροθυμίαν, οὕτως γὰρ εἶπεν· Ἐλεᾶτε ἵνα ἐλεηθῆτε, κ.τ.λ. 46, 7 : μνήσθητε τῶν λόγων Ἰησοῦ τοῦ κυρίου ἡμῶν, εἶπεν γάρ· Οὐαὶ τῷ ἀνθρώπῳ, κ.τ.λ. ; in Acts· xx. 35 : μνημονεύειν τῶν λόγων τοῦ κυρίου Ἰησοῦ, ὅτι εἶπεν, κ.τ.λ. ; in Polycarp, ep. 2 : μνημονεύοντες δὲ ὧν εἶπεν ὁ κύριος διδάσκων· μὴ κρίνετε, κ.τ.λ., and in the Διδαχή (9, 5). This is the oldest formula in quoting the words of the Lord.
10. διδασκάλου. See par. 8. This designation for Jesus (apart from the Gospels) is wanting in Apostolic literature, and is very rare in that of post-apostolic times. It is commoner with the apologists; for this see the text of the App. Const. B. III. 6 : αὐτὸς ὁ διδάσκαλος ἡμῶν καὶ κύριος. III. 7 : ὁ κύριος καὶ διδάσκαλος ἡμῶν εἶπεν. III. 19 ; II. 20, V. 12, Methodius.

SOURCES OF THE APOSTOLIC CANONS 23

εἴδετέ με πεινῶντα καὶ οὐκ ἐθρέψατέ
με. οἱ γὰρ καλῶς διακονήσαντες
καὶ ἀμέμπτως τόπον ἑαυτοῖς περιποιοῦνται τὸν ποιμενικόν.

works, in consideration of the words of our teacher: 'Ye saw me hungry, and did not feed me'; for those who have been deacons of good report and blameless purchase to themselves the pastorate.

7. Ὁ λαϊκὸς τοῖς λαϊκοῖς
πράγμασι περιπειθέσθω ὑποτασσόμενος τοῖς παρεδρεύουσι τῷ
θυσιαστηρίῳ. ἕκαστος ἐν τῷ ἰδίῳ

Let the layman confine himself to the work of the laity, yielding obedience to those who sit at the altar. Let every one please

11. εἴδετέ με. See Matt. xxv. 37 (πότε σε εἴδαμεν πεινῶντα καὶ ἐθρέψαμεν) not quoted quite literally (see xxv. 42). Compare the similar quotation in Const. App. V. 1, p. 124, 24.

12. οἱ γὰρ καλῶς διακονήσαντες. See 1 Tim. iii. 13: οἱ γὰρ καλῶς διακονήσαντες βαθμὸν ἑαυτοῖς καλὸν περιποιοῦνται. With this passage seems to be blended 1 Clem. 44, 3, 5: λειτουργήσαντας ἀμέμπτως.

13. τόπον . . . ποιμενικόν. Thus is the bishop's office placed in view of the deserving deacons (on ποίμην as equivalent to ἐπίσκοπος, see par. 2). This is an extremely important notice; for it affords direct evidence of a proceeding at which we otherwise could only guess. See my *Analecten* to Hatch's *Gesellschaftsverfass.*, p. 246, and fol. The deserving deacons had the prospect of attaining to the bishopric. Nothing is said about their gaining the rank of presbyters.

7. 1. Ὁ λαϊκός, κ.τ.λ. See 1 Clem. 40, 5: ὁ λαϊκὸς ἄνθρωπος τοῖς λαϊκοῖς προστάγμασιν δέδεται. Also Clem. Hom. (ep. Clem. ad Jacob. 5, p. 7, 38, ed. Lagarde): οὗτος ἑκάστῳ λαϊκῷ ἁμαρτία ἐστίν. Clem. Alex. Strom. III. 12, p. 552: κἂν πρεσβύτερος ᾖ κἂν διάκονος κἂν λαϊκός. V. 6, p. 665: κώλυμα λαϊκῆς ἀπιστίας. Euseb. Hist. Ecc. V. 28, 12. Frequent in Tertullian; for example, de Bapt. 17, de Fuga, 17, de Praescr. 41; also very frequent in the App. Const.

2. περιπειθέσθω. Thus has Lagarde conjectured (the manuscript has περιποιθέσθω); even this word is unusual: 'let the layman confine himself to the work of the laity.'

ὑποτασσόμενος. Thus obedience to the priests is demanded. The expression οἱ παρεδρ. τ. θυσ. arises perhaps from 1 Cor. ix. 13: οἱ τῷ θυσιαστηρίῳ παρεδρεύοντες. The clergy are thereby designated as the priesthood (see 1 Clem. 40 fol., especially c. 41, 2): παρεδρεύειν, also par. 5; on θυσιαστήριον, see par. 2.

4. ἕκαστος, κ.τ.λ. See 1 Clem. 41, 1: ἕκαστος ἡμῶν ἐν τῷ ἰδίῳ τάγματι εὐαρεστείτω (thus the Cod. Constant. and the Syriac; the Alexandrine has εὐχαριστείτω) θεῷ, μὴ παρεκβαίνων τὸν ὡρισμένον τῆς λειτουργίας αὐτοῦ κανόνα. This passage follows in the Epistle of Clement immediately after the above quoted c. 40, 5 (ὁ λαϊκός, κ.τ.λ.); see also in the same beginning: τῷ γὰρ ἀρχιερεῖ ἴδιαι λειτουργίαι δεδομέναι εἰσίν, καὶ τοῖς ἱερεῦσιν ἴδιος ὁ τόπος προστέτακται. Thus our author has read the epistle, and consequently decides for us also the disputed passage of the Epistle of Clement. εὐαρεστείτω was

5 τόπῳ ἀρεσκέτω τῷ θεῷ, μὴ φιλεχ-   God in the place appointed to him,
θροῦντες ἀλλήλοις περὶ τῶν   not striving against one another
τεταγμένων, ἕκαστος ἐν ᾧ ἐκλήθη   in respect of what is commanded
(ἐν τούτῳ μενέτω [θεέτω]) παρὰ   (in relation to their calling and
τῷ θεῷ. ὁ ἕτερος τοῦ ἑτέρου τὸν   rank, by God). Every one shall
10 δρόμον μὴ παρατεμνέτω. οὐδὲ   (remain ? or run ?) in the path in
γὰρ οἱ ἄγγελοι παρὰ τὸ δια-   which he is called according to
τεταγμένον αὐτοῖς οὐδὲν ἕτερον   God's will, and no one shall ob-
ἐξελίσσουσιν.   struct the course of another, for
the angels also do nothing but
what is commanded them.

8. ... εὔχρηστον ταῖς γυναιξὶ   **8.** ... It is profitable to order

written by Clement. Clement gives '*ἐν τῷ ἰδίῳ τάγματι*,' while our author has '*ἐν τῷ ἰδίῳ τόπῳ*' (the *ἐν* is my conjecture); but he has immediately after it '*τὰ τεταγμένα*,' and the '*τόπος*' comes also from the Epistle of Clement (see above).

5. μὴ φιλεχθροῦντες, κ.τ.λ. See 1 Clem. 41, 3: οἱ οὖν παρὰ τὸ καθῆκον τῆς βουλήσεως τοῦ θεοῦ ποιοῦντές τι, c. 44, 1: οἱ ἀπόστολοι ἡμῶν ἔγνωσαν, ὅτι ἔρις ἔσται ἐπὶ τοῦ ὀνόματος τῆς ἐπισκοπῆς.

6. τῶν τεταγμένων. What is commanded in relation to calling and rank (by God); see the common use of τάσσειν, διατάσσειν, ἐπιτάσσειν, ὑποτάσσειν, τάγμα, τάξις in the first Epistle of Clement.

7. ἕκαστος, κ.τ.λ. See 1 Cor. vii. 24: ἕκαστος ἐν ᾧ ἐκλήθη, ἐν τούτῳ μενέτω παρὰ θεῷ. It is to be supposed that in the MS. in our passage ἐν τούτῳ μενέτω has fallen out after ἐκλήθη. To such omission seems to point also the παρὰ τῷ θεῷ, for otherwise we should expect παρὰ τοῦ θεοῦ. It is possible also, according to the Oriental versions ('currat unusquisque prout datum est ei a domino') that θεέτω has fallen out after θεῷ, for—1st, beside the θεῷ it might easily disappear; 2nd, in the following sentence a 'course' is spoken of. See 2 Clem. 7, 3: ὥστε θέωμεν τὴν ὁδὸν τὴν εὐθεῖαν, and see also Lightfoot in his Commentary (p. 453) on this passage, on τρέχειν as well as on θέειν. But even if we suppose that θεέτω has fallen out, the παρὰ τῷ θεῷ still offers some difficulties. For the description see also 1 Cor. ix. 24 and follg.

9. τὸν δρόμον μὴ παρατεμνέτω. A warning not to press forward ambitiously to influential places, and obstruct the promotion of others; the antithesis is in Rom. xii. 10: τῇ τιμῇ ἀλλήλους προηγούμενοι (see the Exhortations of Hermas); for δρόμος see Acts, xiii. 25, xx. 24, 2 Thess. iv. 7; 1 Clem. 6, 2: ἐπὶ τὸν τῆς πίστεως βέβαιον δρόμον κατήντησαν. Ignat. ad Polyc. 1, 2: προσθεῖναι τῷ δρόμῳ σου.

10. οὐδὲ γὰρ ἄγγελοι, κ.τ.λ. This concluding sentence also points to a dependence on the first Epistle of Clement; see c. 34, 5: κατανοήσομεν τὸ πᾶν πλῆθος τῶν ἀγγέλων αὐτοῦ, πῶς τῷ θελήματι αὐτοῦ λειτουργοῦσιν παρεστῶτες; c. 20, 3: ἥλιός τε καὶ σελήνη ἀστέρων τε χοροὶ κατὰ τὴν διαταγὴν αὐτοῦ ἐν ὁμονοίᾳ δίχα πάσης παρεκβάσεως ἐξελίσσουσιν (see Lightfoot on this passage) τοὺς ἐπιτεταγμένους αὐτοῖς ὁρισμούς. For διατεταγμένον see 1 Clem. 37, 2.

8. 1. εὔχρηστον. See 2 Tim. iv. 11: ἔστι γάρ μοι εὔχρηστος εἰς διακονίαν (see c. ii. 21, Philemon 11).

SOURCES OF THE APOSTOLIC CANONS 25

διακονίαν καταστῆσαι. . . . ὅτε	a service from the women. . . .
ᾔτησεν ὁ διδάσκαλος τὸν ἄρτον	When the master asked for the
καὶ τὸ ποτήριον καὶ ηὐλόγησεν	bread and the cup and blessed
5 αὐτὰ λέγων· τοῦτό ἐστι τὸ σῶμά	them with the words 'This is my
μου καὶ τὸ αἷμα, οὐκ ἐπέτρεψε	Body and Blood,' he did not grant
ταύταις συστῆναι ἡμῖν—Μάρθα	to them (the women) to stand

3. ὅτε ᾔτησεν, κ.τ.λ. Here begins the apocryphal evangelical fragment. There is no parallel in the canonical gospels to the ᾔτησεν.

διδάσκαλος. Of Jesus, see par. 6 and below: ὅτε ἐδίδασκεν.

4. ποτήριον. Thus it is called in Matt. xxvi. 27, also with its parallel in 1 Cor. x. 11.

ηὐλόγησεν. See Matt. xxvi. 26 with parallel passages.

5. τοῦτό ἐστιν, κ.τ.λ. See Matt. xxvi. 27, 28, but the words are brought close together in the text.

6. ἐπέτρεψε. See 1 Tim. ii. 12 : γυναικὶ δὲ διδάσκειν οὐκ ἐπιτρέπω. 1 Cor. xiv. 34 : οὐ γὰρ ἐπιτέτραπται αὐταῖς λαλεῖν. Apoc. ii. 20 : 'Ιεζάβελ, ἡ λέγουσα ἑαυτὴν προφῆτιν καὶ διδάσκει, κ.τ.λ.

7. συστῆναι. Here in the literal sense; see Luke ix. 32 : εἶδαν τοὺς δύο ἄνδρας τοὺς συνεστῶτας αὐτῷ. What is meant is the standing at the altar for the purpose of blessing and distributing the sacred food. On this point see Const. App. III. 9, p. 105 (especially the sentence on p. 105, 22 : εἰ δὲ ἐν τοῖς προσλαβοῦσι διδάσκειν αὐταῖς οὐκ ἐπιτρέπομεν, πῶς ἱερατεῦσαι ταύταις παρὰ φύσιν τις συγχωρήσει). In this chapter the women are refused baptism (see Tertullian de Baptismo, c. 17). In Const. App. VIII. 27, p. 266, 15 it says : διακόνισσα οὐκ εὐλογεῖ, ἀλλ' οὐδὲ τι ὧν ποιοῦσιν οἱ πρεσβύτεροι καὶ οἱ διάκονοι ἐπιτελεῖ. From the second to the fourth century regulations were necessary to secure passive worship in regard to the women ; see Canon 44 of Laodicea : 'That the women may not go up to the altar' (see the enigmatical Canon 11 on female presbyters, see Epiphanius 79, 4), and his commentaries on it, Haer. 79 (κατὰ Κολλυριδιανῶν), c. 2 : Θεῷ μὲν ἀπ' αἰῶνος οὐδαμῶς γυνὴ ἱεράτευσεν, especially ch. 3-7 : παρατηρητέον δὲ ὅτι ἄχρι διακονισσῶν μόνον τὸ ἐκκλησιαστικὸν ἐπεδεήθη τάγμα.

ἡμῖν. This reading is the compiler's, but in this section we cannot dispense with it.

Μάρθα, κ.τ.λ. These words as far as ἐγέλασα are in the sense of the compiler of the 'Apostolic Canons' probably a side remark made by the apostle, and thus do not belong to the regular discourses of the apostles, although they are likewise introduced by εἶπεν. This is decided, 1st, because according to the introduction of the whole work only the apostles were assembled to a conference ; 2nd, because the sentence προέλεγε γὰρ ἡμῖν, κ.τ.λ., can only be referred to the οὐκ ἐπέτρεψε, κ.τ.λ. Martha complains of Mary, as in Luke x. 40. Compare, in this matter, the Apost. Const. III. 6 : οὐκ ἐπιτρέπομεν οὖν γυναῖκας διδάσκειν ἐν ἐκκλησίᾳ, ἀλλὰ μόνον προσεύχεσθαι, καὶ γὰρ αὐτὸς ὁ διδάσκαλος ἡμῶν καὶ κύριος 'Ιησοῦς ἡμᾶς τοὺς δώδεκα πέμψας μαθητεῦσαι τὸν λαὸν καὶ τὰ ἔθνη—συνῆν δὲ ἡμῖν Μαρία ἡ Μαγδαληνὴ καὶ Μαρία ἡ 'Ιακώβου καὶ Μαρία ἑτέρα—οὐκ ἐξαπέστειλεν εἰς τὸ κατηχεῖν σὺν ἡμῖν τὸν λαόν. The Recension has : συνῆν γὰρ ἡμῖν ἥ τε μήτηρ τοῦ κυρίου καὶ αἱ ἀδελφαὶ αὐτοῦ, ἔτι δὲ Μαρία ἡ Μαγδαληνὴ καὶ Μαρία ἡ 'Ιακώβου καὶ Μάρθα καὶ Μαρία, αἱ ἀδελφαὶ Λαζάρου, Σαλώμη καὶ ἕτερα ἵτινες. Epiph., h. 79, 7 : . . . 'Women were never

εἶπεν· διὰ Μαριάμ, ὅτι εἶδεν αὐτὴν   with us — Martha said : 'For
μειδιῶσαν, Μαρία εἶπεν· οὐκέτι   Mary's sake, because he (she?) had
ἐγέλασα — προέλεγε γὰρ ἡμῖν,   seen her smile'; Mary said : 'I
ὅτε ἐδίδασκεν, ὅτι τὸ ἀσθενὲς διὰ   did not laugh again,' for he

deemed worthy of the priesthood, οὐκ εὐδόκησεν ὁ θεὸς τοῦτο ἐν Σαλώμῃ γενέσθαι, οὐκ ἐν αὐτῇ τῇ Μαρίᾳ. Οὐκ ἐπέτρεψεν αὐτῇ δοῦναι βάπτισμα, οὐκ εὐλογῆσαι μαθητάς . . . οὐ τὴν καλουμένην μητέρα Ῥούφου, οὐ τὰς ἀκολουθησάσας ἀπὸ Γαλιλαίας, οὐ τὴν Μάρθαν τὴν ἀδελφὴν Λαζάρου καὶ Μαρίαν . . . τοῦτο ποιεῖν προσέταξε τὸ ἀξίωμα. There is very little in the extra-canonical literature known of the two sisters of Lazarus. In the catalogue of Christian sects which Celsus had given (Origen. contra Celsum v. 62) it is said : 'Some are also Sibyllists ; also I know some Simonians, Marcellians from Marcellina, Harpokratians from Salome, and others from Mariamne (= Mary), and others from Martha ; Marcionites who put Marcion at their head.' This account is illustrated by what Hippolytus (Philos. v. 7, p. 95, also x. 9) tells us, that the Naassenes appealed to a tradition about James, the Lord's brother, which had reached them through Mariamne. In the 'Pistis Sophia,' a writing preserved in Coptic, a Mary holds discourse with our Lord ; she has the place of honour beside John, but is not the mother of Jesus, but is identified with Mary Magdalene (ed. Schwartz and Petermann, p. 182), and probably also with Mary the sister of Martha. For Martha sometimes appears in the book beside her. The pair of sisters appears thus in Egyptian gnostic circles, and it is this authority of the sisters, especially of Mary, which our fragment seems to combat. Another tradition of Mariamne (= Mary) is found in the Gnostic Acts of Philip (see Tischendorf, *Acta Apocryph.* p. xxxii., etc. ; Lipsius, *Apocryph. Apostelgesch.* ii. 2, p. 1 and fol.). Here she is introduced as the sister of Philip, who accompanies him in his wanderings in man's dress. (Salmon, *Dictionary of Christian Biography*, iii. p. 830).

9. μειδιῶσαν, κ.τ.λ. See Genesis xviii. 12 and fol. (Sarah). μειδιᾶν is the soft soundless smile, γελᾶν the ringing laugh (see the ascending scale, h. Hom. Cer. 204, μειδῆσαι γελάσαι τε). The change is here thus an intentional one.

οὐκέτι, 'no more,' 'not again.' The word would have been explained by the connection which is wanting. At what did Mary laugh ?

10. προέλεγε. When ? Probably when they were sent forth.

ἡμῖν, that is, 'us apostles.'

11. ἐδίδασκεν. See the 'διδάσκαλος' above, and in par. 6.

ὅτι τὸ ἀσθενὲς, κ.τ.λ. An apocryphal expression of the Lord, I believe, not found elsewhere. It is possible that it comes from the Gospel of the Egyptians, for in this there must have been much about male and female. See the fragments in Hilgenfeld, Nov. Test. extra can. fasc. iv. ed. ii. p. 43 and fol. However, in these fragments the question is never of saving the woman by the man, but of a neutralisation of the sexes. This salvation through the male ('sealing') played a part among the Marcionites, but never occurs otherwise in the ancient church. Hence it may be doubted whether, according to the original sense of the Lord's word, τὸ ἀσθενές can mean the woman and τὸ ἰσχυρόν the man (see 1 Peter iii. 7 : ὡς ἀσθενεστέρῳ σκεύει : 1 Clem. vi. 2 : γυναῖκες . . . αἱ ἀσθενεῖς τῷ σώματι, Eusebius, Hist. Evan. V. i. 18). It is indeed very possible that under τὸ ἀσθενές, 'the flesh,' and under τὸ ἰσχυρόν, 'the spirit,' are to be understood, that thus the saying may have

SOURCES OF THE APOSTOLIC CANONS

τοῦ ἰσχυροῦ σωθήσεται . . . ταῖς
γυναιξὶ μὴ ὀρθαῖς (πρέπει) προσεύχεσθαι, ἀλλὰ ἐπὶ τῆς γῆς
15 καθεζομέναις . . . πῶς. οὖν
δυνάμεθα περὶ γυναικῶν διακονίας
ὁρίσαι, εἰ μή τι διακονίαν ἵνα
ἐπισχύσωσι ταῖς ἐνδεομέναις;

had (already) said to us, when he used to teach, that the weak shall be saved by the strong. It is not proper for the women to pray standing, but sitting on the ground. How then can we, concerning women, order them services, unless perchance that of coming to the help of necessitous women?

been used by the author in a sense foreign to him. Perhaps he was thinking of 1 Tim. ii. 15 : γυνὴ σωθήσεται διὰ τῆς τεκνογονίας?

13. μὴ ὀρθαῖς, κ.τ.λ. A new reason why the women should not be allowed to perform deacons' services ; it becomes them to pray sitting on the ground, but in those services they would have to stand. So far as I am aware there is nothing known elsewhere of the sitting of women while praying. Bingham in his Orig. Eccl. lib. xiii. ch. 8 says nothing about it. A woman *standing* in· prayer is of common occurrence in early Christian painting.

17. διακονίαν ἵνα ἐπισχύσωσι, κ.τ.λ. The only ecclesiastical service with which women can be trusted is the nursing of women needing help.

CHAPTER III

CHURCH GOVERNMENT ACCORDING TO SOURCE A OF THE APOSTOLIC CANONS.

1. *Order of precedence of the Offices.*—The fragment of Source A which the editor of the Apostolic Canons has introduced treats first of the bishop and the presbyters, *then of the reader*, and after that of the deacons. The answer to the question as to whether this striking order is by chance or no, can only be settled in connection with an investigation on the origin of the readership in the church. Such an investigation, however, leads necessarily to the discussion of the more comprehensive problem which the 'lower orders,' especially in their origin, offer to the church historian. As this problem has not as yet been undertaken, I have felt myself compelled to take it in hand in order to bring light on our Source A. In the treatise supplemental to this work, 'On the Origin of the Readership and of the other lower Church Orders,' will be found a complete answer to the questions which are raised by the striking position of the reader in this document, and by the qualities which are demanded of him. The high importance of our Source will by these very instructions relating to the reader come out in a strong light.

2. *The Government of the Congregation: the Bishop and the College of Presbyters.*—At the head of the congregations, which the author has here in view, stood everywhere already one bishop[1], who is also called 'pastor.' Further, the difference between 'ordo' and πλῆθος[2] in the ἀδελφότης[3] is already clearly marked. Among the former (without there being a collective name for

---

[1] Par. 1, and especially 2, ll. 15 and 17. The plural τῶν ἐπισκόπων (par. 2, l. 19) does not contradict this. See the remarks on the passage.

[2] This word occurs in the Source several times; see also the designation οἱ πολλοί (par. 1, end), οἱ πάντες (par. 2, end).   [3] Par. 2, l. 13.

them) are reckoned the presbyters, the reader, the deacons, and the widows. Even the presbyters are bound to a willing disposition towards the bishop [1], they are further designated as consecrated with and fellow-combatants with the bishop [2]. From these statements it appears without doubt that the bishop at least in one view, although *primus inter pares*, is considered the superior of the presbyters. From the conception 'consecrated with' it follows, however, further that the worship was already in some way advanced in the light of a mystery, and that the difference between clergy and laity had found expression in the different position of the latter in worship. The bishop is the $\mu\acute{v}\sigma\tau\eta\varsigma$, the presbyters are the $\sigma\upsilon\mu\mu\acute{v}\sigma\tau\alpha\iota$; the laity are, however, called to divine service [3] by the presbyters, and to be instructed in all submission [4].

Of the reader it is said that he should fill the ear of the 'ignorant' by his reading [5]. The immaturity, that is, the want of independence, of the $\pi\lambda\hat{\eta}\theta o\varsigma$, especially in divine service, appears plainly from this source.

As to the abilities of the bishop, the qualities demanded of him in par. 1 do not allow us to form a sure judgment. The requirements that he 'should be faultless, a friend of the poor, honourable, no drunkard, no adulterer, not avaricious, nor a slanderer, or a partisan, or suchlike' appear as quite common. However, we may perhaps be able to gain a certain knowledge from these requirements. Besides, four other points must be considered. *First*, it is required of the bishop alone that he should have a good report *among the heathen* [6]; *second*, there is no fixed age demanded for him [7]; *third*, marriage is allowed him [8]; *fourth*, a certain amount of education is credited to him (competence to expound the scriptures), not yet positively as necessary for him, but only as very desirable. The first regulation is only intelligible, if the bishop, in circumstances in his position

---

[1] Par. 2, l. 17.   [2] 2, ll. 15, 16.   [3] 2, l. 16.   [4] 2, l. 25.   [5] Par. 3, end.

[6] Any analogous regulation for the presbyters is wanting. As to the deacons we read (par. 4), $\mu\epsilon\mu\alpha\rho\tau\upsilon\rho\eta\mu\acute{\epsilon}\nu o\iota\ \pi\alpha\rho\grave{\alpha}\ \tau o\hat{\upsilon}\ \pi\lambda\acute{\eta}\theta o\upsilon\varsigma$. Here there is only required a testimony from the congregation.

[7] It is expressly stated for the presbyters (par. 2) that they must be advanced in age.

[8] Celibacy is indeed already desirable; but as to the presbyters it is distinctly said that they are to have no connection with women.

as bishop, had to have intercourse with the non-Christians. We conclude from this (see the parallel regulation 1 Tim. iii. 7), and from the want of such a regulation in the case of the presbyters and deacons, that the bishop alone had to represent the congregation to the outer world. The two following points are interesting on this account, that they do *not* harmonise with the instructions binding on the presbyters. From the bishop neither a certain age nor celibacy is required, though both are necessary to the presbyters. Even here we are reminded of the question raised in more modern times, as to whether the bishop had been originally anything other than a presbyter. Whence then the difference of qualifications? But this question presses still more, when we reflect that in our Source, as also in 1 Tim. iii., the qualities required for the bishop and the deacons show a much greater resemblance than those required for the bishop and the presbyters. Lastly, as to the fourth point, it appears plainly here that education and teaching capacity were not yet considered as a *necessary* requisite of the bishop. However desirable it appears to the author of our Source that the bishop should be also the one who edifies the congregation out of the Holy Scriptures, he cannot have recognised in this function the *peculiar* activity and significance of the bishop.

Where then is this to be sought for? Now we have already learnt two regulations: 1. the bishop represents the congregation to the outer world (hence he is also its ἐπίμαχος); 2. he is the μύστης of the congregation, that is, the conductor of the worship. Now let us return to the general qualities which are demanded in paragraph 1 for the bishop (εἰ ἀναμάρτητος ὑπάρχει, εἰ φιλόπτωχος, εἰ σώφρων, μὴ μέθυσος, μὴ πόρνος, μὴ πλεονέκτης ἢ λοίδορος ἢ προσωπολήπτης καὶ τὰ τούτοις ὅμοια): we are struck by the fact that among them there is really only one positive and concrete: φιλόπτωχος; the remaining ones are comprised together in the conception 'blameless in manners [1].' Thus this quality must be decidedly important, and on that account shows an important function of the bishop.

[1] A special weight cannot be laid on the μὴ προσωπολήπτης, as it stands beside πλεονέκτης and λοίδορος in a list which is subordinated to the chief conception, σώφρων. It is therefore to be explained according to the regulation found in par. 4 for the deacons: μὴ πρόσωπον πλουσίου λαμβάνοντες. (See also par. 6, μήτε πλούσιον προσωπολητποῦντες.) The case in par. 2 is a different one. Here the 'respect of person' in a *judicial* act is considered.

He is the administrator for the poor; the φιλόπτωχος corresponds to the above-mentioned technical term for the bishop, ποιμήν, and explains it clearly. The bishop is the head of the congregation as far as he is its administrator and pastor; that is, he cares for all the needs of the congregation, especially for those of the poor. He represents the congregation to the outer world, and he is at the same time director of the worship. In these relations all the members of the congregation, including the presbyters and deacons, are bound to him in willing service.

That these two functions, direction of the charitable administrations [1], and direction of the worship, are not foreign to one another, but rather are connected in the closest manner, has been known for a long time. But our Source shows this also in the closest connection, and indeed in one sentence, which, as short as it is, contains one of the most valuable accounts which we possess from the oldest time of the church in relation to the organisation of congregations. The sentence runs: οἱ ἐκ δεξιῶν πρεσβύτεροι προνοήσονται τῶν ἐπισκόπων πρὸς τὸ θυσιαστήριον, ὅπως τιμήσωσι καὶ ἐντιμηθῶσιν, εἰς ὃ ἂν δέῃ. In order to estimate it justly, we have first to consider what the Source especially orders concerning the presbyters.

The introduction of the section can unfortunately no longer be restored with certainty. Above all, we can no longer make out whether, how, and by whom, according to the author, the presbyters should be appointed [2]. So much, however, is clear, that the presbyters of the Apocalypse were in the mind of the author. He has accordingly laid stress on the number 24, because it is an even number, and consequently desires an even number because the functions of the presbyterate necessitate two divisions [3]. To the Apocalypse, however, the author has simply transferred the two functions of the presbyters. From this it follows that they really existed in the congregations which the author has in view. The one part of the presbyters

---

[1] Par. 1, 1. 20 : τῇ ἀγάπῃ εἰς πάντας περισσευέτω.
[2] See in pars. 3, 4, 5 the καθίστασθαι.
[3] The author has (see also par. 1) small congregations in view. For these, *two* presbyters are sufficient. Larger congregations must naturally have more presbyters. The number, however, must remain an even one. Thus I think the author is to be understood.

has (in divine service) a function in relation to the bishop, the other one in relation to the congregation [1]. The qualities demanded for them characterise them, *first*, as a college of worthy persons, standing at the side of the bishop. They shall be advanced in years, they shall keep from marriage, and they shall be the willing συμμύσται καὶ συνεπίμαχοι of the bishop, supporting [2] him in the assembly of the congregation; *second*, as a directing counsel and juridical council [3] to the congregation. Here are thus two separate courts of justice within the college. The one half of the presbyters has to look after the order in the πλῆθος [4] during divine service and warn the disturbers [5]. If, however, a member of the congregation opposes the warning and shows himself disobedient, the whole college (as a supreme court) has to meet together and decree unanimously the suitable punishment on such a one [6]. But what has the other half of the presbyters, what have the presbyters on the right, to do? Here stands the important problem, the sense of which is explained and thoroughly treated in the note at the passage 'they shall bear the cares for the bishop at the altar, so that they may distribute the gifts of honour and even receive there the necessary amounts (or in regard to all needs).'

This passage is of immense importance for understanding the function of the presbyters as well as that of the bishop.

First it is to be observed that of the relation of the presbyters to the bishop the same word is used (προνοεῖσθαι), which shows their relation to the congregation. This is the technical term for the function of the care and of the 'rule,' and that

---

[1] This separation occurs in no other source.

[2] Thus are to be understood the words συναθροίζοντας τὸ πλῆθος standing between συμμύστας τοῦ ἐπισκόπου καὶ συνεπιμάχους and προθυμουμένους τὸν ποιμένα. On account of their position they must also have a relation to the bishop, and this can be found in the σύν, although συναθροίζειν signifies, as a rule, little more than ἀθροίζειν. But if this meaning were to be accepted here, how did the sentence receive the position in which we find it, and how was it to be thought that the presbyters alone had to assemble the congregation?

See the twice occurring μὴ πρόσωπον λαμβάνειν in par. 2, ll. 14 and 31.

[4] Par. 2, l. 22: οἱ ἐξ ἀριστερῶν πρεσβύτεροι προνοήσονται τοῦ πλήθους.

[5] This function fell to the deacons later. There is also here an archaism.

[6] See the end of par. 2. The congregation is not a participator in administering discipline.

among the presbyters[1]. Thus also the bishop stands under the care of the presbytery. That is information of the first importance; for what we hitherto might only have guessed at, we now receive incontestable proof of. We discover that even in the time in which from a plurality of bishops there has come to be only *one*, a kind of supervision of the presbyters over the bishop's actions has continued. The episcopal monarchy has thus not yet had, even at the beginning, the significance of an autocracy; rather has the supreme control of the presbyters continued at times (at least in certain countries). There were πρεσβύτεροι οἱ προϊστάμενοι τῆς ἐκκλησίας[2] in the full sense of the word, when as yet there were no ἐπίσκοποι, but only one bishop (a single pastoral office). The directing council (or, more strictly, the council bearing the cares) which had to superintend the bishop, and the bishop who was the pastor, the liturgist and representative of the congregation to the outer world, raising by these functions a claim on all sides to good will and obedience, are not excluded. We have rather to recognise a peculiar dyarchy (the presbyterian council and bishop) in the congregation, within which authority and subordination prevail. We know also from another source that our document presupposes such a state. In paragraph 5 it says of the serving congregational widows: τὰ δέοντα ἀπαγγέλλουσα τοῖς πρεσβυτέροις. If this passage stood isolated, the upholders of the theory of the original identity of the presbyters and bishops in early times might take it as a plain witness in their favour, and certainly with great probability; for in instructions of a later date we find in similar cases: τὰ δέοντα ἀπαγγέλλουσα τῷ ἐπισκόπῳ[3]. See my remark on paragraph 5. Our author, however, distinguishes particularly between the one bishop and the council of presbyters. If he now in spite of this tells the widows to announce what was necessary to the latter and not to the bishop, it follows undoubtedly that formerly the pres-

---

[1] As, for example, on profane and on church inscriptions; see Le Bas and Waddington, Inscrip. Grecq. et Lat., etc., III. No. 2558, p. 582 (in Deir-Ali, about three miles south of Damascus, λχ' aer. Seleucid = 318-19 A.D.): Συναγωγὴ Μαρκιωνιστῶν κώμ(ης) Λεβάβων τοῦ κ(υρίο)υ κ[α]ὶ σ(ωτῆ)ρος Ἰη(σοῦ) Χριστοῦ προνοίᾳ Παύλου πρεσβ(υτέρου).

[2] For this expression see the Shepherd of Hermas and other witnesses.

[3] The epistle of James agrees here with our document, as does also the epistle of Polycarp (see 6. 1): οἱ πρεσβύτεροι . . . ἐπισκεπτόμενοι πάντας ἀσθενεῖς.

byters had been always in reality οἱ προϊστάμενοι τῆς ἐκκλησίας. Such a position could not last long, as the necessary conflict between the bishop and the council must arise. But that there was a time in which the episcopal-diaconal organisation of the congregation had been of equal weight with that of the presbyterian, consequently it can no more be denied that one or other of their roots had withered. I have remarked in the Analecta to my translation of Hatch's *Early Christian Churches*, p. 229 : ' The later fixed government of the Church (Bishop, Presbyterian Council, Deacons), is a combination of two different organisations. As far as the congregation was divided into those that guided and those that were led, and the congregation would be sufficient for this separation for each sphere of action [1], the distinction of οἱ πρεσβύτεροι and οἱ νεώτεροι (πλῆθος) was originally given. So far as the congregation embraced a system of functions (looking after the poor, worship, correspondence,—in short, economy in the widest sense of the word), and formed an active brotherhood, special officials for government were necessary '; and this is confirmed by our Source. This fixes sufficiently the point in the development of both organisations in which the monarchical bishop appears as the single person in his own sphere on the same level with the council of elders. He is still indeed watched over, but otherwise he appears as the pastor, liturgist, and representative of the congregation, whom the presbyters have to *support*, as they are also bound to give him willing service. But wherein are the presbyters the rulers over the bishop? This question is also answered to us by our Source: that is, *in the disposal of the gifts taking place during the divine service*. The bishop is at the θυσιαστήριον not only the liturgist, but also the manager of the congregation ; but his government is subordinated to the care of the council of the elders, that is, to a half of it. This council reveals itself as the judgment court for order and discipline in the congregation, which extends its authority, πρόνοια, as well over the bishop as over the congregation. The bishop is, however, not only ποιμήν,

---

[1] See also Hatch's own explanations on p. 66 : 'The presbyters had the supreme oversight of all matters of adminstration'; and the expositions of the patriarchal organisation of the congregations in its difference from and its relation to the administration in my edition of the Διδαχή, p. 146 and fol.

μύστης, and ἐπίμαχος in the congregation, but also οἰκονόμος. It is certainly no news that he is that, especially in the divine service of the congregation[1]. But it is new to us that he acts independently as steward, however he stands under a kind of supervision of the presbyters. It is not said that this supervision extended to the other functions of the bishop. It is however worthy of observation that in par. 1 and 2 only what is quite essential to the bishop is treated of, as he exercises functions in the assembly of the congregation. Here arises the question, which must especially be raised in regard to the Epistle of Polycarp (c. 6): Has the bishop originally possessed, apart from his office in the worship and as a steward, other functions? Does not the dyarchy in the congregation explain that originally the bishop had been the guide and principal only in the sphere of the regular government of the congregation?

With what we have now explained, all that our Source contains about the bishop and the council of elders is exhausted; but it still brings out a striking and important regulation: that is, on the election of a bishop. The passage runs[2]: 'If there are in one place few men, and not twelve persons who are fit to vote in respect to the election of a bishop, one must write to the neighbouring churches, where there is a settled one, in order that three selected men may come and examine carefully if he is worthy.'

This regulation, for which a parallel is not known to me, is of interest in more than one point of view. (1) It teaches us that a well-ordered form of congregation was considered necessary in all cases: even where there were less than twelve Christians of age of the male sex (these only appear as entitled to vote) present in a town, a bishop must be chosen (what wisdom is expressed in this regulation!). (2) It shows the sovereign right of the congregation to choose their bishop still unfettered. (3) It throws a bright light on the close connections of the congregations with one another, and of their intercourse by letter—the strong congregation shall come to the

---

[1] Just as little is it new that our passage excludes the practice of fixed payments to the bishop and the clergy; see Eus. Hist. Eccl. v. 28, and the reproaches made to the Montanists.

[2] See par. 1.

help of the weak, and assist them to an organisation. (4) It shows us how carefully they went to work in the election of a bishop: a committee of selection of less than twelve members does not evidently offer the necessary guarantees in regard to a right election; a future bishop should receive his testimony of qualification from at least twelve persons. But that where this demand was not to be fulfilled in the single congregation, the episcopal formation of the congregation was not to be abandoned, but rather the neighbouring congregation drawn upon, is a proof as well for the connection of congregations, as also for the beginning of the consideration that the united church had to take an interest in each single bishop, and that accordingly similar ordinances were valid for all bishops. *Here is therefore distinct evidence of the transformation of the episcopate as a congregational office into the episcopate as an ecclesiastical office.* (5) The passage contains nothing as to whether the person chosen must already belong to the order; as there is no definition as to age given, so there is also wanting any instruction in that relation. But still more (and that is perhaps the most interesting), even those three men selected from the neighbouring congregations to strengthen the committee of selection are simply called ἐκλεκτοὶ ἄνδρες. There is nothing said about their being clergymen. The election (there is nothing said, and indeed nothing to be said, about the consecration) is thus represented as an act for which the difference of clergy and laity does not come into consideration.

As remarked, this direction is unique[1], but when we come later in history we are met by an institution which probably arose somehow out of the order which our Source has marked. In the letter of Cornelius of Rome to Fabius of

[1] There is, however, an interesting parallel, which does not exactly refer to the election of a bishop, but still to the conditions of government. When about the year 96 disturbances broke out in the Corinthian church regarding the direction of the congregation (ἔρις ἐπὶ τοῦ ὀνόματος τῆς ἐπισκοπῆς, 1 Clem. ad Rom. 44, 1), the Roman church sent them not only a letter, but also *three* selected men, and tacitly supposed that these three men would be acknowledged by the sister church as authorised. See c. 63, 3 : ἐπέμψαμεν δὲ ἄνδρας πιστοὺς καὶ σώφρονας, ἀπὸ νεότητος ἀναστραφέντας ἕως γήρους ἀμέμπτως ἐν ἡμῖν, οἵτινες μάρτυρες ἔσονται μεταξὺ ὑμῶν καὶ ἡμῶν. C. 65, 1 : τοὺς δὲ ἀπεσταλμένους ἀφ' ἡμῶν Κλαύδιον Ἔφηβον καὶ Οὐαλέριον Βίτωνα σὺν καὶ Φορτουνάτῳ ἐν εἰρήνῃ μετὰ χαρᾶς ἐν τάχει ἀναπέμψατε πρὸς ἡμᾶς.

CHURCH GOVERNMENT

Antioch we read the following[1]: '(Novatian) chose two companions who had given up their salvation, and sent them to a small and quite insignificant part of Italy to deceive there three bishops, peasants, and extremely simple men, by some deceptive representation. He caused them to understand by assurances and protestations that they must betake themselves to Rome hastily, in order that by the mediation of them and of the other bishops that dissension, of which kind there was always something, might be taken away[2]. When they were now come, he caused them, as they were men, who, as already said, were too simple in opposition to the intrigues and cunningness of bad men, to be surrounded by some of the people of his sort commissioned thereto, and compelled them then by force at the tenth hour, when they reeled with drunkenness, to give him, by an apparent and invalid laying on of hands, the episcopal ordination.' This story shows that in the middle of the third century (in Rome) it was the naturalised custom to have bishops consecrated by *three* foreign *bishops*; only such a consecration could be considered as perfect. It shows however, further, that three foreign bishops are cited in order to put down disturbances which troubled the order of the church. Doubtless this fixed practice stands in connection with the arrangement met with in our Source; it has been developed from it. But in place of three 'selected men' we now meet with bishops. In this form, as is known, it has in the Catholic Church, on the ground of the established decrees of the Synods of Arles and Nicaea, been made into an invariable law: the bishop must be consecrated by at least three bishops[3]. Hitherto we were not able to put back the

---

[1] See Eusebius, Hist. Eccl. vi. 43, 8, 9.

[2] Ὡς δῆθεν πᾶσα ἡτισδηποτοῦν διχοστασία γεγονυῖα σὺν καὶ ἑτέροις ἐπισκόποις καὶ αὐτῶν μεσιτευόντων διαλυθῇ.

[3] See the 20th Canon of Arles : De his qui usurpant sibi, quod soli debeant episcopos ordinare, placuit, ut nullus hoc sibi praesumat nisi assumptis secum aliis septem episcopis. Si tamen non potuerit septem, infra tres non audeat ordinare. Can. 4 of Nicaea : Ἐπίσκοπον προσήκει μάλιστα μὲν ὑπὸ πάντων τῶν ἐν τῇ ἐπαρχίᾳ καθίστασθαι· εἰ δὲ δυσχερὲς εἴη τὸ τοιοῦτο, ἢ διὰ κατεπείγουσαν ἀνάγκην ἢ διὰ μῆκος ὁδοῦ, ἐξάπαντος τρεῖς ἐπὶ τὸ αὐτὸ συναγομένους, συμψήφων γινομένων καὶ τῶν ἀπόντων καὶ συντιθεμένων διὰ γραμμάτων, τότε τὴν χειροτονίαν ποιεῖσθαι : besides the 12th Canon of Laodicea, can. 19 of Antioch, Const. App. VIII. 4, 20; see Hefele, *Conciliengesch*, vol. i. 2d ed. p. 384 fol. Custom did not generally observe this law everywhere in the church;

law beyond the time of Cornelius (250 A.D.), and its origin was obscure. Our Source in some measure lightens the darkness.

3. *The Reader.*—The most important points on the position of the reader in our source will be treated of in the supplement, to which we now refer. Still, the following should be remarked. Teachers and prophets, as in the Διδαχή, are not found in our Source [1]. Accordingly the bishop appears as μύστης, the presbyters as συμμύσται [2]. In this conception free speech for edification on the foundation of the holy scriptures is *not* necessarily included; capacity to expound the scriptures was certainly desired of the bishop, but not absolutely demanded. It is the reader who must regularly have this capacity; of him it is said that he must be διηγητικός, εἰδὼς ὅτι εὐαγγελιστοῦ τόπον ἐργάζεται· ὁ γὰρ ἐμπιπλῶν ὦτα μὴ νοοῦντος ἔγγραφος λογισθήσεται παρὰ τῷ θεῷ. The author has chosen the word εὐαγγελιστής as the general designation of the teacher with the *charisma.* The apostles, as well as the prophets and teachers, are all evangelists. We have here thus a reminiscence of a past organisation of the congregation [3]. It has, in fact, passed away; for the reader is an *elected* official. The double position in which he acted did not last long. He would soon have to hand over to the bishop the important function of the exposition of the scriptures, which is shown even in our Source in the regulation that, where possible, the bishop should be παιδείας μέτοχος, κ.τ.λ.[4], and thereby he would sink into the position of a lower church minister, as his service, the mere reading of the scriptures, was

hence it had always to be enjoined afresh. We find also varying arrangements. Thus in the 1st Apostolic Canon it stands: ἐπίσκοπος χειροτονείσθω ὑπὸ ἐπισκόπων δύο ἢ τριῶν; in the 2nd Arabic Canon of Hippolytus: 'One shall be chosen out of the bishops and presbyters, who will lay his hand on the head of the person to be consecrated.' It is possible that in the Irish Church at the episcopal consecration only *one* bishop was invited. See, however, Loofs, *Antiq. Britonum Scotorumque ecclesiae,* pp. 26 and 75; and generally in Hatch's article, 'Ordination,' in the *Christian Antiq.*

[1] Even the Διδαχή notes the fact that *charismatic* (inspired) teachers may be sometimes wanting. See c. 13, 4: ἐὰν δὲ μὴ ἔχητε προφήτην, δότε τοῖς πτωχοῖς.

[2] In the Διδαχή the prophets (13, 3) are designated as the high priests of the congregation.

[3] See my edition of the Διδαχή, p. 93 and fol.

[4] In Rome the bishop was not a teacher until the fifth century; see Sozom. *Hist. Eccl.* vii. 19.

a purely mechanical one. Our Source comes from an earlier time, and its requirements are quite unique. It requires, first, a thorough examination of the person to be chosen; then a list of moral qualities which are in the closest relation to the function of a reader [1]; further, obedience and benevolent intentions, probably in regard to the bishop [2]; lastly, the abovementioned properties of a good delivery, and the capacity to explain what he reads. Between them stands the astonishing regulation that the reader should be the first in the assembly at the Sunday divine services [3]. Why should it be the reader? Are we here to recognise a reminiscence of that past time when the charismatic teachers, whose diminished office the reader had inherited, were the directors of the devotional assemblies in which they preached?

4. *The Deacons.*—The bishop, the council of presbyters, and the reader exercise their functions completely within the solemn assemblies of the congregation. What is said with regard to them in our Source stands therefore thoroughly in connection with those assemblies. It is otherwise with the deacons; *they appear as the maintainers, ministers, and comforters of the congregation in their daily life* [4]. In this activity a certain independence and authority belongs to them. Everything which our Source remarks on the deacons is to be understood from that standpoint. First, the appointment of (at least) three deacons is required. The motive of this is clear. They shall be three in order that they may be able to bear an effective witness in cases of complaint before the disciplinary judgment of the presbyters [5]. The deacons are thus also public accusers; in short, the middlemen between the congregation and their government. In the second place an examination of them is demanded, not only in general, but specially 'in every act of service'. There are many duties of a practical kind that are obligatory on them; and they must

---

[1] Μὴ γλωσσοκόπος, μὴ μέθυσος μήτε γελωτολόγος, εὔτροπος.
[2] See the parallel regulation for the presbyters.
[3] Ἐν ταῖς κυριακαῖς συνόδοις πρῶτος σύνδρομος. A remembrance of this appears to be present in the 37th Arabic Canon of Hippolytus.
[4] That they have also in the divine service fixed obligations is not said in this source; but on the other hand, it is not denied. Besides, the presbyters exercise the discipline during divine service; see above.
See par. 4 : τρεῖς—γέγραπται γάρ. ἐπὶ τριῶν σταθήσεται πᾶν ῥῆμα.

have already proved themselves as experienced in them. In the third place, an approbation on the part of the congregation is desired—not, as in the case of the bishop, a good report from the non-Christians; for the deacons have nothing to do with the connection of the congregation with the outer world. After these general instructions follows a list of single ones, which expose very plainly the functions of the deacons; they must be pattern fathers ($\mu o\nu \acute{o}\gamma a\mu o\iota$, $\tau\epsilon\kappa\nu o\tau\rho\acute{o}\phi o\iota$), besides being honourable, gentle, peaceable, not murmuring, not double-tongued, not passionate. From this we perceive that they take a part in all the details of the life of the congregation, advising one, comforting another, exhorting another; and in this activity it is necessary that they should have earnestness, friendliness, unwearied action, and calm. But, above all, it is important for them to behave justly in the opposition of rich and poor, which is found in the churches: the rich must by no means be preferred, the poor must not be oppressed; indeed one of the chief tasks of the deacons is to compel the rich to give, and to call forth good works which take place in silence. Hence must they be judicious men. As, however, generosity can only be stirred up by one who is generous, they should themselves be willing to give and to communicate [1].

Deacons who thus prove themselves the models and advisers of the congregation have also a claim on honour, esteem, and awe on their side. As the author of the $\Delta\iota\delta a\chi\acute{\eta}$ [2] has named the deacons together with the bishops the $\tau\epsilon\tau\iota\mu\eta\mu\acute{\epsilon}\nu o\iota$ of the congregation, so has our author reckoned them among the honoured ones [3]. But, in conclusion, he remarks expressly that a kind of police power belongs to them over those 'walking disorderly [4].' The means which they have to use for this are warning, exhortation, threatening; despisers, however, must they leave completely to themselves [5]. Of course there is here no reference to excommunication, but a rule is given for the conduct of the deacons. No more is said; but we

[1] The words $\mu\eta\delta\grave{\epsilon}$ $o\check{\iota}\nu\omega$ $\pi o\lambda\lambda\hat{\omega}$ $\chi\rho\omega\mu\epsilon\nu o\iota$ are evidently interpolated, being foreign to the sense of the passage.
[2] See c. 15.   [3] See par. 4, 1. 16 f.
[4] See par. 4, at end.
[5] The $\pi a\rho a\pi\acute{\epsilon}\mu\pi\epsilon\sigma\theta a\iota$ answers to the regulation in the $\Delta\iota\delta a\chi\acute{\eta}$; c. 15, 3: $\kappa a\grave{\iota}$ $\pi a\nu\tau\grave{\iota}$ $\grave{a}\sigma\tau o\chi o\hat{\upsilon}\nu\tau\iota$ $\kappa a\tau\grave{a}$ $\tau o\hat{\upsilon}$ $\grave{\epsilon}\tau\acute{\epsilon}\rho o\upsilon$ $\mu\eta\delta\epsilon\grave{\iota}s$ $\lambda a\lambda\epsilon\acute{\iota}\tau\omega$ $\mu\eta\delta\grave{\epsilon}$ $\pi a\rho$' $\grave{\upsilon}\mu\hat{\omega}\nu$ $\grave{a}\kappa o\upsilon\acute{\epsilon}\tau\omega$, $\acute{\epsilon}\omega s$ $o\hat{\upsilon}$ $\mu\epsilon\tau a\nu o\acute{\eta}\sigma\eta$.

might conclude from the introduction to the whole section that the deacons in such cases would have to make an announcement to the council of presbyters.

5. *The Widows.*—The division of work among the widows, the number of whom is to answer to the number of the deacons, is completely new to us. That the widows of the congregation were to be the intercessors for the congregation, and the nurses of the women, we knew long ago. But that these obligations were to be divided is surprising. According to our Source two widows are appointed for intercessory prayer and (what is also new) for the reception of revelations, and have nothing to do with the nursing of women. This order (πρὸς τὰς ἀποκαλύψεις περὶ οὗ ἂν δέῃ) is extremely ancient, and reminds us of a still earlier state of things. In the Διδαχή we read[1] of prophets who speak 'in the spirit,' who order 'in the spirit' a meal for others, who 'in the spirit' beg for money for the needy, and demand gifts. Of such prophets our Source does not speak, but it has introduced to us in the bishop the mystic; in the presbyters the companion mystics; in the reader the representative of the charismatic teacher. These have shared in the inheritance of the prophets and teachers. Should not the widow also have her share, and should not the revelations which were expected for her be the residuum of those revelations of the prophets who have died out? No doubt the selected apocalyptic widows died out likewise, and in a very short time—selection and apocalypse are not compatible; but even here we are shown that as with the reader and as with the bishop and council of presbyters, so here our Source does not exhibit to us the complete Catholic Church government, but its vestibule. This entrance hall stands incomparably nearer to the Catholic government, than it does to the early Christian; it contains, however, features drawn from the latter. Our Source shows us the middle step between the organisation which we find in the Διδαχή, and that which we find at the end of the second century: it is in this that consists its inestimable value[2].

[1] Chapter 11.
[2] We still possess a writing whose accounts on the ordinances of government agree with those of the Διδαχή, however, in such a manner that it shows the progress in the dying out of the old enthusiastic organisation. I mean the

What this Source says of the widow as a nurse, has already been partly spoken of[1]; partly it is without any particular interest.

Ascensio Jesaiae, that is the latest recension, which also belongs to the second century (see Dillmann's *Ascensio Jesaiae*, 1877, and my review of the work in the Theol. Lit. Zeitung, 1878, no. 4). The passage referred to, and which is exceedingly instructive runs, (c. iii. 23-31): Et iis diebus multi erunt amatores munerum quamquam denudati sapientia, et erunt multi seniores inique agentes et pastores oppressores ovium suarum et erunt rapaces socordia sua pastores sancti. Et commutabunt multi honorem vestitus sanctorum cum vestitu amatoris auri, et erit personarum acceptio multa illis diebus et amatores honoris huius mundi. Et erunt calumniatores et calumniantes multi et inanis honor sub appropinquationem domini et secedet spiritus sanctus e multis. Nec erunt illis diebus prophetae multi nec qui loquentur res confirmatas nisi singuli singulis locis, propter spiritum mendacii et fornicationis et inanis honoris et amoris auri, qui futurus est in iis qui dicentur servi istius iisque qui recipient istum. Et erit inter eos odium magnum, in pastoribus et in senioribus inter sese. Nam invidia magna erit ultimis diebus, nam quivis quod ei libitum est coram oculis suis loquetur. Et negligent prophetiam prophetarum, qui ante me fuerunt, et meas quoque visiones negligentes, ut ebullitionem cordis sui loquantur.

[1] See above, on the words τὰ δέοντα ἀπαγγέλλουσα τοῖς πρεσβυτέροις, and the notes to par. 5.

CHAPTER IV

THE HISTORICAL CONTENTS OF SOURCE B.

IN comparison with the rich historical contribution which Source A has brought us, what is offered us by Source B must be called trivial. In addition to this in the second half the order of words of the torn document is by no means to be depended on, and the apocryphal evangelical fragment which is communicated in it offers us an insoluble problem. What can be remarked on this subject is done in the note to the passage. On that account we leave it on one side.

Source B is, as announced above, incontestably a document by itself; that is proved by the duplicate passage A (ordinance in relation to the deacons)[1]. B gives regulations for deacons, laity, and women in relation to the obligations laid upon them in the church, and is probably a fragment of the conclusion of a treatise of canon law. But in spite of certain peculiarities in the form[2], and in spite of the designation of Jesus as the 'Teacher,' B stands in the closest relations, one might say kinship, to A. This is shown, first, in the sources of both documents[3]; second, in the striking agreement of the constitution of the deacons; third, even in the selection of words[4]. Thus

---

[1] The duplicate is partly a very perfect one; compare par. 6: μήτε πένητα ὑπεροπτεύοντες μήτε πλούσιον προσωπολημπτοῦντες with par. 4: μὴ πρόσωπον πλουσίου λαμβάνοντες μηδὲ πένητα καταδυναστεύοντες; also par. 6: ἐπαναγκάσουσι τοὺς δυναμένους ἀποθησαυρίζειν εἰς ἔργα ἀγαθά with par. 4: ἐπαναγκάζοντες τοὺς ἔχοντας τῶν ἀδελφῶν ἁπλοῦν τὰς χεῖρας.

[2] In A, par. 3-5, at the beginning καθιστανέσθωσαν is always used. (In par. 2, the beginning is not found.) In B there is no question of appointing.

[3] See the following paragraphs.

[4] The material is really very small, so much the more important is the agreement. The symbol of the angels is used in A (par. 2) and in B (par. 7); ἐπαναγκάζειν (of the deacons), pars. 4 and 6; θυσιαστήριον, pars. 2 and 7;

the two sources must stand closely together even in point of time.

Now, as far as relates to the section on the deacons (par. 6), it is worthy of remark that, like A, par. 4, it contains nothing on the function of the deacons at worship; rather, exactly as in A, they appear as those moving about in the congregation, the acknowledged helpers and exhorters of the members. The expression, ἐργάται τῶν καλῶν ἔργων, νυχθήμερον ἐπιλεύσσοντες πανταχοῦ, characterises them especially well. There are two single points which are important to us: first, it is said that the deacons shall not exclude the poor from the division of the λογία; second, it is promised them that after a blameless holding of their office they may attain the office of bishop. As far as relates to the first, our Source offers by the side of 1 Cor. xvi. the only witness for the word λογία, and is one of the few witnesses in Christian antiquity for the existence of a congregational treasury. As touching the second, the passage confirms the special affinity between the bishops and the diaconate. The deserving deacon is promised, not the presbyter's office, but that of the bishop. This agrees completely with the references which Hatch[1] has given[2]. It should be observed (as we have shown above) that even in the third century the presbyters were completed out of the number of the readers. Thus in this advancement within the catholic church government (the deacon to bishop, the reader to presbyter) we see the reminiscence of an older pre-catholic form of government. Already in the third century in connection with the abasement of the presbyters and the readers, this practice begins to be naturalised, that the deacon should ascend to the presbyter, the presbyter to the bishop, the reader however to the acolyte or sub-deacon. In the section on the laity (par. 7), which is gathered together from bits of older writings, the only thing worthy of remark is the designation of the clergy as

παραπέμπεσθαι, pars. 4 and 6; παρεδρεύειν, pars. 5 and 7; ποιμήν (for the bishop), par. 2, and τόπος ποιμενικός for the bishop's office, par. 6; προσωπολήπτης, par. 1, and προσωποληπτεῖν, par. 6, τόπος (for a position of rank), pars. 3, 6, and 7.

[1] *Organization of the Early Christian Churches*, 3rd ed., p. 52 note 59, and p. 54.

[2] See also my notes in the *Analecta*, p. 246, and in my edition of the Διδαχή, p. 140 and follg.

παρεδρεύοντες τῷ θυσιαστηρίῳ. They are thereby designated as priests, or, more correctly, there is only one step from this to the designation of 'priest.'

Lastly (par. 8) from the constitution on the women, in which every public office in the church is forbidden them (they have simply to busy themselves with the nursing of sick women), it appears that formerly there must have been some expression of a desire for a public service for the women. If we consider what part women play as priestesses in many heathen religions we cannot wonder at this desire.

CHAPTER V

THE SOURCES LYING AT THE FOUNDATION OF DOCUMENTS A AND B.

IN regard to their sources and the manner of their application, our fragments, which must here be judged together, offer quite a pattern type for the pre-catholic time. There are quoted as absolutely authentic authorities, *first*, with γέγραπται (par. 4), an Old Testament passage, Deut. xix. 15; *second*, three times words of our Lord, that is (par. 6), Matt. xxv. 37, (par. 8) Matt. xxvi. 26 and follg., and also an apocryphal saying of our Lord, τὸ ἀσθενὲς διὰ τοῦ ἰσχυροῦ σωθήσεται. The first passage is introduced by προορῶντες τοὺς λόγους τοῦ διδασκάλου ἡμῶν, the second by ὁ διδάσκαλος . . . λέγων, the third by προέλεγεν, ὅτε ἐδίδασκεν—these are the very oldest forms of quotation; *third*, the Revelation of St. John (par. 2), in so far as in the situation depicted it is represented as suitable for the order in the church. We find besides a reminiscence of the text of an apocryphal evangelical sermon. Thus the Old Testament, the words of our Lord, and an apocalypse form the important cases. The words of our Lord are made use of in the synoptical setting, but our synoptical gospels are still not considered as alone authoritative, as is proved by the apocryphal quotation. A canon of the New Testament is to our authors unknown; this is so much the plainer as (apart from the pastoral epistles, which require here a peculiar examination) reminiscences of New Testament writings are not completely wanting. Their significance is really doubtful. We can only assert with safety that our author has read St. Paul's Epistle to the Corinthians [1]. Very probably knowledge of the Epistle to the Thessalonians is shown in A [2]. On the other hand, the parallels to 2 Cor-

---

[1] Compare 1 Cor. v. 11 with par. 1, 1 Cor. vii. 1 with par. 1, 1 Cor. vii. 24 with par. 7, 1 Cor. ix. 13 with par. 7, 1 Cor. xvi. 1-2 with par. 6.

[2] Compare 1 Thess. iii. 12 with par. 1, 1 Thess. v. 14 with par. 4. See also 2 Thess. iii. 6, 11.

inthians, Galatians, and James do not allow us to form a judgment on them [1]. There is no doubt that *B* must have read the first epistle of Clement to Corinth [2]. There is no trace of a knowledge of the gospel of St. John. The relation of our documents to the pastoral epistles is of extraordinary interest. Firstly let us here collect together the materials:—

1 Tim. ii. 11: γυνὴ ἐν ἡσυχίᾳ μανθανέτω ἐν πάσῃ ὑποταγῇ.
1 Tim. ii. 12: διδάσκειν γυναικὶ οὐκ ἐπιτρέπω [3].
1 Tim. iii. 2 f.: δεῖ τὸν ἐπίσκοπον ἀνεπίλημπτον εἶναι, μιᾶς γυναικὸς ἄνδρα, νηφάλιον, σώφρονα, κόσμιον, φιλόξενον, διδακτικόν, μὴ πάροινον, μὴ πλήκτην, ἀλλὰ ἐπιεικῆ, ἄμαχον, ἀφιλάργυρον ... δεῖ δὲ καὶ μαρτυρίαν καλὴν ἔχειν ἀπὸ τῶν ἔξωθεν.

1 Tim. iii. 3.
1 Tim. iii. 8 f.: διακόνους σεμνούς, μὴ διλόγους, μὴ οἴνῳ πολλῷ προσέχοντας ... καὶ οὗτοι δὲ δοκιμαζέσθωσαν πρῶτον, εἶτα διακονείτωσαν ... διάκονοι ἔστωσαν μιᾶς γυναικὸς ἄνδρες, τέκνων καλῶς προϊστάμενοι καὶ τῶν ἰδίων οἴκων.
1 Tim. iii. 8: μὴ οἴνῳ πολλῷ προσέχοντας, μὴ αἰσχροκερδεῖς.

Par. 2: ὅπως εὐσταθήσῃ καὶ ἀθόρυβον ᾖ, πρῶτον μεμαθηκὸς ἐν πάσῃ ὑποταγῇ.
See Par. 8.

Par. 1: (ἐπίσκοπος) εἴ τις φήμην καλὴν ἔχει ἀπὸ τῶν ἐθνῶν, εἰ ἀναμάρτητος ὑπάρχει, εἰ φιλόπτωχος, εἰ σώφρων, μὴ μέθυσος, μὴ πόρνος, μὴ πλεονέκτης ἢ λοίδορος ... καλὸν μὲν εἶναι ἀγύναιος, εἰ δὲ μή, ἀπὸ μιᾶς γυναικός· παιδείας μέτοχος ... εἰ δὲ ἀγράμματος, πραΰς.
Reminiscences also in par. 4.

Par. 4: διάκονοι ἔστωσαν δεδοκιμασμένοι πάσῃ διακονίᾳ ... μονόγαμοι, τεκνοτρόφοι, σώφρονες ... μὴ δίγλωσσοι ... μηδὲ οἴνῳ πολλῷ χρώμενοι.

Par. 5 (of the widow): μὴ αἰσχροκερδής, μὴ οἴνῳ πολλῷ προσέχουσα.

---

[1] Compare 2 Cor. xiii. 1 with par. 4, 2 Cor. xi. 25 with par. 6, Gal. v. 21 with par. 1, James ii. 6 with par. 4, James ii. 9 with par. 6.
[2] See the remarks on par. 6 end, and par. 7.
[3] In Tit. ii. 4 it is demanded of the female presbyters that they must be καλοδιδάσκαλοι; this striking demand is explained by the context.

48 SOURCES OF DOCUMENTS *A* AND *B*

1 Tim. iii. 13 : οἱ καλῶς διακονήσαντες (διάκονοι) βαθμὸν ἑαυτοῖς καλὸν περιποιοῦνται.

1 Tim. v. 5 : ἡ ὄντως χήρα καὶ μεμονωμένη . . . προσμένει ταῖς δεήσεσιν καὶ ταῖς προσευχαῖς νυκτὸς καὶ ἡμέρας.

1 Tim. v. 10 : ἐν ἔργοις καλοῖς μαρτυρουμένη . . . εἰ ἐθλιβομένοις ἐπήρκεσεν, εἰ παντὶ ἔργῳ ἀγαθῷ ἐπακολούθησεν.

1 Tim. v. 20 : ἵνα καὶ οἱ λοιποὶ φόβον ἔχωσιν (with regard to discipline).

1 Tim. vi. 17, 18 : ἀγαθοεργεῖν, πλουτεῖν ἐν ἔργοις καλοῖς, εὐμεταδότους εἶναι, κοινωνικούς, ἀποθησαυρίζοντας, ἑαυτοῖς θεμέλιον καλόν.

2 Tim. ii. 17 : ἐπὶ πλεῖον προκόψουσιν ἀσεβείας, καὶ ὁ λόγος αὐτῶν ὡς γάγγραινα νομὴν ἕξει. . . . iii. 6 : αἰχμαλωτίζοντες γυναικάρια.

2 Tim. iv. 2 : ἐπιτίμησον, παρακάλεσον.

2 Tim. iv. 5 : ἔργον ποίησον εὐαγγελιστοῦ.

Par. 6 : οἱ καλῶς διακονήσαντες (διάκονοι) . . . τόπον ἑαυτοῖς περιποιοῦνται τὸν ποιμενικόν.

Par. 5 : αἱ χῆραι . . . προσμένουσαι τῇ προσευχῇ.

Par. 5 : ἵνα δύνηται νήφειν πρὸς τὰς νυκτερινὰς ὑπηρεσίας καὶ εἴ τις ἕτερα βούλοιτο ἐργαγαθεῖν.

Par. 2 : ἵνα καὶ οἱ λοιποὶ φόβον ἔχωσιν (with regard to discipline).

Par. 5 : ἐργαγαθεῖν, par. 4 : τῶν κρυφίων ἔργων καλοί προτρεπτικοί . . . εὐμετάδοτοι, κοινωνικοί, par. 6 : ἀποθησαυρίζειν εἰς ἔργα ἀγαθά, par. 5 : θησαυρίσματα ἀγαθά, par. 6 : ἐργάται τῶν καλῶν ἔργων.

Par. 2 : καὶ ἐπὶ πλεῖον νεμηθῇ ὡς γάγγραινα, καὶ αἰχμαλωτισθῶσιν οἱ πάντες.

Par. 4 : οὓς δὲ παρακαλοῦντες, οὓς δὲ ἐπιτιμῶντες.

Par. 3 : εὐαγγελιστοῦ τόπον ἐργάζεται.

At the first glance our documents appear as a speaking supplement for the justice of the well-known sentence of the Muratorian Fragment regarding the pastoral epistles: 'in ordinatione ecclesiasticae disciplinae sanctificatae sunt.' The pastoral epistles, especially the First Epistle to Timothy, appear to have formed the basis for the canon law definitions of our author. We possess from the oldest times no other documents in which the service, which the pastoral epistles have afforded to the settlement of ecclesiastical order and discipline, appears to come out as plainly as here. The Apostolic Canons which, as far as I know, have not yet been used for the history of the pastoral epistles, thus prove themselves a very important monument with regard to the early history of the New Testament Canon. But does a use of the epistles of Timothy really occur here? The question is not, in my opinion, a simple one. That a literary connection exists is without doubt; but do our documents presuppose the pastoral epistles in their present form, and is it really to be made out whether the priority should be given to them or to *A* and *B*?

The next impression, derived from the consideration of the parallel passages, after the literary relation is affirmed, is this, that we have before us in the sections of the First Epistle to Timothy and in our documents two independent recensions on the foundation of a common material. It can be no question of slavish dependence and mechanical copying of the ordinances on the one side or the other. It is sufficiently clear that what is said on the bishop, on the deacons, and on the widows is the same; and yet it is quite different. So much is thus at least plain: if our author had read the canonical regulations in the Epistles to Timothy, they were of no binding authority on him. The freedom with which they have been treated puts this without doubt. But still more: the First Epistle to Timothy requires plainly of the bishop that he should be διδακτικός (ch. iii. 2); in *A* this requirement only appears as a wish; however, it says of the reader, who is not mentioned in the pastoral epistles, that he should be διηγητικός, εἰδὼς ὅτι εὐαγγελιστοῦ τόπον ἐργάζεται. In *A* it is said of the widows that they should wait on the revelations, περὶ οὗ ἂν δέῃ, while we find in the Epistle to Timothy no trace of this ancient regulation. On the other hand, there are undoubtedly traces of the highest antiquity in the First Epistle to Timothy; thus it is there said quite simply of the bishop, μιᾶς γυναικὸς ἄνδρα, while it stands in *A*, καλὸν μὲν εἶναι ἀγύναιος, εἰ δὲ μὴ ἀπὸ μιᾶς γυναικός. If we miss the regulations in the First Epistle to Timothy and in *A B* about the original organisation of the congregations, the proportion of the archaistic element is about the same in both—(there is indeed something greater in the former, as it brings to light the position which is given to Timothy himself),—but it comes out in different ways and in various places. One has the impression that the author of the pastoral epistles and our authors must have written about the same time, that the ecclesiastical circumstances in which they stood were about the same, that they had essentially the same body of canonical ordinances and to some extent the same order of words, but that they had conceived their regulations quite independently on the same ground. There is still one observation to be emphasised: according to $A\,B$ we can form to ourselves a picture of the government which the authors wished to see affirmed, while it is hardly possible to do so from the pastoral epistles. The canonical regulations in the First Epistle to Timothy are wanting in order, and disconnected; in chapter iii. the question is of the bishop and deacons, in chapter v. of the widows and presbyters; between these, and scattered here and there, are regulations on the competency of the person addressed. In many of the ordinances we see references to an earlier time than that shown by $A\,B$, and by others we are led into a later epoch.

If we were sure that the pastoral epistles are in every point of view integral and original pieces of writing we could rest satisfied in spite of everything (that will have to be conceded) with the opinion that they had been read and taken advantage of by the authors of our documents. But that certainty by no means exists; it exists for none of the three epistles. In regard to the Second Epistle to Timothy, it is generally admitted; in regard to the Epistle to Titus quite lately Otto Ritschl[1] has made valid arguments against the originality of Ch. i. 7-9 which deserve every consideration; with regard to the First Epistle to Timothy the section Ch. iii. 1-13 must raise a doubt of its position between Ch. ii. 1 follg. and Ch. iii. 14 and follg. It does not belong to an epistle, but to a law book. However, it is not permitted us at this time to continue our investigations on the pastoral epistles as if it were certain that the varied material which they contain lies before us in its original form and in its original connection.

Bearing this in mind, we are not in a position to continue further our considerations on the relations of our documents with the pastoral epistles and bring them to a conclusion.

As we do not possess any other writings which will throw light on the sections of the pastoral epistles relating to the government of the church, the question thus arises whether

[1] *Theol. Lit. Zeitung*, 1885, No. 25.

we shall make any sure progress in the positive criticism of these unique compilations of the time when the transition of the enthusiastic organisation of the church into the Church Catholic took place.[1]

[1] It is also to be remarked that our documents *A B* show a certain relation to the text of the first six books of the Apostolic Constitutions. However, this can only be treated of after a searching investigation of this hitherto strangely neglected writing.

CHAPTER VI

THE DATE OF THE COMPOSITION OF DOCUMENTS A AND B

THE indications of date have been shown as completely as possible in chapters 2-5. Thus there is only needed here a short recapitulation. In my edition of the Διδαχή I had shown document A as belonging to the beginning of the third century, and B to the end of the second. The first statement was really caused by what I find was a false though common opinion on the origin of the readership. I see now no cause to separate the two documents from one another, and to assume that the time of their authorship was later than the end of the second century,—it appears to me rather that even the end of the second century is excluded. Instead of a closer determination of the time in figures, giving somewhere between 140 and 180, which must, however, be always uncertain, because the development in various provinces proceeded with varying rapidity, I must content myself with affirming that our documents have thus the closest parallels in the pastoral epistles and in the description of the church organisation by Justin, and that the circumstances of composition which they presuppose are to be held as the immediate introduction to the Catholic Church government; while reminiscences of the organisation for which the Διδαχή offers us a witness are not wanting. There is no presumption of the existence of a New Testament Canon in the documents; but even in the third century there were in all probability provinces in which such a thing was unknown, so that here also nothing is gained as to the time. It may be granted that a fixed divine service and congregational order existed in the time at which our documents arose. Here we have in the description which Justin has given in his Apology the best parallel. If the fragments originated in Egypt we could place their authorship comparatively late between the years 140-180. If we place value on the use made of the Pauline and of the Roman Epistle to the Corinthians, and on that account remove the documents to Greece, we dare not put their authorship much later than the middle of the second century. That we cannot fix the time of authorship within a generation is, particularly in relation to our knowledge of early Christian literature, of little importance. Every student will rejoice with us at the addition of two such instructive documents to the valuable treasures of this literature.

Our knowledge of the history of the pre-catholic government has really been most considerably increased thereby, for—1. They have given us the key by which to open up a series of hitherto not understood and hence not considered problems on the original nature of the office of reader in its full significance. 2. They have given us a sure hint in relation to the origin of the hitherto mistaken so-called 'lower orders.' 3. They have shown us a condition of church government in which so to speak there existed a dyarchy of the presbyterian council and of the one bishop, and have shown us the presbyters as the comptrollers of the bishop's management of the gifts. 4. They have brought us an incontestably plain evidence of rising from the diaconate to the episcopate. 5. They have shown us the last remains of the enthusiastic constitution, already nearly extinct, as it stood immediately before the complete establishment of the catholic church constitution; they have, in one word, introduced us to the last step but one in the development which has taken place from the government of the $\Delta\iota\delta\alpha\chi\acute{\eta}$ to the old catholic constitution. 6. Lastly, they have thrown a peculiar light on the pastoral epistles; for they are the only documents which offer us in their regulations real parallels to the canonical ordinances of the pastoral epistles in early church history.

ON THE ORIGIN OF THE READERSHIP AND OF THE OTHER LOWER ORDERS.

Source A[1] contains regulations on the appointment of the clergy, and in the following order: bishop, presbyter, reader, deacons (and widows). On the reader it says: Ἀναγνώστης καθιστανέσθω (εἷς), πρῶτον δοκιμῇ δεδοκιμασμένος, μὴ γλωσσοκόπος, μὴ μέθυσος μήτε γελωτολόγος, εὔτροπος, εὐπειθής, εὐγνώμων, ἐν ταῖς κυριακαῖς συνόδοις πρῶτος σύνδρομος, εὐήκοος, διηγητικός, εἰδὼς ὅτι εὐαγγελιστοῦ τόπον ἐργάζεται· ὁ γὰρ ἐμπιπλῶν ὦτα μὴ νοοῦντος ἔγγραφος λογισθήσεται παρὰ τῷ θεῷ.

The arrangement of the order of the offices here is surprising. If we did not know that nearly every document of the oldest time (especially any concerning the government) contains something singular, we might be inclined to consider the precedence of the reader before the deacons as an indifferent incident not further to be explained. Hitherto, as far as I know, there is no indication in any of the sources known to us, that the reader possessed[2] a superior position to

[1] See above, p. 7 and follg.
[2] In Bingham, *Orig.* vol. ii. (1725) p. 29 and f., we find nothing on the subject, just as little in the Dictionary of Christian Antiquities, in Kraus, *Real-Encyklop. d. Christ. Alterthümer* (see the article 'Lector,' by Peters), and in the older and in the more modern text-books of Church Law, as far as I know. The older monographs (but which were not accessible to me) on the reader's office are J. A. Schmid, de primitivae ecclesiae lectoribus, Helmst. 1696; Celsius, de anagnostis vet. eccl., Upsal. 1718; Frommann, de hermeneuta vet. eccl., Altorf 1747. Probst, in more modern times, has treated fully (*Kirchl. Disciplin in den 3 ersten christl. Jahrh.*, 1873, p. 60 and follg., and pp. 108-119) of the lower *ordines*, without, however, sifting critically the (very incomplete) material offered. That he should have treated of the readers together with the '*cantores*' (p. 113 and follg.), is an arbitrary proceeding, doubly striking in a Roman Catholic scholar; for the '*cantores*' have in the West never belonged to the lower *ordines*. Hatch, in his lectures on the Organization of the Early Christian Churches, has paid no attention to the lower orders.

ORIGIN OF THE READERSHIP 55

the deacons, and in the passage which even now is still considered as the oldest witness for the existence of a special reader's office in the Catholic hierarchy, the superiority of the deacons over the reader is, as it appears, plainly presumed [1]. We thus find also in most Roman Catholic and Protestant text-books the assertion that the readership and the other lower church orders, since the end of the second or the beginning of the third century, have *arisen out of the diaconate*; that is, it is acknowledged that it must find its origin [2] in the new

[1] Tertullian, de Praescr. 41 : 'Itaque' (in the heretical [Marcionite] communities) 'alius hodie episcopus, cras alius; hodie diaconus qui cras lector, hodie presbyter qui cras laicus.' Besides, De Rossi has discovered in the catacombs of St. Agnes an inscription 'Favor Lector,' and thinks that this is older than the testimony of Tertullian to the existence of the office of reader.

[2] Thomas Aquinas was, I believe, the first to assert definitely that it had its origin in the diaconate, quoting a passage in Dionysius the Areopagite (Summa Suppl. Part III. Quaest 37, Art. 2 : 'In primitiva ecclesia propter paucitatem ministrorum omnia inferiora ministeria diaconibus committebantur. . . . Nihilominus erant omnes praedictae potestates, sed implicite in una diaconi potestate').. As we see, it is a dogmatic theory which influenced him. While all the lower orders are conceived as contained implicitly in the diaconate, they must be all dated back to the Apostolic Age. On the strength of the authority of Thomas this view has become the prevailing one in the Roman Catholic Church (in more ancient times it was opposed by Cardinal Bona, *Rer. Liturg.* l. 1, c. 25, c. 16, who only allowed it as valid for the sub-deacons, and by Morinus, *De Ordin.* P. III. exerc. 14 c. 1). It has now been repeated without hesitation by teachers of canon law and of dogmatics (see also C. Trident. Sess. XXIII. de sacr. ord. c. 2, and the Catechism. rom. Pars II. qu. XII. XV.-XIX.); see B. Phillips' *Kirchenrecht*, 3rd ed. vol. i. (1855), pp. 284 and 310, etc., as well as his *Lehrb. d. Kirchenrechts*, 3rd ed. 1881, p. 101 : 'Out of the diaconate have proceeded the orders of sub-deacons, acolytes, exorcists, readers, and doorkeepers.' P. 106 : 'In the Divine institution of the three hierarchical orders, especially of the diaconate, and therewith also in its sacramental significance, the remaining five degrees dependent on it, although singly they only belong to the *jus ecclesiasticum*, have mediately their share, in so far as the functions which are connected with them originally belonged all to the diaconate.' But even the Protestant canonists and teachers have accepted, as a decided truth, the conclusion that the lower orders, including the readership, sprung from the diaconate; that is, that they arose first in the third century. J. Delitzsch, in his *Lehrsystem d. röm. Kirche*, i. 129, writes thus: 'At the first there proceeded out of the diaconate various minor offices and degrees of consecrated orders—such as sub-deacons, acolytes, exorcists, readers, and doorkeepers.' Friedberg is more careful in his *Lehrbuch des Kirchenrechts*, 2d ed. p. 104, and denies any such derivation ; and so does Richter-Dove, *Lehrb. d. Kath. u. Evang. Kirchen-Rechts*, 6th ed. 8vo, p. 289. Kurtz too (*Lehrb. d. Kirchengesch.* 9th ed. vol. i.) has been silent on the origin of the 'ordines minores'; however, he expressly

requirements of the divine service and of church order, and has naturally its position after that of the much older diaconate. Our passage however, in which the reader stands *before* the deacon—(I call in what follows the whole piece referred to [c. 16-21] 'Source *A* of the Apostolical Canons ')—requires that we should examine the testimony which we possess bearing on the nature and history of the readership, and convince ourselves whether this office really existed from its earliest origin as one related to the diaconate and subordinate to it, or not rather as one of an entirely different kind. Such an examination is so much the more necessary, as our passage offers us a problem not only in the representation of the reader before the deacon, but also in what is required of the reader ($\delta\iota\eta\gamma\eta\tau\iota\kappa\acute{o}\varsigma$, $\epsilon\dot{\iota}\delta\grave{\omega}\varsigma$ $\ddot{o}\tau\iota$ $\epsilon\dot{v}\alpha\gamma\gamma\epsilon\lambda\iota\sigma\tau o\hat{v}$ $\tau\acute{o}\pi o\nu$ $\dot{\epsilon}\rho\gamma\acute{a}\zeta\epsilon\tau\alpha\iota$). This is very striking, but beside this there is one other thing remarkable. Our fragment contains, besides the three well-known Catholic 'ordines,' the readership *alone*. But wherever after the middle of the third century we find this office, we find (at least in the West) also regularly subdeacons, acolytes, exorcists, and doorkeepers, and in this group the readers stand (in Rome) very low in the list, that is, between the exorcists and doorkeepers[1]. Thus is it called, even in the famous passage of the letter of the Roman bishop Cornelius to the Antioch bishop Fabius in the year 250, according to Eusebius (Hist. Eccl. vi. 43, 11): $o\dot{v}\kappa$ $\dot{\eta}\pi\acute{\iota}$-

claims the office of the reader as the oldest. Hinschius (*System d. Kathol. Kirchenrechts*, I. 1869, p. 2) declares: 'The fact that with the spread of Christianity the deacons fitted for the service were not sufficient, so much the less as they maintained the number seven, owing to the circumstance that the apostles in Jerusalem appointed seven, gave a reason for the separation of the further offices.' Hase (*Kirchengeschichte*, I. 1885, p. 419) writes: 'The lesser church service was looked after by the laity, out of whom were formed the four grades of semi-clerics.' Planck (*Geschichte d. christl.-kirchl. Gesellschaftsverfassung*, 1803, i. pp. 141-177), finds that the services performed by the new officials had previously been done by the presbyters and deacons, and he concludes from this that the origin of the new offices arose from the possessors of the older offices advancing from ministers into rulers of the congregation, and hence they needed fresh special *servants*.

[1] We find the offices given together, with the exception of that of the doorkeepers, in the Epistles of Cyprian; see O. Ritschl, *Cyprian v. Karthago u.s.w.* (1885), p. 235 and fol. Ritschl has correctly laid no stress on the absence of the doorkeepers.

ORIGIN OF THE READERSHIP 57

στατο, ἕνα ἐπίσκοπον δεῖν εἶναι ἐν καθολικῇ ἐκκλησίᾳ, ἐν ᾗ οὐκ ἀγνοεῖ πρεσβυτέρους εἶναι τεσσαράκοντα ἕξ, διακόνους ἑπτά, ὑποδιακόνους ἑπτά, ἀκολούθους δύο καὶ τεσσαράκοντα, ἐξορκιστὰς δὲ καὶ ἀναγνώστας ἅμα πυλωροῖς, δύο καὶ πεντήκοντα. Thus—there can be no doubt of this—as an office in the circle of higher and lower hierarchical offices, the readership took a very low position in the second half of the third century (at Rome). But how is it to be explained that the other lower church offices do not occur in our fragments, and that the readership, which is the only one named, stands before the diaconate? Does the origin of our fragment (perhaps for the East) explain the problem, or *has* (this question must necessarily arise) *the readership, before it was a part of the hierarchy, experienced a history of its own? has it, in a word, not had originally a totally different nature and significance, but of which it has now been deprived*?

As soon as this question is asked, there is no more need to complain of the silence of our certainly meagre sources. They were hitherto only dumb because they had not been questioned. We possess, in fact, still the means to justify, in some measure, the singular attitude of our Source in regard to the reader, and to dig out its crumbling primitive history. It will be shown that this history has stood in connection with the history of the enthusiastic organisation of the congregations. In what follows we will try to bring the primitive history of the readership to light, and therewith to connect a research on the origin of the lower orders in general, and on their engrafting into the hierarchy.

Cornelius of Rome has in the passage quoted, as it appears, collected in *one* group exorcists, readers, and doorkeepers[1], while he has mentioned the remaining offices singly. Doubtless this group has appeared to him as the lowest within the hierarchy. At the first glance it appears as somewhat heterogeneous, for more varied functions than the driving out of the devil, reading of the scripture, and church doorkeeping, can hardly be imagined. But, compelled to seek for something to unite them, we easily find the agreement: that the first (the exorcists) have to speak a *sacred formula* (the formula of devil-exorcising); the second (the readers) read the *holy scrip-*

---
[1] However, it is possible that the number 52 only refers to the ostiarii.

ture; and the third have to watch the *holy building*; that is, the holy assembly. It is thus a service in holy things which combines the clergy in this group, but a mechanical service; just on that account they have the lowest rank. The task of the reader in Rome must have been considered mechanical, and for that reason a lower service in things holy.

All developments in the region of church government were completed most speedily at Rome. It might therefore happen that at Carthage still older circumstances and arrangements existed at the same time. In fact we meet with such in the collection of Cyprian's letters.

We should next determine its agreement with the Roman order described by Cornelius. Besides the bishop, presbyters, and deacons there were, according to Cyprian, other *ministeria* among the clergy[1], and these are the exorcists, the readers, the sub-deacons, and the acolytes. These are not seldom mentioned by Cyprian, specially as letter carriers, and are designated as clergy expressly by him and other Carthaginians[2]. As in the official writing, ep. 23[3], the exorcist precedes the reader, so we may take it for granted that the same arrangement was accepted in Carthage as in Rome[4].

But on the other side Cyprian betrays a view of the readership which lets us see this office in another light, and adds thereto some problems which deserve the highest consideration. In the 39th letter he reports to his congregation that he has appointed certain worthy people as readers, and then continues (c. 5): 'ceterum presbyterii honorem designasse nos illis iam sciatis, ut et sportulis idem cum presbyteris honorentur et divisiones mensurnas aequatis quantitatibus partiantur, sessuri nobiscum provectis et corroboratis annis suis,' etc. Thus these readers were not to become mere exorcists, or sub-deacons or deacons, but they were to be immediately appointed to be *presbyters*. Hence Otto Ritschl rightly remarks[5]: '... and thus we

[1] See, for example, Ep. 43, 1.
[2] See especially the letter of the confessors to Cyprian where it says (Ep. 23): 'praesente de clero et exorcista et lectore.'—Ritschl, p. 208 f. 235 f.
[3] See the preceding remark.
[4] That according to Cyprian the readership with the sub-diaconate and the office of exorcist belongs to the lower orders, thus that it is under the diaconate, is plain, and proved so by Ritschl.
[5] Also on p. 185.

see here also, how Cyprian had in view laymen, whom he first nominated readers, as future presbyters. Perhaps, besides this course, there was the other that a sub-deacon should rise to be a deacon[1].' Besides, it is to be observed that in Carthage at the time of Cyprian there had been not only ' presbyteri doctores[2],' but also *lectores doctorum audientium*[3], and that these, both presbyters and readers, stood in the closest connection. The latter, doubtless, supported the former while teaching[4]. But these '*lectores doctorum audientium*' *were not clergymen, but only clero proximi*; further, this passage shows us that the laity were trusted with the reading in divine service, but they still remained laity. Lastly, Cyprian gives in the 39th Epistle (chap. iv.), a description of the significance of the readership, and at the same time a notice on the position which the reader took during the divine service in the church; both show again, as it seems, a certain relationship of the presbyterate with the readership. ' Quid aliud,' it says of the reader, ' quam super pulpitum id est super tribunal ecclesiae oportebat imponi, ut loci altioris celsitate subnixus et plebi universae pro honoris sui claritate conspicuus legat praecepta et evangelium domini quae fortiter ac fideliter sequitur ? vox dominum confessa in his cottidie quae dominus locutus est audiatur. Viderit an sit ulterior gradus ad quem profici in ecclesia possit.' As the presbyters form the ecclesiastical judges, and as the tribunal of the church have their seat in the apse of the church, so does the reader also stand ' super tribunal,' and as the presbyters exhort and practise discipline on the ground of the *Divine word*, so has the reader also to cause the *vox domini* to sound forth[5].

Thus the lowest of the ordines minores appears accord-

[1] See also Ritschl, p. 236.

[2] See on this Dodwell's Dissertatio Cypr. VI. in Migne's *Patr. Lat.* tom. v. pp. 33-48, and the remarks of Ritschl thereon on pp. 171 f. 232 f.

[3] The explanation given by Ritschl on p. 171 to the 29th Epistle seems to me correct ; see also p. 232 f.

[4] See Cypr., ep. 29 : ' fecisse me autem sciatis lectorem Saturum et hypodiaconum Optatum confessorem, quos iam pridem communi consilio clero proximos feceramus, quando aut Saturo die paschae semel atque iterum lectionem dedimus aut, modo cum presbyteris doctoribus lectores probaremus, Optatum inter lectores doctorum audientium constituimus,' etc. etc.

[5] But certainly, even according to Cyprian, the lector is simply a reader, not even a homilist ; and it must besides not be overlooked that Cyprian in

ing to this description as a very high one[1]; from the reader-ship one can rise direct to the office of a presbyter: there is something quite special, readers associated with special presbyters (the *lectores doctorum audientium* by the side of the *presbyteri doctores*); they have to do with the higher education, but they are not members of the clergy, but are reckoned as laymen; lastly, the reading in the church during divine service can be handed over by the bishop to accomplished laymen. All these facts are of the highest importance; they show that the position within the hierarchy to which the readership has fallen does not show the significance which the function of the reader must have possessed in more ancient times, or (more correctly expressed) they show that the readership could not possibly have developed out of the diaconate as a ramification of it; rather must it have had its own proper roots by the side of the episcopal-diaconal organisation of the congregation[2].

But beyond this general acknowledgment the announcements in the Cyprian correspondence will not carry us. Let us pass

other places tries to reduce the significance of the reader as much as possible. The most important and most detailed passage on the readers in the time before Constantine which we possess is in the 'Gesta apud Zenophilum' (Routh, *Reliquiae Sacr.* tom. iv. ed. II. pp. 322-325), for the congregation at Cirta. We there discover that the readers kept the sacred codices in their houses. In the church itself was only one codex, pernimius maior, under the care of the sub-deacons. On the other hand, with the seven readers which the church at Cirta had at the time of the Diocletian persecution, were found 32 codices and 5 quinions. Of those seven readers, one was a tailor, one a grammarian, one an Imperial servant (Caesarianensis). Among the signatures of the Canons of Arles (314) we find the names of 7 exorcists and 2 readers (see Routh, p. 312).

[1] Compare also the contemporary poem of Commodian, 'lectoribus' (Instruct. II. 26). In this it stands: 'Vos flores in plebe, vos estis Christi lucernae, Servate quod estis et memorare potestatis.'

[2] The recognition of this fact is further strengthened by observing that the reader, together and in close connection with the exorcist, suddenly appears among the clergy (at Rome and Carthage). That, however, the exorcists had originally signified something quite different from the ordo minor of the exorcists needs hardly to be proved. However in the older time the 'exorcismos agere' is generally joined to the 'docere' (see, for example, Pseudoclem. de virgin. I. 10; Tertullian de praescr. 41: 'Ipsae mulieres haereticae quam procaces! quae audeant docere, contendere, exorcismos agere, curationes repromittere.' Now if the ordo minor of the exorcists is the phlegma of the old demon-exorcists, who possessed the 'Spirit,' the ordo minor of the readers is the phlegma of the older teachers who were filled with the Spirit. This assertion is purely an hypothesis; but the wonderful connection in Cyprian and Cornelius of 'exorcista et lector' must certainly lead to it.

on to Tertullian. In the first place, it is to be admitted that, if we leave out of view *one* passage, we must acknowledge that Tertullian only knew as within the clergy the bishop, presbyter, and deacon (and the widows[1]); thus he knew nothing yet of the so-called ordines minores [2]. But the passage already quoted (*De Praescript.* 41) shows that in his time at Carthage there were readers, and that they stood *in rank* below the deacons. Still with the latter too much has already been asserted. Tertullian writes: 'Itaque alius hodie episcopus, cras alius; hodie diaconus qui cras lector, hodie presbyter qui cras laicus.' According to this it appears, at the first glance, as if Tertullian in this recognised as a disorder among the heretics, that any one among them could rise from the diaconate to the readership, and one appears to be justified in asserting that, in the sense of Tertullian, the reversed order was that in the church, and then the prevailing one. Thereby would it be proved that in the year 203 at Carthage within the clergy there was at least a fourth grade subordinate to the diaconate; that is, the readership. This conclusion is compulsory on all those who still maintain that already, about the year 200, all ἡγούμενοι in the congregations, as well as all those who exercised spiritual functions, had received their fixed position within the hierarchical episcopal organisation. Whoever is not, however, of this opinion, and is ready to be convinced otherwise—for example, out of the history and works of Origen, or out of the valuable notice in Eusebius, Hist. Eccl. vi. 19 to end—must necessarily be surprised that Tertullian in one single passage should have distinguished indirectly four orders in the clergy, while everywhere else he only speaks of three.

But must this passage be really thus understood, that at Carthage at that time there was existing the *ordo minor of the readership*, and that Tertullian blames the heretics for their rising from the diaconate to the readership (instead of from the readership to the diaconate)? By no means; rather is a totally different explanation of this passage offered. The complete passage runs as follows: 'Ordinationes haereticorum temerariae, leves, inconstantes. Nunc neophytos conlocant,

---

[1] See, for example, de praescript. 3 : 'episcopus, diaconus, vidua.'
[2] See, for example, de bapt. 17, also de fuga 11 ; de exhort. 7 ; de monog. 11, 12. Tertullian separates (de corona 10) 'sacerdotes,' 'ministri' in heathen worship, but not in the Christian.

nunc saeculo obstrictos, nunc apostatas nostros, ut gloria eos obligent, quia veritate non possunt. Nusquam facilius proficitur quam in castris rebellium, ubi ipsum esse illic promereri est. Itaque alius hodie episcopus, cras alius; hodie diaconus qui cras lector, hodie presbyter qui cras laicus. Nam et laicis sacerdotalia munera iniungunt.' Tertullian has a much more serious reproach to make against the heretics than that they did not correctly observe the degrees of order within the clergy. He reproaches them with this, that their 'ordinationes' are especially 'temerariae, leves et inconstantes.' This reproach he grounds in a double way. First, he asserts that they put unqualified persons into the clergy; and secondly, he says, *that the boundary between the 'ordo' and the members of the congregation is not a fixed one but fluctuating*. He illustrates this last sentence, which he concludes with the general reproof, 'nam et laicis sacerdotalia munera iniungunt,' by three examples—(1) The bishops among the heretics change from one day to another; (2) That he who is a deacon to-day may be a reader to-morrow; (3) That he who is a presbyter to-day is a layman to-morrow. Thus, according to Tertullian, the *reader belongs as little to the 'ordo' as does the layman*. He does not blame them because an ordained person (the deacon) must descend and accept a *lower* ordination, but rather because the ordained deacon gives up his ordination, and returns to a position which does not belong to the position of the ordained (the clergy).

Thus we may conclude that Tertullian (as all other passages of his writings show) knew of only *three 'ordines'* in the clergy[1]. There were certainly at his time readers; Tertullian would have perhaps considered their position as subordinate to that of bishops, priests, and deacons, but they did not belong to the clergy.

But to what then did they belong? We may here answer by the counter-question, To what did the 'martyrs,' the 'confessors,' the 'virgins of both sexes,' the 'doctors,' the '*prophetae et prophetissae*' belong? We find all these in Tertullian [2]. They were very important, honourable persons, but they did not belong to the clergy.

We have thus to decide that the readers (and with them the

---

[1] If we leave out of view the 'viduae.'
[2] Doctor: de praescr. 3. 14; adv. Prox. 1. See my edition of the Διδαχή, pp. 131-137, on teachers.

exorcists) first came into the clergy in the time between Alexander Severus (c. 222) and Philippus Arabs in Carthage and Rome, and were attached to the deacons as lower officers [1]. There were there, about the year 200, undoubtedly special readers. But if this was the case, and if we consider that they, together with the exorcists, were added afterwards to the clergy, while at Cyprian's time they possessed a certain affinity to the presbyters, especially to the *presbyteri-doctores*, and on the other hand laymen could still be always intrusted with the reading, there must exist the well-grounded supposition that their function earlier had not been a mere mechanical one, or was at least not held to be so. So far as they by the reading of the holy scriptures according to their vocation had *edified* the congregation, they must (just as the exorcists) have been brought into a special relation *to the Holy Spirit*. It is easily to be supposed that they probably besides reading had possessed also the right of expounding the scriptures. But in this passage we have no ground to adopt this hypothesis. It suffices for us to remember that in the older time, in the second century, the functions of reading the scriptures and of preaching were often quite closely connected, because both had the same end and the like success, that is, the edification of the congregation [2]. The spiritually filled teacher and prophet did not

---

[1] For the Roman church the silence of Hippolytus is of significance. From the Philosophumena, which were written soon after the death of Callistus, thus soon after the year 222, there is evidence that then *only* bishops, presbyters, and deacons were reckoned in Rome among the clery. See IX. 12: Ἐπὶ Καλλίστου ἤρξαντο ἐπίσκοποι καὶ πρεσβύτεροι καὶ διάκονοι δίγαμοι καὶ τρίγαμοι καθίστασθαι εἰς κλήρους. Εἰ δέ τις ἐν κλήρῳ ὢν γαμοίη, μένειν τὸν τοιοῦτον ἐν τῷ κλήρῳ ὡς μὴ ἁμαρτηκότα. Thus the year 222 marks the *terminus a quo* for the increase of the clergy by the lower clergy. Just so far do the last writings of Tertullian lead us. Hagemann indeed (*Römische Kirche*, 1864, p. 64 and follg.) quite arbitrarily refers to the sentence εἰ δέ, κ.τ.λ., on lower clergy, to free Callistus from the reproach that he suffered marriage of the priests; so does Probst (*Kirchl. Disciplin*, 1873, p. 61). This view was first given out by Döllinger (*Kallist. u. Hippolyt*, p. 150 and follg.); it is however refuted by Langen (*Gesch. d. röm. K.* i. p. 252 and follg.; see Tert. de Monog. 12). Even De Rossi (*Bullet.*, 1886, p. 33) has not adopted it.

[2] See, for example, 1 Tim. iv. 13: ἕως ἔρχομαι πρόσεχε τῇ ἀναγνώσει, τῇ παρακλήσει, τῇ διδασκαλίᾳ. The sense is that the evangelist of the congregation, Timothy, should exercise these three functions until the apostle should come and undertake them. From a later time, we may be reminded of Tertullian, De anima 9 : 'Scripturae leguntur aut psalmi canuntur aut allocutiones

give out their own, but that which the Holy Spirit laid on their lips. Thus there consisted no real difference between them and those who put in efficacy the written word of the Holy Spirit. If we add to this that the art of reading [1] and a good delivery could not have been common among the uncultivated congregations of Christians in the second century (there were even among the bishops Analphabeti), it can thus be perfectly understood that the readers of the second century would have stood in the highest esteem. That there was, however, in Rome even in the middle of the second century a reader distinct from the overseer and from the deacons is shown in the famous 67th chapter of the First Apology of Justin, in which the congregational divine service is depicted. Here it is said:—Καὶ τὰ ἀπομνημονεύματα τῶν ἀποστόλων ἢ τὰ συγγράμματα τῶν προφητῶν ἀναγινώσκεται, μέχρις ἐγχωρεῖ. Εἶτα παυσαμένου τοῦ ἀναγινώσκοντος ὁ προεστὼς διὰ λόγου τὴν νουθεσίαν καὶ πρόκλησιν τῆς τῶν καλῶν τούτων μιμήσεως ποιεῖται. And at the end: τοῖς οὐ παροῦσι διὰ τῶν διακόνων [the sacred food] πέμπεται.

Thus about the year 150 the 'sermon' was in Rome the regular affair of the overseer, but there was (at least) one special reader. The western sources lead us no further. We possess, however, fortunately eastern sources which strengthen our conjectures on the original significance and the oldest history of the reader, which we have already indicated above, and give us a more sure introduction to it.

In the eastern churches the lower orders are never so distinctly marked out and in such a fixed order (five) as in the west. Also the holders of these offices, from the moment when they appear as lower church officers, appear to have played if possible a still

proferuntur aut petitiones delegantur.' Compare Origen c. Celsum III. 50: καὶ δι' ἀναγνωσμάτων καὶ διὰ τῶν εἰς αὐτὰ διηγήσεων προτρέποντες. Pseudo-Clem. de Virgin. I. 10 : 'legere scripturas aut exorcizare aut docere.'

[1] The *scriptio continua* in which the books were then written made the reading of them extraordinarily difficult. Thus Hermas says, Vis. II. 1, 4: μετεγραψάμην πάντα πρὸς γράμμα (that is the whole book handed to him), οὐχ ηὕρισκον γὰρ τὰς συλλαβάς. Compare also Isidore, de Offic. II. 10, 2 (see Wasserschleben *Die irische Kanonensammlung*, 2d ed. p. 24): 'Qui ad lectoris provehitur gradum, ista erit doctrina: in libris inbutus, sensuque verborum scientia ornatus ita, ut in distinctionibus sententiarum intelligat, ubi finiatur iunctura, ubi adhuc pendeat oratio, ubi sententia extrema concludatur et his similia.'

ORIGIN OF THE READERSHIP

more subordinate part than in the western. On the other hand some of these orders have been retained effectively in the life of the church in the west, while in the east they have been practically as good as extinguished. In what follows I shall first give a short survey of the state in which we find them in the fourth century, when the lower orders may first be observed within the clergy in the west, and from that point work backwards.

In the so-called Apostolic Canons[1] there are reckoned in many passages, besides the bishop, presbyter, and deacon, other persons in the κατάλογος ὁ ἱερατικός, and general directions given for them[2]. In three passages they are in fact introduced: (ch. 27, 69) readers and psalm-singers, (ch. 43) sub-deacons, psalm-singers, and readers; in Dionysius Exiguus the readers stand here also first. Marriage was permitted to readers and psalm-singers in their office. Acolytes, exorcists, and doorkeepers are not mentioned. In the Canons of the Synod of Laodicea[3] it is said, ch. 15, 'that besides the psalm-singers appointed thereto, who mount the ambo and sing out of the book, no others should sing in church'; in chapter 17 that psalm-reading and lesson should alternate in divine service; then follow from ch. 20 some regulations on the servants (ὑπηρετῶν), and all (the lower) clergy. Sub-deacons are justly understood among them. The regulations show what subordinate officials these clergy had been[4]. The second Canon contains a sufficient announcement on the clerical degrees of rank in the following order: presbyters, deacons, ministers (sub-deacons), readers, psalm-singers, exorcists, doorkeepers. Acolytes are not known, and psalm-singers are added to the readers (a proof how low they stand); otherwise the said order lies before us as in the letter of Cornelius. But before everything, it is important that we read in the twenty-sixth Canon: 'Whoever is not ordained by the bishop may not exorcise either in

---

[1] See Hefele, *Conciliengeschichte*, i., 2d ed., p. 793 and follg. These canons may be named here, although their last editing is later than the fourth century.

[2] See the canons 9, 15, 17, 18, 26, 51, 63, 70, according to the Roman numbering.

[3] Hefele, p. 746 and follg.

[4] See ch. 21: the ministers (sub-deacons) shall not move the sacred vessels. Ch. 22: they may not carry the orarium, just as little (ch. 23) may the readers and psalm-singers. See also ch. 25.

E

the church or in the houses.' Such a regulation was thus still necessary; that is, there were still laymen who practised as exorcists [1]. Lastly, it may be remarked that the Synodal Canons in several places (see 27, 30, 36, 41, 42, and 54) distinguish between the higher (ἱερατικοί) and the lower (κληρικοί) clergy, and acknowledge by their side a special class of ascetics (see 24, 30). In the forged recension of the Ignatian epistles, which arose in the middle of the fourth century [2], the following order is given: presbyters, deacons, sub-deacons, readers, psalm-singers, doorkeepers, grave-diggers, exorcists, confessors, deaconesses, virgins, lay brethren, lay sisters [3]. This is the completest list which we possess of the fourth century. Again we observe, as everywhere in the east, the connection of readers and psalm-singers, while in the west it is the exorcists and readers who stand together. The same Syro-Palestinian cleric who in the fourth century forged the Ignatian epistles edited also older canonical law books, and out of them restored the collection of eight books of Apostolic Constitutions [4]. Accordingly we find also in the eighth book of this collection, chapters 4, 5, 15-17, the following clerical stages: bishop, presbyter, deacon,—deaconesses,—sub-deacons, readers, confessors,—virgins, widows,—exorcists; in chapter 27 at the end, however, by the side of the readers, psalm-singers are specially mentioned. It is seen that there are wanting only the doorkeepers and the gravediggers who were certainly not consecrated [5]. A complete and strict order of rank of the ministering clergy did not exist as it did at Rome. Epiphanius [6] gives the following order: bishop, presbyter, deacon,

[1] I quote here the remark of Hefele, and refrain from any commentary on it: 'Balsamon here concludes that this exorcising is identical with "catechising the unbelieving," and Van Espen remarks on this: "there is a double power of the demons on man, an outer and an inner; by the latter man is, among other things, fast held in unbelief, and for that purpose catechetical instruction is also an exorcism."'

[2] See my edition of the Διδαχή, p. 241 and follg.

[3] See the Pseudo-Ignat. ad Antioch. 12.

[4] See my edition of the Διδαχή, etc.

[5] Const. App. III. 11, the editor has the following order: bishop, presbyter, deacon: οἱ λοιποὶ κληρικοὶ οἷον ἀναγνῶσται ἢ ψάλται ἢ πυλωροὶ ἢ ὑπηρέται and immediately after ἀναγνῶσται, ὑπηρέται, ᾠδοί, πυλωροί. The 'servants' are the sub-deacons. II. 28: bishop, presbyter, deacon, reader, psalm-singers, doorkeeper; VI. 17: bishop, presbyter, deacon, minister, psalm-singers, readers, doorkeepers.

[6] Panarion, *Expos. fidei*, c. 20.

sub-deacon; these four ranks he reckons for the ἱερωσύνη, for which he gives special duties and positions in regard to marriage, and who hence can only be recruited from certain classes of men. Then he continues: μετὰ ταύτην τὴν ἱερωσύνην λοιπὸν ἀναγνωστῶν τάγμα ἐξ ὅλων τῶν ταγμάτων, τουτέστι παρθένων καὶ μοναζόντων καὶ ἐγκρατευομένων καὶ χηρευσάντων καὶ τῶν ἔτι ἐν σεμνῷ γάμῳ, εἰ δὲ εἴη ἀνάγκη, καὶ ἀπὸ τῶν μετὰ θάνατον τῆς πρώτης γυναικὸς δευτέρᾳ συναφθέντων. Καὶ γὰρ οὐκ ἔστιν ἱερεὺς ὁ ἀναγνώστης, ἀλλ' ὡς γραμματεὺς τοῦ λόγου. Hereupon he mentions the deaconesses, then (ἑξῆς τούτων) the exorcists, and the interpreters[1] (ἐπορκισταὶ καὶ ἑρμηνευταὶ γλώσσης εἰς γλῶσσαν ἢ ἐν ταῖς ἀναγνώσεσιν ἢ ἐν ταῖς προσομιλίαις). Gravediggers and doorkeepers make up the end. We have here manifestly present the same relations and the same order as in the pseudo-Ignatius (and pseudo-Clement).

If we pass on as far as the beginning of the fourth century we find accounts of the lower clergy very rare. But that there were such about 325 in the east is shown by the sixteenth canon of Nicaea, for we there meet with a regulation for presbyters and deacons, and thereto τοῖς ἐν τῷ κανόνι ἐξεταζομένοις. Under this expression, which occurs twice, only the lower clergy can be understood[2]. The canons of the Synod of Neo-Caesarea carry us still further back. Here it says (ch. 10) that a deacon, who has sinned, τὴν τοῦ ὑπηρέτου τάξιν ἐχέτω. He should thus be degraded to the *clerici minores*, that is, to a sub-deacon[3]. The name 'sub-deacon' occurs besides in the east for the first time in Athanasius[4].

In what we have hitherto said we have given a survey of the *clerici minores* in the oriental churches in the fourth century.

[1] The interpreters of the speakers of tongues is not meant, as a closer consideration makes plain.

[2] See Hefele.

[3] On ὑπηρέτης in the sense of a collective designation of the lower clergy see the second Canon of Arles. It equals sub-deacon in the Canons of Laodicea (see above and Routh, *Reliq. Sacr.* iv. p. 199). The fifteenth Canon of Neo-Caesarea is also instructive for the origin of the sub-diaconate: Διάκονοι ἑπτὰ ὀφείλουσιν εἶναι κατὰ τὸν κανόνα, κἂν πάνυ μεγάλη εἴη ἡ πόλις· πεισθήσῃ δὲ ἀπὸ τῆς βίβλου τῶν πράξεων.

[4] Epist. ad solitar. vitam ag. tom. i. p. 380, Paris edition, 1698: Εὐτύχιον ὑποδιάκονον ἄνδρα καλῶς ὑπηρετοῦντα τῇ ἐκκλησίᾳ. Here also we recognise the identity of ὑποδιάκονος and ὑπηρέτης. The deacons were in reality no longer 'servants'; hence for the performance of services ὑπηρετεῖν is used instead of διακονεῖν.

It has shown us that their order was not a very strict one, but that the readers had received their position by the side of the psalm-singers, who do not occur in the west[1]. It teaches us us further that acolytes did not exist as clergy in the east, and it shows lastly that even in the fourth century the occurrence of unordained laymen as exorcists had to be opposed. Basil has, however, given us the most important difference between the κατάλογος τῶν ἱερωμένων ἀνδρῶν and the lower clergy when he designated the latter as προσκαρτεροῦντες ἐν ἀχειροτονήτῳ ὑπηρεσίᾳ[2]. They must be *appointed* by the bishop, but they were—at least according to Basil—not *consecrated*, as were the presbyters and deacons[3].

Hitherto we have been left in darkness as to the origin of these offices. But might not perhaps something be made of such passages where the appointment of readers and exorcists is described? The Apostolic Constitutions contain, as is well known, some very old fragments in all their books. They communicate to us the prayer, which was to be spoken during the consecration of the reader[4], and this is, in fact, extremely remarkable. It runs:—Ὁ θεὸς ὁ αἰώνιος, ὁ πολύς ἐν ἐλέει καὶ οἰκτιρμοῖς, ὁ τὴν τοῦ κόσμου σύστασιν διὰ τῶν ἐνεργουμένων φανεροποιήσας καὶ τὸν ἀριθμὸν τῶν ἐκλεκτῶν σου διαφυλάττων· αὐτὸς καὶ νῦν ἔπιδε ἐπὶ τὸν ἐγχειριζόμενον τὰς ἁγίας σου γραφὰς ἀναγινώσκειν τῷ λαῷ σου, καὶ δὸς αὐτῷ πνεῦμα ἅγιον, πνεῦμα προφητικόν· ὁ σοφίσας Ἔσδραν τὸν θεράποντά σου ἐπὶ τὸ ἀναγινώσκειν τοὺς νόμους σου τῷ λαῷ σου, καὶ νῦν παρακαλούμενος ὑφ' ἡμῶν σόφισον τὸν δοῦλόν σου καὶ δὸς αὐτῷ, ἀκατάγνωστον διανύσαντα τὸ ἐγχειρισθὲν αὐτῷ ἔργον, ἄξιον ἀναδειχθῆναι μείζονος βαθμοῦ διὰ Χριστοῦ, μεθ' οὗ σοι ἡ δόξα κ.τ.λ.

[1] On their origin see Fertsch in the *Denkschrift d. Predigerseminars zu Friedberg*, Giessen, 1839, p. 70. [2] Basil. ep. canon 51.

[3] We find in Origen no account of lower clergy in the church. There were of course readers as well as 'doctores' during his time in Alexandria, but they did not belong to the 'ordo.'

[4] According to VIII. 21 he should be consecrated by the laying on of hands, not so according to Basil. In the Διατάξεις τῶν ἁγίων ἀποστόλων περὶ χειροτονιῶν διὰ Ἱππολύτου (*Reliq. jur. eccles.*, ed. Lagarde, p. 5 and follg.), which give in a shorter form the eighth book of the Constitutions, and belong at any rate at the earliest to the fourth century, it says: ἀναγνώστης καθίσταται, ἐπιδιδόντος αὐτῷ βιβλίον τοῦ ἐπισκόπου, οὐδὲ γὰρ χειροθετεῖται. The consecration prayer is on this account also wanting.

ORIGIN OF THE READERSHIP 69

Can this prayer—apart from its unfitting and ugly conclusion, ἄξιον κ.τ.λ.—have been composed in the fourth century? Certainly not, as little as most of the other consecration prayers in the eighth book of the Constitutions. Like these it shows its dependence on the great prayer in the first Epistle of Clement [1], and while the Holy Spirit, the prophetic spirit, is entreated to descend on him who is to be consecrated, his function appears in a different light from that which rests on the reader joined to the psalm-singer of the fourth century. We are rather reminded of passages like that in 1 Tim. iv. 14: μὴ ἀμέλει τοῦ ἐν σοὶ χαρίσματος, ὃ ἐδόθη σοι διὰ προφητείας μετὰ ἐπιθέσεως τῶν χειρῶν τοῦ πρεσβυτερίου. The prophetic spirit shall be apportioned to the reader. God himself shall instruct him (σοφίζειν); as Ezra shall he stand in the congregation; he is consecrated to a special work, not to an office. This prayer belongs to Christian antiquity, or at least it points back to it [2]. *It shows us that the reader was once reckoned among the persons who had the charisma.*

Nor is it otherwise with the exorcists according to the Const. App. VIII. 25: Ἐπορκιστὴς οὐ χειροτονεῖται [3]· εὐνοίας γὰρ ἑκουσίου τὸ ἔπαθλον καὶ χάριτος θεοῦ διὰ Χριστοῦ ἐπιφοιτήσει τοῦ ἁγίου πνεύματος· ὁ γὰρ λαβὼν χάρισμα ἰαμάτων δι' ἀποκαλύψεως ὑπὸ θεοῦ ἀναδείκνυται, φανερᾶς οὔσης πᾶσιν τῆς ἐν αὐτῷ χάριτος. ἐὰν δὲ χρεία αὐτοῦ γένηται εἰς ἐπίσκοπον ἢ πρεσβύτερον ἢ διάκονον χειροτονεῖται.

According to this regulation—again apart from the conclusion—the exorcist does not yet specially belong to the clergy. He has a charisma received from God, and by his exercise of it he is *ipso facto* announced by God as an exorcist [4].

This view is also represented in the instructive fragment which opens the eighth book of the Constitutions; it is however

---

[1] See 1 Clem. 60, 1 : σὺ τὴν ἀέννασν τοῦ κόσμου σύστασιν διὰ τῶν ἐνεργουμένων ἐφανεροποίησας . . . ἐλεήμων καὶ οἰκτίρμος . . . (59, 2) : ὅπως τὸν ἀριθμόν τῶν ἐκλεκτῶν αὐτοῦ ἐν ὅλῳ τῷ κόσμῳ διαφυλάξῃ.

[2] Probst (*Kirchl. Disciplin i. d. 3 ersten Jahrh.*, p. 119) believes that this prayer was composed *after* the middle of the third century; but his arguments are very vague.

[3] Thus it is said also (ch. 53) for the confessor.

[4] In relation to the practice of exorcism among the possessed and the sick in the middle of the third century, compare Cornelius in Eusebius, H. E. VI. 43, 14, Firmilian in Cyprian, Ep. 75, 10, and Pseudo-Clem. de Virgin. I. 12.

also especially in MSS. under the title Διδασκαλία τῶν ἁγίων ἀποστόλων περὶ χαρισμάτων [1]. Here the charismata, exorcism, healing of the sick and prophecy are all acknowledged as gifts bestowed on certain laymen by God, but the possessors of them are warned not to exalt themselves above their office. But at the same time these gifts are greatly lowered in their significance; they are only given to the church for its mission-activity and bring no gain to the congregation; they would therefore cease if there were no more unbelievers; much higher than the χαρίσματα τὰ διὰ τῶν σημείων stands the χάρισμα πνευματικόν, which every Christian, in so far as he is believing, has attained. 'Rejoice not'—this gospel saying is quoted—'that the spirits are subject to you, but rejoice rather that your names are written in heaven.' Here we see plainly in an original source of the apostolic constitutions of the third century, how in the course of that century the gifts of grace and their possessors, the prophets and exorcists, were deposed until they became regular clergy *ordinis minoris*, and therewith were transformed into something quite new [2].

The Apostolic Constitutions, however, bring us one more important notice. In Book II. Ch. 28 there is an account of the share that the various clergy should receive out of the church treasury, and of the reader it says: εἰ δὲ καὶ ἀναγνώστης ἐστι, λαμβανέτω καὶ αὐτὸς μοῖραν μίαν εἰς τιμὴν τῶν προφητῶν. The deacons are compared with Christ, the presbyters with the apostles, *the readers with the prophets*. Have we not here a reminiscence that the reader was formerly considered as one gifted with the Holy Spirit? Does not the εἰς τιμὴν τῶν προφητῶν agree with that πνεῦμα προφητικόν which, according to the old consecration prayer, was prayed to be sent down on the reader?

We possess, however, still three documents of canon law which are older than the Apostolic Constitutions, and have served them partially as a basis: that is, 1st, the Διδασκαλία, only preserved in the Syriac, the foundation of the first six

[1] Lagarde, *Reliq.* p. 1 and follg.
[2] Origen speaks several times in his books against Celsus of the dying out of the charismata. See also the fragment out of the Commentary on the Proverbs (Opp., ed. Delarue, iii. p. 5): μὴ θαυμάσῃς δέ, εἰ νῦν ὁ ἀληθῶς κατὰ θεὸν σοφὸς οὐχ εὑρίσκεται· ἐκλέλοιπε γὰρ τὰ πλεῖστα τῶν ἐξαιρέτων χαρισμάτων, ὡς ἢ μηδαμῶς ἢ σπανίως εὑρίσκεσθαι.

books of the Apostolic Constitutions; 2nd, the Canons of Hippolytus in Arabic, which is the most correct version,—the old source which lies at their basis here comes into consideration; and 3rd, the Διδαχὴ τῶν δώδεκα ἀποστόλων. The last, the oldest document, unfortunately for our purpose, yields nothing *direct*, for neither readers nor exorcists are mentioned in it. However, the two first named deserve our attention in a high degree. Lagarde has made accessible to us in the most thankworthy manner the Didaskalia, which exist in Syriac, in Bunsen's *Analecta Ante-Nicaena* (vol. ii., 1854). He has printed them also in a Greek re-translation, as well as the first six books according to the vulgar Greek edition, with double type, so that at once the original and the work of the editor can be easily distinguished. The foundation which lies before us in the Syriac translation, not without small omissions and additions [1], belongs rather to the first than to the second half of the third century. That is shown also in the order of government. *The Didaskalia does not yet know of the sub-deacons, the psalm-singers, and the ostiarii, it knows besides the bishop, the presbyters, the deacons, and the widows, only the reader.* Thus it shows us the same condition within the clergy as our Source *A*. But still more: one passage throws a bright light on the significance and position of the reader. In Book II. 20, it says [2] :—Ἀφοριζέσθω δὲ ἐν τῇ δοχῇ τὸ τῷ ποιμένι ἐθίμιον, κἂν μὴ παραδέχηται, εἰς τιμὴν θεοῦ τοῦ τὴν ἱερατείαν αὐτῷ ἐγχειρίσαντος. ὅσον δὲ ἑκάστῃ τῶν χηρῶν δίδοται, διπλοῦν διδόσθω τοῖς διακόνοις εἰς γέρας Χριστοῦ. εἰ δὲ τις θέλοι καὶ τοὺς πρεσβυτέρους τιμᾶν, διπλοῦν διδότω αὐτοῖς ὡς καὶ τοῖς διακόνοις. τιμᾶσθαι γὰρ ὀφείλουσιν ὡς ἀπόστολοι καὶ ὡς σύμβουλοι τοῦ ἐπισκόπου καὶ τῆς ἐκκλησίας στέφανος. εἰσὶ γὰρ συνέδριον καὶ βουλὴ τῆς ἐκκλησίας. εἰ δὲ καὶ ἀναγνώστης ἐστί, λαμβανέτω καὶ αὐτὸς ὡς οἱ πρεσβύτεροι [εἰς τιμὴν τῶν προφητῶν [3]]. ἑκάστῳ οὖν ἀξιώματι οἱ λαϊκοὶ τὴν προσήκουσαν τιμὴν νεμέτωσαν ἐν τοῖς δόμασι.

[1] The additions are for the most part anti-Novatian; by them contradictions have come into the text of the Didaskalia. Omissions are not very rare.
[2] We have introduced above part of the passage, but as it was revised by the editor of the fourth century.
[3] These words are wanting in the Syriac, but their existence is attested by Greek, and they are required by the context. It is quite improbable that they have been added by the editor.

Thus the office of the reader is an ἀξίωμα: it belongs, as it does in our Source A, to the clergy; but it is not an absolutely necessary ἀξίωμα in the clergy; the reader may also be wanting. Where there is a reader, he should have as much as the presbyters, that is, double what the widow receives, for he has the position of a *prophet*.

What is so eminently instructive in this regulation is this, that the reader appears here among the clergy, but not as a *servant*—there were not yet any *ordines minores*—but in an equal position to the presbyters and deacons. Here we have a real parallel to the regulation in Source A on the reader; the λαμβανέτω ὡς οἱ πρεσβύτεροι reminds us of the affinity of readers and presbyters in Cyprian, and the εἰς τιμὴν τῶν προφητῶν points out that the function of the reader was not yet considered as a purely mechanical duty in holy things. But still plainer does the importance of our passage come out if we compare it with its re-edition in the second book of the Apostolic Constitutions. It runs:—Εἰ δὲ καὶ ἀναγνώστης ἐστί, λαμβανέτω καὶ αὐτὸς μοῖραν μίαν εἰς τιμὴν τῶν προφητῶν, ὡσαύτως καὶ ψαλμῳδὸς καὶ πυλωρός. ἑκάστῳ οὖν ἀξιώματι, κ.τ.λ.

Thus the editor has changed the double share of the reader into a single one; he has therefore omitted the words ὡς οἱ πρεσβύτεροι, and has lastly by adding to the reader the psalm-singer and door-keeper thereby degraded him into a quite subordinate sphere.

There lies, as we see, quite a piece of the history of the reader between the definition of the Didaskalia and the definition of its editor in the fourth century. It is not the first phase of the history of the reader but the second. The first was already past at the moment in which the reader found a position, still a high one, in the *clergy*.

With the gain which the Didaskalia has procured for the history of the reader anything we can learn from the Arabic canons of Hypolytus is not to be compared, but it is still not without importance. We certainly require a thorough examination of these canons[1], and until we have received this any consideration of single points can only promise an hypothetical

---

[1] The disquisition given by Haneberg in his valuable publication (1870) cannot be considered as such.

value. As the Canons exist in Arabic, they form a law book which has got into disorder and been disfigured by very late additions. But an old foundation is unmistakable, and can indeed be proved, as this is shown already in its close relations with the original text of the 8th book, especially in the first half of the Constitutions. The canons recognise, besides the bishop, presbyters, and deacons, only readers and sub-deacons. Of the first, however, we read (chapter 7)[1]: 'Qui eligitur Anagnostes, ornatus sit virtutibus diaconi, neque manus ipsi imponatur primo, sed liber evangelii ab episcopo ipsi porrigatur'; and chapter 37[2]: 'Etiam Anagnostae habeant festiva indumenta sicut diaconi et sacerdotes et stent in ambone et alter alterum excipiat, donec totus populus congregetur.'

Here it strikes us that the reader has to be adorned with the virtues of the deacon, and that he is not to be specially consecrated. If he has to possess the qualities of a deacon *before* he is appointed reader, he appears at least equal in rank to the deacons. We only point here to this remarkable passage, and reserve to ourselves further explanations. But we remember here the above mentioned saying of Tertullian that in the heretic (Marcionite) churches, 'hodie diaconus est qui cras lector.' Tertullian has judged this as a punishable disorder; but we may now say it was no disorder, but the retention of an older order. Should it be shown that a deacon possessed the gift of reading, he could also act as reader to the congregation. *Reader and deacon were not yet distinct orders, but had quite different functions*[3].

Let us return now to our Source *A*. It places the reader between the presbyters and deacons, and thus determines: 'Ἀναγνώστης καθιστανέσθω (εἷς) πρῶτον δοκιμῇ δεδοκιμασμένος ... εὐήκοος, διηγητικός, εἰδὼς ὅτι εὐαγγελιστοῦ τόπον ἐργάζεται. ὁ γὰρ ἐμπιπλῶν ὦτα μὴ νοοῦντος ἔγγραφος λογισθήσεται παρὰ τῷ θεῷ.' The reader shall, according to this, be appointed on the ground of an examination: this characterises

[1] See Haneberg, p. 67 and fol. [2] *Ibid.* p. 94.
[3] It is worth mentioning that we possess also a notice on readings in the Marcionite, or more strictly in the Apelleian Church. Of Apelles it is said in the Pseudo-Tertullian, in the spurious supplement to the Praescriptiones: 'Solo utitur (evangelio) et apostolo, sed Marcionis, id est non toto. Habet praeterea privatas, sed extraordinarias lectiones suas, quas appellat Phaneroseis.'

him as an official like the deacon. But as an official he appears in the Didaskalia, and indeed, as here, as a *higher* official, and not yet as a servant in the proper sense of the word. Our Source places him between the presbyters and deacons; but also according to the Didaskalia he was to receive the same portion (τιμή) as the presbyters; according to the Arabic canons he was to be adorned with the virtues of a deacon; and even from the epistles of Cyprian there appears a closer affinity of the reader to the presbyters, especially to the presbyteri-doctores. Lastly, in our Source *A* it says that the reader must be mindful that he occupies the place of an evangelist[1]. By the evangelists are to be understood charismatic teachers. Of these Source *A* says nothing, but it contains, just in this designation of the reader, a rudiment of them. The reader appears in it by no means as one intrusted with a lower mechanical service in holy things, but he is in it a charismatic teacher. But it is this manner of considering it which we find in the old consecrating prayer for the reader : δὸς αὐτῷ πνεῦμα ἅγιον, πνεῦμα προφητικόν; we find it in the regulation that the reader should receive his portion εἰς τιμὴν τῶν προφητῶν; we may, lastly, in all probability surmise this to be the case in the Marcionite congregations where the reader in Tertullian's time was not reckoned in the *ordo*, and where a layman or even a deacon could act as reader. We see thus that the regulations hitherto considered in our Source are not absolutely unprecedented. We have found for them various and important parallels. It is at any rate now manifest that the reader is shown in our Source to be in a position in which it would be impossible to reckon on any continuance. In the 'ἀναγνώστης καθιστανέσθω πρῶτον δοκιμῇ δεδοκιμασμένος,' and in the 'εἰδὼς ὅτι εὐαγγελιστοῦ τόπον ἐργάζεται,' there lies a deep contradiction: it is the contradiction of the future and past in the government of the church. If the reader is an

---

[1] Even if ἐργάζεσθαι were to be translated by 'to acquire,' which is improbable, the reference to the evangelist would still be significant. According to the Irish Collection of Canons, Book V. (Wasserschleben, die irische Kanonensammlung, 2d Aufl. p. 24), a Synodus Romana (in truth the statuta ecclesiae antiq. c. 8) has determined that at the consecration of a reader, the bishop, while he hands him the sacred codex, shall say: 'Accipe et esto verbi dei revelator, si fideliter et utiliter impleveris hoc officium, *habiturus partem cum his, qui ministraverunt verbum domini.*'

evangelist appointed by God, he cannot be at the same time an official appointed by the congregation. As soon as he became the latter, he could not long continue to be the former. But if he was *only* an official without being at the same time a priest, without being able to receive consecration like a deacon, he must become a *lower* official, and that so much the more as the function of edification passed more and more into the hands of the priests. The change of the bishops and presbyters into a priesthood which stood high above the congregation put an end to all charismata, and forced their possessors— they were now valued only according to to their relationship to the priesthood—into a low position [1].

Our Source, however, contains yet *one* regulation for which we have hitherto found no parallel. It requires that the reader should be 'διηγητικός,' and has added specially to this quality the following words : ' εἰδὼς ὅτι εὐαγγελιστοῦ τόπον ἐργάζεται.' Capacity of teaching, the capacity of *expounding* the holy scriptures can alone be understood by the word 'διηγητικός,' and this explanation is confirmed by the fact that this capacity was not yet demanded in all circumstances of the bishop [2] : the reader is thus here brought nearer to the *doctor*, the old διδάσκαλος, than is hitherto to be found in any other source. We have seen how close the ἀνάγνωσις and the διδασκαλία were brought together in the oldest time—1 Tim. iv. 13 : ἕως ἔρχομαι πρόσεχε τῇ ἀναγνώσει, τῇ παρακλήσει, τῇ διδασκαλίᾳ —we also saw that even in the time of Cyprian the nonclerical lectores doctorum audientium were in connection with the presbyteri-doctores; we heard that gifts were to be bestowed on the readers εἰς τιμὴν τῶν προφητῶν ; but a direct assertion that the charisma of the Anagnosis could include its related charisma of exposition and teaching was wanting. The reverse case certainly needs no proof. There is no doubt that the free teachers, such as there were in the third,

---

[1] As soon as the episcopal organisation had established itself—even before the bishop received priestly qualifications—the significance of all possessors of the charismata was destroyed. The sentence of Ignatius (ad Smyrn. viii. 1) : Μηδεὶς χωρὶς τοῦ ἐπισκόπου τι πρασσέτω εἰς τὴν ἐκκλησίαν, is here decisive.

[2] It is said of the bishop in Source *A* of the Apostolic Canons : παιδείας μέτοχος, δυνάμενος τὰς γραφὰς ἑρμηνεύειν· εἰ δὲ ἀγράμματος, πραῢς ὑπάρχων.

and even in the fourth century [1], used also to read aloud the texts which they expounded. In this sense each doctor was also a reader; but the reverse cannot at least have been the rule,—rather, it must have been extremely rare, otherwise the functions of the reader and of the doctor would not have been so definitely differentiated in ordinary church language. Thus the demand of our Source A is at any rate a striking one; it does not correspond with the rule; it is explained by this, that at the time of the author the prophets and teachers were conceived as dying out, or at least were very rare (he does not name them), and that the taking up of their functions could not be in all cases required of the bishops, because they were too uneducated (ἀγράμματοι, see above,—what our Source still presupposes in regard to the bishops). There it was better to intrust with the power of instructive exposition the man who offered certain sureties by the gift of the Anagnosis and of a good delivery. It was a period of transition—reading aloud is one thing, and exposition and free speech another; the situation could not last long, and certainly many congregations did not pass through it. The instructive speech for edification, as a rule, passed rather, as Justin relates, from the doctores to the 'overseer,' that is, to the presbyters. We therefore could not wonder if we cannot show a parallel for our passage out of the scanty literature of the second century.

But we do possess a parallel. It is contained in one of the two passages which are the oldest of those which stand especially at our service for the reader, and which on that account I have kept back until the end. The first is Apoc. i. 3, and the second the so-called 2d Epistle of Clement. The first shows us in a surprising manner, what position the reader possessed even at the end of the first century, and *the second is a sermon preached by a reader* [2].

The Revelation of St. John, as it lies before us, begins,

[1] See the references in my edition of the Διδαχή, p. 131 and fol., and besides the 98th Canon of the fourth Council of Carthage of the year 399: 'Laicus praesentibus clericis, nisi ipsis rogantibus, docere non audeat.'

[2] We leave aside the passage of Hermas, Vis. II. 4, 3; the layman Hermas is here asked to read to the Roman presbyters a book of revelations handed to him: 'σὺ δὲ ἀναγνώσῃ εἰς ταύτην τὴν πόλιν μετὰ τῶν πρεσβυτέρων τῶν προϊσταμένων τῆς ἐκκλησίας. For our question the passage has hardly any weight.

chapter i., verses 1 and 2, with a short announcement of the contents, origin, and communication of the book; then it says (verse 3): μακάριος ὁ ἀναγινώσκων καὶ οἱ ἀκούοντες τοὺς λόγους τῆς προφητείας. This distinction would have been an empty pedantry if the reader had not then possessed a peculiar and prominent position in the congregations. Thus is the verse of significance for the date, and for the original position of the reader. There were certainly readers about the year 100, and at that time congregations could, in view of edification, be divided into *reader* and hearers.

But what we seek the 2nd Epistle of Clement provides for us. This writing, now that it has been made completely accessible to us by Bryennios, has, as is well known, claims to give us the copy of a sermon, and that of the *oldest* sermon which we possess (not later than the middle of the second century). That it was not delivered by the bishop or a presbyter [1] was to be seen from chapter xvii. 3, and still plainer from chapter xix. 1. The preacher comes here to a conclusion, and says: "Ὥστε, ἀδελφοὶ καὶ ἀδελφαί, μετὰ τὸν θεὸν τῆς ἀληθείας ἀναγινώσκω ὑμῖν ἔντευξιν εἰς τὸ προσέχειν τοῖς γεγραμμένοις, ἵνα καὶ ἑαυτοὺς σώσητε καὶ τὸν ἀναγινώσκοντα ἐν ὑμῖν. On the strength of this passage I had in my edition (1876) ascribed the sermon to a 'διδάσκαλος.' As I was certain that a presbyter or the 'overseer' could not have preached the sermon, and as I then knew nothing of the significance of the readers in the oldest time, there remained to me no other alternative. But even then I remarked that the author expressly stated that he *read* his sermon, and that this statement was contrary to what had elsewhere been conjectured on the oldest sermons.

Now for the first time, after the reader has come into clearer light, is it possible to decide on this passage. The author announces (1) that before his sermon he read a portion of the Holy Scriptures ; he remarks (2) casually that he also

[1] Καὶ μὴ μόνον ἄρτι, says the preacher, δοκῶμεν πιστεύειν καὶ προσέχειν ἐν τῷ νουθετεῖσθαι ἡμᾶς ὑπὸ τῶν πρεσβυτέρων, ἀλλὰ καὶ ὅταν εἰς οἶκον ἀπαλλαγῶμεν μνημονεύωμεν τῶν τοῦ κυρίου ἐνταλμάτων. One who is himself a presbyter would not speak like this, although it is so assumed not only by Bryennios, but also by Lightfoot ; see Clement of Rome, Appendix, p. 304.

[2] Thus all critics and exegetes after the example of Bryennios understand the difficult words : 'μετὰ τὸν θεὸν τῆς ἀληθείας ἀναγινώσκω.' They are explained by the following τοῖς γεγραμμένοις.

read his sermon relating to this portion, and he calls himself (3) 'ὁ ἀναγινώσκων ἐν ὑμῖν,' and makes the same distinction (you, the hearers—he who is reading among you) which we have found in the Revelation of St. John [1]. Our author is thus no διδάσκαλος, *but he is the reader to the congregation, who follows up his lesson with a thorough exposition, and this he also reads.*

Here we have thus the ἀναγνώστης διηγητικός, εἰδὼς ὅτι εὐαγγελιστοῦ τόπον ἐργάζεται. Our elaborate and read sermon is separated in its performance and its character very decidedly from the free discourses of the διδάσκαλοι, as we must surmise these to be. Our author does not rely on the 'Spirit,' he sets up no spiritual personal quality as *preacher*, he does not speak ὡς ὤν τις, as we know the old διδάσκαλοι did [2], but he speaks rather of himself in the most depreciating manner [3], includes himself everywhere with his hearers [4], and ranks himself below the presbyters [5]. Thus we may conclude *that we have in the second epistle of Clement not the unrestrained speech of a spiritual teacher, but the elaborate sermon intended for delivery of a congregational reader, like those which Source A has made known to us* [6].

We may thus characterise the information which Source A gives us on the reader as neither needing correction, nor accidental or altogether unique. We have rather to acknowledge

---

[1] The words ἵνα καὶ ἑαυτοὺς σώσητε καὶ τὸν ἀναγινώσκοντα ἐν ὑμῖν can also so be understood, as if the author only called himself the reader on account of the momentary situation; but the absolutely laid down ' ὁ ἀναγινώσκων ἐν ὑμῖν,' makes the explanation given in the text far more probable.

[2] The διδάσκαλος writes, speaks, and gives instructions (διατάσσεται) ὡς ὤν τις—like an apostle. His attitude towards the congregation is as of one appointed by God. See the manner of expression in Barnabas I. 8, IV. 9 ; Ignat. ad Ephes. III. 1 ; Dionys. Alex. ep. ad Basil., when they speak of the activity of the διδάσκαλοι. The exact opposite of this is found in our author.

[3] See c. 18, 2 : καὶ γὰρ αὐτὸς πανθαμαρτωλὸς ὢν καὶ μήπω φυγὼν τὸν πειρασμόν, ἀλλ' ἔτι ὢν ἐν μέσοις τοῖς ὀργάνοις τοῦ διαβόλου, σπουδάζω τὴν δικαιοσύνην διώκειν, κ.τ.λ. Similarly in other passages.

[4] See especially c. 17 and 19.

[5] See c. 17.

[6] It is worthy of remark, as a parallel, that the martyr Procopius had exercised in the church at Scythopolis the office of a reader, interpreter, and exorcist. See Ruinart, *Acta Mart. Sinc.* ii. 1, p. 318. Whether the catechists and readers have ever belonged together remains dark. Hom. Clem. III. 71 forms a conception of the presbyters and catechists.

that in it an important historical announcement is preserved to us. The Source is shown in this piece—in its arrangement and in that which it says on the reader—as an extremely valuable document, which casts a bright light on hitherto unconsidered witnesses, which being fragmentary had been declared to be false, and challenges and renders possible an explanation of their details.

The preceding references may justify the following attempt to give the primitive history of the reader in the church in consideration of his place among the other lower orders [1].

I. A completely organised congregation at the end of the apostolic age possessed:—1. Prophets and teachers, who were awakened by the spirit, and announced the word of God; 2. a circle of elders who in all emergencies which affected the congregation could come forth to guide them, and who had to watch over especially the life and the evangelical character of the congregation, and hence admonished, punished, and comforted; 3. the administrative officials—bishops and deacons—who possessed the charisma of government and of public service,

[1] The following conclusions are based partially on the researches which I have published in the Analecta to Hatch, *Gesellschaftsverfass. d. christl. Kirche*, 1883, as well as in my edition of the Διδαχή, pp. 88-170 on the oldest history of church government. It may also be remarked that the appointment of *special* readers in Christian congregations cannot be explained by the synagogal worship. See Schürer, *Gesch. d. jüd. Volkes im Zeitalter Christi*, Part II. p. 364 : 'By the side of the elders who had to direct in general the services of the (Jewish) congregation, *special* officers had to be appointed for special objects. But the peculiar thing here is, that just for the ordinary divine service, *reading of the scriptures*, sermon, and congregational prayer, no special officers were appointed. These acts were performed in the time of Christ more often by the members of the congregation alternately.' But for the fixing of the origin of the lower orders we must completely disregard the synagogal worship and the Jewish officers. The appointment of the lower church offices falls in a time in which nothing more was learned or taken from Judaism on the part of the church. Hence we must not be misled by observing that the church fathers and the canons of later date refer times without number (see, for example, Isidor. de Offic. II. 10, or the collection of Irish canons in Wasserschleben, p. 22 and follg.) the appointment of the lower orders to the Old Testament (sub-deacons = Levites, etc.). This practice is only a special instance out of an innumerable number of similar cases which have arisen from certain altogether misleading conceptions of the relations of the church to the 'Old Testament church.' On this conception and its consequences I have treated in my edition of the Διδαχή, p. 239 and follg., and in my *Lehrb. d. Dogmengesch.* Bk. I. p. 220 and follg.

and who had to act especially in divine service and in the care of the poor; the bishops were also members of the presbytery. But besides these there were active in the congregations the most varied charismata: δυνάμεις, χαρίσματα ἰαμάτων, γένη γλωσσῶν, etc., etc. (see 1 Cor. xii., Mark xvi. 17, 18). Each individual gift or talent which aimed at the edification of the congregation (in the fullest sense of the word) was considered as a charisma of the Holy Ghost; but among the possessors of these only the (apostles), prophets and teachers held a *special rank* in the congregations, for they were the spirit-bearers κατ' ἐξοχὴν, in so far as their efficiency was absolutely necessary for the congregation.

Among the various 'men of gifts' there were even in the earliest times readers and exorcists. As regards the former, we may safely surmise that the public reading of the Old Testament took place from the beginning in the heathen-Christian congregations. It formed an integral part of divine service. Also other writings, apocalypses, epistles, and soon even gospels were to be read in the church. Not many, however, were fitted for this, and there must have been many highly esteemed prophets and teachers who could edify by free speech who were not able to read the holy scriptures. Thus readers were necessary, and the existence of such we find presupposed even in the Apocalypse of St. John. The art of reading and of delivery for the object of edification of the congregation was considered a gift of the Holy Spirit. So far as the reader served for this edification he approximated to the prophets and teachers; for ἀνάγνωσις of the word of God, παράκλησις and διδασκαλία belonged closely together (1 Tim. iv. 13). In an old consecration prayer for the reader which is preserved to us, the πνεῦμα προφητικόν is prayed to be sent down on him, and even, in comparatively later times, what is paid to the reader out of the congregational treasury is designated as given εἰς τιμὴν τῶν προφητῶν. But the capacity and the right to free speech for edification in which the Holy Spirit spoke direct and *ad hoc* to the congregation always formed the fixed boundary between the prophets and teachers on the one side the readers on the other. The former came forth with a peculiar indisputable authority in the congregations, while the reader possessed no personal authority. The former must be maintained by the congregation; with regard to the readers such a duty was considered as little as it was with the exorcists [1] and other possessors of spiritual gifts.

II. In the course of the second century the organisation of congregations was thoroughly altered : the foundations of the government of the Catholic Church were formed. The alterations are shown principally by three developments. 1st, The prophets and teachers died out more and more, or were deprived of their original significance. 2nd, The worship and other relations made it necessary to place *one* man at the head of the administration of the congregation—the ἐπίσκοποι were fused into the bishop. 3rd, The directing college of elders was more and more degraded to the position of an advising college for the support of the bishop. Thus was the ruling order developed in the congregation: bishop, presbyters, deacons; and these officials formed a special body of consecrated persons above the laity. This development was accomplished in the various provinces with different degrees of rapidity, and accordingly we find various transitional forms in different churches. These transitional forms must have been specially present in regard to the function of spiritually edifying the congregation [2]. As far as it was possible, the free speech for edification passed over to the bishop, partly also to the presbyters, the latter of whom had always exhorted and punished in accordance with the gospels. In Justin the 'overseer,' that is, the bishop, appears as the homilist. But by his side until the end of the second century there were probably everywhere free teachers—laymen to whom permission was given not only to speak in the divine service but also to exercise the work of teaching. Such people enjoyed by the side of the officials, just the same as the confessors, virgins,

[1] In ancient Christian literature we hear very much of exorcisms and exorcists, from St. Paul down to Origen (and still further), especially in Justin and the apologists. However, it is not necessary for our purpose to collect and bring out these passages. Only this may be remarked : that exorcism at a very early period played a part in baptism, and that accordingly the exorcists as well as the readers received a function in the divine, that is, the public services of the church. That one could not be appointed an exorcist, or at least consecrated as such, comes out in the regulation of the eighth book of the Apostolic Constitutions, chap. 25, but as a remnant of a system that had passed away.

[2] Similarly uncertain and different must have been for about two generations the relations of the πρεσβύτεροι οἱ προϊστάμενοι to the bishop until the bishop became perfect monarch. It is not our part to give here any further details.

widows, and exorcists, a more or less high esteem. They possessed rank but not an office. The position of the reader appears to have been the most uncertain one. As a rule, in the second century he had stood outside the newly formed *ordo*, as did the doctor or the exorcist, and his duties were restricted to the Anagnosis. Thus it appears from Justin and Tertullian that the reader belonged to the laity. In the Marcionite congregations it was not yet considered a disorder if, for example, a deacon undertook the function of the Anagnosis in divine service. And in single catholic congregations of the east dispositions were not wanting to include the reader in the *ordo* as well as also to extend his functions. The oldest Christian sermon which we possess is that which was specially prepared for reading by an old reader who must have been more than a mere reader. In the Didaskalia which exist in Syriac the reader alone stands beside the presbyters and deacons as an official of the congregation, and it was settled that he should receive the same portion out of the congregational treasury as they —εἰς τιμὴν τῶν προφητῶν. In Source *A* of the Apostolic Canons the reader is placed, according to his rank, between the presbyters and deacons : it was expected of him that he should be διηγητικός, and he is reminded that he holds the place of an evangelist. Here it is plainly to be seen that the reader was to step into the blank, which was the consequence of the general dying out or rather the drawing back of the 'teachers.' He was certainly peculiarly a makeshift, for the same Source considers it very desirable that the bishop should be παιδείας μέτοχος, δυνάμενος τὰς γραφὰς ἑρμηνεύειν. The function of the Anagnosis might be considered in a twofold manner. Its possessor might approximate to those filled with the Spirit and become an ἡγούμενος in the congregation, but he might also sink to a lower sphere, becoming an elected minister, and limited to the function of Anagnosis. In the change of the original orders in the second century, and the departure of the enthusiastic teacher, the reader might have had a high future, and in fact he must certainly have had such in some single congregations in the east for some time, but the new episcopal organisation of the congregation in the end excluded and deeply degraded him.

III. In the first half of the third century the new church organisation reached its final form in the congregations.

ORIGIN OF THE READERSHIP

This finality is characterised by four moments: 1st, by the quality of the sacrificing priesthood, who now took the position of higher clergy, and were settled in it by a solemn consecration; 2nd, by a comprehensive adoption of the complicated forms of the heathen worship, of the temple service, and of the priesthood, as well as by the development of the idea of a magical power and real working of sacred actions [1]; 3rd, by the *strict* and *perfect* carrying out of the clerical organisation in the sense that everything, however old, of dignities, claims, and rights should be excluded, or at any rate made over and subordinated to them; 4th, by the dying out, that is, by the extermination of the last remains of the charismata, which under the new relations were dangerous, seldom appearing, and often besides compromising and discrediting, as far as they rose above the rank of the harmless.

As now the exorcist and reader were necessary for certain acts in the divine service, a certain rank by the side of the priests and deacons might exist in the church, but not any more as independent. Thus in the time between Alexander Severus and Philip the Arabian, that is, in the years 222 to 249, which were most decisive for the consolidation of the churches, first at any rate in Rome, then also in the west [2], the appointment of *clerici minores* is met with, and exorcist and reader are remitted to this position [3]. In this separation of higher and lower, acting and ministering clergy, of priests and of servants in holy things, we see at once a striking agreement with the Roman sacrificial system [4].

---

[1] See on the significance of the alterations named under 1 and 2, Tzschirner, *Fall d. Heidenthums*, p. 606 and follg.

[2] Of course gradually, but quickest in the large towns. Perhaps it is not by chance that even by Commodian in his Instructions only readers were named and honoured with a special poem, while he is silent as to the other *ordines minores*. Commodian has, as is well known, much that is ancient. On the other hand, it is to be observed that Cyprian (Ep. 55, 8) says in praise of Cornelius: 'non ad episcopatum subito pervenit, sed per omnia ecclesiastica officia promotus . . . ad sacerdotii sublime fastigium cunctis religionis gradibus ascendit.' Thus the appointment of *clerici minores* had before 249 taken place in Rome for several years.

[3] There were, however, as is plain from Cyprian's letters, at least in Carthage for a time, remembrances of the former different position of the reader; for instance, the affinity of the reader to the presbyters, and the practice of letting him be advanced to a presbyter is instructive.

[4] See on this Marquardt, *Röm. Staatsverwaltung*, vol. iii. (1878), especially p. 203 and follg.

It is still a question whether the necessity of lowering the exorcist and the reader had given an impulse in the Roman church to accept the Romish-sacrificial separation, or if the position of the *clerici minores* had already been settled when the former had to have their rank determined. In order to decide it, attention must be drawn to the other *clerici minores* which, at least for us, arise suddenly in the clergy at Rome and Carthage. They are the five classes, which are first mentioned by BishopCornelius: 'sub-deacons, acolytes, exorcists, readers, and door-keepers.'

What a difference there was between the exorcist and the reader on one side, and the sub-deacon, acolyte, and doorkeeper on the other! The former had already a *history* in the church when they became *clerici minores*, and were certainly not developed out of the diaconate; with the latter it is, however, quite different. *Their names and functions only appear before us with certainty for the first time in the year* 250. Whence do they arise?

In regard to the sub-deacons the answer, as it seems, is a simple one. Here the name itself points to its origin. The subdeacons have really developed out of the diaconate. Two causes have here been at work. At first it was thought, on the strength of the account in the Acts of the Apostles, not right to over-step the number of seven for the deacons, while in larger towns a larger number of deacons was necessary[1]. In the second place the deacons became so dignified that they sought to rid themselves of the lower ministerial services.

The sub-deacons are thus in their origin the superfluous deacons (over seven) and are at the same time the διάκονοι ὑπηρέται[2]. This double character explains the fact that they took the *highest* place among the *clerici minores*, they even gravitated more and more towards the higher clergy, until once for all Innocent III. numbered them among the higher

[1] Cornelius in his list of the Roman clergy gives the number of deacons in Rome as restricted to seven. See the above quoted fifteenth canon of Neo-Caesarea : Διάκονοι ἑπτὰ ὀφείλουσιν εἶναι κατὰ τὸν κανόνα, κἂν πάνυ μεγάλη εἴη ἡ πόλις· πεισθήσῃ δὲ ἀπὸ τῆς βίβλου τῶν πράξεων. See for Rome Sozom. H. E. vii. 19. Of the Roman bishop Symmachus (end of fifth century) it is said that he was chosen ὡς ἕνα τῶν ἑπτὰ διακόνων ὄντα (see Photius, Erotem., in Routh's *Reliquiae Sacr.* ed. 2. T. III., p. 61). At a later time the restriction of the number to seven was not retained.

[2] See Const. App. VIII. 28 : Ὑποδιακόνῳ οὐκ ἔξεστιν ἀφορίσαι . . . ὑπηρέται γάρ εἰσι διακόνων. Ignatius (Trall. 2. 3) calls the deacons themselves ὑπηρέται.

ordines in the west[1]. But the necessity of appointing sub-deacons by no means explains the institution of the *clerici minores* in the church. These officials could always, as being related to the deacons, be reckoned as belonging to the one *ordo* in the church. We must, therefore, direct our attention to the acolytes and doorkeepers. Here we find in fact the key to the historical understanding of the whole momentous institution of the *clerici minores*.

Exorcists and readers there had been in the church from old times: sub-deacons are not essentially strange, as they participate in a name (deacon) which dates from the earliest days of Christianity. But acolytes and door-keepers ($\pi v \lambda \omega \rho o i$) are quite strange, are really novelties. And these acolytes even at the time of Cornelius stand at the *head* of the *ordines minores*: for that the sub-deacons follow on the deacons is self-evident. Whence do they come? Now if they do not spring out of the Christian tradition, their origin must be explained from the Roman. It can in fact be shown there with desirable plainness.

Marquardt in his exposition of the Roman sacrificial system [2] depicts on p. 203 and follg. the state temple, and on p. 212 and follg. the state-priest.

1. The temples have only partially their own priests, but

[1] See the article 'Sub-deacon' by Friedberg in Herzog's *Real-Encyklopädie*, 2d ed. vol. xv., p. 7 and follg. According to Cornelius and Cyprian sub-deacons were mentioned in the thirtieth canon of the Synod of Elvira (about 305), so that the sub-diaconate must then have been acknowledged as a fixed general institution in the whole west (see Dale, *The Synod of Elvira*, Lond., 1882). The same is seen in the 'gesta apud Zenophilum.' As the appointment of the lower orders took place at Rome between about the years 222-249, the announcement in the Liber Pontificalis (see Duchesne's edition, fasc. 2, 1885, p. 148) is not to be despised, as according to it Bishop Fabian appointed seven sub-deacons: 'Hic regiones dividit diaconibus et fecit vii sub-diaconos.' The Codex Liberianus indeed (see Duchesne, fasc. 1, pp. 4 and 5; Lipsius, *Chronologie d. röm. Bischöfe*, p. 267) only contains the first half of the sentence, and what the *Liber Pontif.* has added of the account of the appointment of sub-deacons (. . . qui vii notariis imminerent, ut gestas martyrum in integro fideliter colligerent) is, in spite of the explanation of Duchesne not convincing. According to Probst and other catholic scholars the subdiaconate existed in Rome a long time before Fabian (*Kirchl. Disciplin*, p. 109), but Hippolytus is against them. Besides, it should be observed that the officials first, even in Carthage, are called hypo-deacons, though the word sub-diaconus was by degrees used in the west. This also points to a Roman origin of the office, for in the Roman church in the first part of the third century the Greek language was the prevailing one, but not at Carthage.

[2] See *ante*.

86 ORIGIN OF THE READERSHIP

they all have a superintendent (*aedituus* = *curator templi*). These *aeditui*, who lived in the temple, fall again into two classes. At least 'in the most important brotherhoods the chosen *aedituus* was not in a position to undertake in person the watching and cleaning of the *sacellum*. He charged therefore with this service a freedman or slave.' 'In this case the *sacellum* had two *aeditui*, the temple-keeper, originally called *magister aedituus*, and the temple-servant, who appears to be called the *aedituus minister*.' 'To both it is common that they live in the temple [1], although in small chapels the presence of the servant is sufficient. The temple-servant *opens, shuts* [2], *and cleans the sacred place, and shows to strangers its curiosities* [3], *and allows according to the rules of the temple those persons to offer up prayers and sacrifices to whom this is permitted, while he sends away the others* [4].'

[1] Suetonius, Domit. 1, Tac. Hist. III. 74, L. Pomponius Bononiensis in Nonius, p. 75, 15, and Gellius XII. 10, 7, Macrob. X. 2, 12, Plut. q. R. 35, Varro de l. L. 22 (note by Marquardt).

[2] Plaut. Curc. I. 3, 46, Liv. XXX. 17, 6, Capitolin., Pert. IV. 9 (note by Marquardt).

[3] Plin. n. h. 32, 17, Horat. Epist. II. 1, 230. Friedländer, Darstell., I. p. 170, ff. 1 (note by Marquardt).

[4] This function, which the Greek νεωκόρος also had, is made known to us best by the inscription of Arcesina in Amorgos, edited by R. Weil in the Mittheilungen des arch. Instituts in Athen, vol. i. p. 342 : "Ἔδοξε τῇ βουλῇ καὶ τῷ δήμῳ "Αγ[ναν] εἶπε· Μελίτων ἐ[πεστ]άτει. μὴ ἐξεῖναι κατά[ρχ]εσθαι εἰς τὸ ʽΗραῖ[ον] ξένῳ μηδενί, ἐμπιμελε[ῖσ]θαι δὲ τὸν νεωκ[όρο]ν καὶ ἐξείργειν· ἐὰν δὲ μὴ ἐξείργῃ, ἀποτίνειν αὐτὸν τῆς ἡμέρας ἑκάστης δέκα δρα[χ]μὰς ἱερὰς τῇ ʽΗρᾳ. On the Roman aeditui see Seneca ep. XLI. 1 : ʽ Non sunt ad caelum elevandae manus nec exorandus aedituus, ut nos ad aurem simulacri, quasi magis exaudiri possimus, admittat ' (note by Marquardt). On the existence and significance of a lower clergy in the oriental religions see Réville (*La Religion à Rome sous les Sévères*, p. 53) : A côté du clergé régulièrement constitué, c'est-à-dire chargé du sacerdoce par une association régulièrement organisée et attaché à un sanctuaire particulier, il y avait encore dans la plupart de ces religions orientales une sorte de bas clergé irrégulier, qui colportait sa marchandise religieuse à peu près partout.' These wandering irregular clergy are, however, to be compared chiefly with the old apostles, prophets and teachers, not with the *ordines minores*. On the other hand the Mithras-religion, whose confessors formed a close society, possess an organised hierarchy, wherein are various lower grades, that is, stages. On the number of these grades investigators are not clear. (See Réville's *Religion*, p. 100, and Marquardt, p. 86 and follg.) Some count 12, others 8, others 7 grades. These are known to us from the inscriptions (see Henzen C. I. L. VI. p. 754), and from Jerome ep. 57. Marquardt accepts seven grades—that of the ravens (κόρακες), that of the initiated (κρύφιοι), that of the fighters (milites), that of the lions, that of the Persians,

ORIGIN OF THE READERSHIP

2. 'Besides the endowment, the colleges of priests were also supplied with a body of servants'—the under officials—'they were appointed to the priests . . . by all of whom they were used partly as letter-carriers (tabellarii), partly as scribes, partly as assistants at the sacrifices.' Marquardt reckons (page 218 and fol.) the various categories of them among the sacerdotes publici (lictores, pullarii, victimarii, tibicines, viatores), sixthly, the calatores, in the priests' colleges free men or freed men, not slaves, *and in fact one for the personal service of each member* [1].

that of the sun-coursers (ἡλιοδρόμοι), and that of the patres. He expressly remarks on these: 'the ravens are the beginners, they still serve as ὑπηρετοῦντες.' [This is the same expression which is used in the east from the fourth century for the sub-deacons and especially for the lower offices. See above.] 'The soldier, however, receives in humility the crown.' We may therefore acknowledge in the Mithras-worship five upper and two lower orders. Here then we have a true parallel to the Christian Institution; yet, the differences are unmistakable. On the 'flamines maiores et minores' see Marquardt p. 314 and follg.

[1] Serv. ad Ge. I. 268 : 'Pontifices sacrificaturi praemittere calatores suos solent' (note by Marquardt). Mommsen, *Röm. Staatsrecht*, vol. i. (2nd ed.), p. 344 : 'Among the priests we find the institution of the calatores. Originally these appear to have been those slaves who were at hand when the master commanded, and generally to execute his commands. Later to the higher colleges of priests there was given to each member a freedman, who was chosen and dismissed by him, and appointed for his special personal service.' In general it is to be remarked that it is just that Roman priesthood, as to which we are by far the best informed, the Fratres Arvales (see Henzen, Acta fratrum Arvalium quae supersunt restituit et illustravit, 1874 ; and Marquardt, p. 428 and fol.), which in its constitution offers the most striking parallel to the ecclesiastical hierarchy. The superintendent of the Arvales is a magister ; and beside him, and as an assistant to him, we find in the sacrifices a flamen. On solemn occasions appear further four *pueri* ingenui patrimi et matrimi, senatorum filii, . . . they are the ministri at the sacrifice during the meal of the Arvales, place the fruits from the table upon the altar, but they take part in the meal at tables by themselves, sitting on chairs, and receive, like the priests, their sportulae.' Here we have the companion picture to the bishop, the priest, and the deacons. But Marquardt thus continues: 'To these now come the servants, that is, first, a number of *servi publici* . . . whom the magister takes charge of (allegit). . . . They were afterwards required for other services, or performed at the same time other services, as at one time a tabularius rationis castrensis appears at the sacrifices of the Arvales ; secondly, the aedituus, who seems to be a servus collegii ; and lastly, the calatores. Each member chooses out of his freedmen a calator.' Any one acquainted with Church history must here be reminded of subdeacons, doorkeepers, and acolytes. The hitherto discovered registers of the Arvales reach from 14 to 241 A.D.

Here we have the forerunners of the church doorkeepers and acolytes. Thus says the fourth Council of Carthage, as far as refers to the former: 'Ostiarius cum ordinatur, postquam ab archidiacono instructus fuerit, qualiter in domo dei debeat conversari, ad suggestionem archidiaconi, tradat ei episcopus claves ecclesiae de altari, dicens: Sic age, quasi redditurus deo rationem pro his rebus, quae hisce clavibus recluduntur.' The ostiarius (πυλωρός) is thus the aedituus minister. He had to look after the opening and shutting of the doors, to watch over the coming in and going out of the faithful, to refuse entrance to suspicious persons, and, from the date of the more strict separation between the missa catechumenorum and the missa fidelium, to close the doors, after the dismissal of the catechumens, against those doing penance and unbelievers[1]. He first became necessary when there were special church buildings (there were such even in the second century), and they like the temples, together with the ceremonial of divine service, had come to be considered as holy, that is, since about 225.

The church acolytes[2] are without difficulty to be recognised in the under officials of the priests, especially in the 'calatores,' the personal servants of the priests. According to Cyprian the acolytes and others are used by preference as tabellarii. According to Cornelius there were in Rome forty-two acolytes. As he gives the number of priests as forty-six, it may be concluded with something like certainty that the rule was that the number of the priests and of the acolytes should be equal, and that the little difference may have been caused by temporary vacancies. If this view is correct, the identity of the calator with the acolyte is strikingly proved. But the name 'acolyte' plainly shows the acolyte was not, like the doorkeeper, attached to a sacred thing, but to a sacred person[3].

[1] See Krüll in Kraus, *Real-Encyclop.*, vol. ii. p. 572 and fol. ; and Armfield in the *Dictionary of Christian Antiquities*, vol. ii. p. 1528.

[2] On their later history see Krüll's article in Kraus, *Real-Encyclop.*, vol. i. p. 30; and Butler in the *Dictionary of Christian Antiquities*, vol. i. p. 13.

[3] Cornelius uses in his letter the Greek names ἀκόλουθος and πυλωρός, because he writes in Greek (ἀκόλουθος is every attendant, scholar, follower, adherent, especially the servant or boy who accompanies his master when he goes out; see Passow). But Cyprian says 'acoluthi,' and no other name. This name has become in the West a technical term. Thus the institution of the acolytes was adopted in Rome at a time in which the congregation was

The new requirements of the sacerdotal and religious church system in Rome, enriched after the heathen pattern, called forth the acolytes and doorkeepers as antitypes to the calatores and aeditui ministri. Thus a foundation was laid for the ordo clericorum minorum. But that from them was created *an effective and closely confined ordo of the second rank*, and that in this ordo the sub-deacons, the readers and the exorcists found their places[1], and that thus a well-linked chain was

mostly a Greek-speaking one. On the other hand, 'ostiarius' became the technical term, and not 'πυλωρός'; the name 'aedituus' was specially avoided; for the church building was not an 'ædes.' Besides, the sub-deacons, and not the deacons, appear to answer to the magister aedituus, as plainly appears from the Gesta apud Zenophilum (Routh, iv. p. 323 and fol.). I only know of two passages in which acolyte is rendered by 'sequens,' and these are in the Liber Pontificalis (see Duchesne's edition, fasc. 2, pp. 137, 161). Speaking of the Roman bishop Gaius (283-296) it says : 'Hic constituit ut ordines omnes in ecclesia sic ascenderetur (sic): si quis episcopus mereretur, ut esset ostiarius, lector, exorcista, *sequens* (Probst, *Kirchl. Disciplin.*, p. 75, translates this word by 'so then'!) subdiaconus, diaconus, presbyter, et exinde episcopus ordinaretur.' Duchesne remarks here correctly : 'Sequens a ici le sens d'acolythe. Il y aurait un exemple épigraphique de cette acception si le sens du mot "sequentibus," dans une inscription de Narbonne, était sûrement celui que propose M. Le Blant, *Inscr. Chrét. de la Gaule*, Tom. II. No. 617.' Besides we find in the *Liber Pontif.* in the parallel, although much fuller, regulation of Pope Sylvester (p. 171) not 'sequens,' but 'acolitus.' It may be remarked, in passing, that the acolyte soon lost his original function—he gave it up to non-clerical functionaries, and in worship employed himself with services, indeed, which would not accord with his position above that of reader, such as kindling the lights in church. In some provincial churches he disappears entirely for a time. Thus in *one* document of the Irish collection of canons (see Wasserschleben, 2nd ed. pp. 22-26) only four lower orders are fixed ; though in the last recension (26 and fol.) the acolyte has been added. We have above fixed the time for the institution of the clerici minores in Rome in the years 222-249 (the time between the composition of the Philosophumena and Cyprian). We may fix the time more precisely if we consider (1) that Cornelius, according to the witness of Cyprian, had gone through all the church orders ; (2) that the names of the offices are all Greek ; (3) that the *Liber Pontif.* traces the appointment of sub-deacons to the time of Bishop Fabian. Hence, with great probability it may be asserted that the appointment of the clerici minores in Rome took place in the first years of the government of Fabian, thus soon after the year 236. The announcement in the *Lib. Pontif.*, p. 137, that Victor had appointed the 'sequentes,' cannot be correct, at least in the strict sense (as an ordo).

[2] The order in which the five offices is arranged is thoroughly transparent. It is easily to be understood that the sub-deacons should occupy the first place, and that the exorcist and reader should stand together. Neither is there anything remarkable in the position of the doorkeeper at the end. But it is not easy to see the meaning of the rank accorded to the acolyte. May we con-

formed, is not one of the least of the great actions of the Roman Church for the building up of the ecclesiastical constitution, but rather one of the greatest[1]. Thus the church created a nursery for the higher clergy; thus it allured the ambitious by means of numerous stages; thus it could for years thoroughly sift from among the clergy of the second order, and only advance to the influential higher dignities men well proved. Thus at last had it fortunately debased the old, as one may say, palæontological dignities, those of the exorcists and readers, that is, rendered them harmless. Many churches of the west very speedily followed their example, and accepted the institution of an effective, five-membered, strictly closed *ordo clericorum ministrorum*. This institution, as it is now plain, did not proceed out of the diaconate: it is a complicated picture; it includes three categories, which in their origin had nothing in common, exorcists and readers[2], sub-deacons, acolytes and doorkeepers.

The last mentioned offices appear indeed as if their fundamental idea was the imitation of the Roman sacrificial arrangements: but in carrying out this idea in the creation of an effective spiritual rank of the second order, and in the founding of a preparatory school for the priestly office it rises high above a mere imitation: it is the most striking witness of the way

clude from the position which he takes that he gave the impulse for the formation of the whole class of ordines minores? At any rate it is to be observed (see above) that Cornelius only really points out three categories : sub-deacons —acolytes—exorcists, readers, and doorkeepers. The last category is for him a single one, because those reckoned in it, as above shown, appear to be intrusted with a more or less *mechanical* service in holy things. The acolytes must have had a greater responsibility. The number 52, which Cornelius has given as the total number of the exorcists, readers, and doorkeepers in Rome, can unfortunately not be differentiated.

[1] It is on this account very striking that Langen, in his exhaustive History of the Roman Church, vol. i. (1881), has not mentioned it.

[2] That there were parallels to be found even for the readers in the heathen worship is partly to be considered as a coincidence, partly a consequence of the later, that is of the special, development of the readership. Such readers as had the custody of the holy scriptures, and also interpreted them, remind one of the fifteen viri sacris faciundis, who had to preserve under lock and key the sibylline books, write them out and explain them ('interpretes'); see Marquardt, p. 366 and fol. Also for the origin of the sub-diaconate, as above shown, there is no necessity to turn to the Roman religion, although even here many parallels appear of considerable importance; see further the Supplementary Chapter.

in which the Roman church understood how to overcome the dangers which still always threatened her from a dead organisation of the church, to build up her episcopal-presbyterian constitution, and to adopt the useful elements of the religious and civil conditions of Roman life [1]. So far as she made it possible for every one, even the least, to reach the highest dignity of a priest from the lowest position of a sexton, and on the other side required, as a rule, every one to begin to serve the church from the lowest step, so far, I say, she broke with the ancient view that the priesthood should be accessible to certain classes only, and also tore down the wall of separation between the priests and the temple servants. The

[1] The organising genius of the leaders of the Roman church in the third century comes out plainly when we follow the origin and development of the clerici minores in the East. Everything was settled there much later. The number of stages remained fundamentally just as uncertain as did the relations of rank; even the conception of a real ordo of the second grade was not strictly marked. Thus, for example, we do not find the acolytes as an 'ordo' in the East, although they were not wanting (see the description of Paul of Samosata, Metropolitan of Antioch, in Eusebius, Hist. Ecc. vii. 30, 8: βαδίζων δημοσίᾳ καὶ δορυφορούμενος τῶν μὲν προπορευομένων, τῶν δὲ ἐφεπομένων πολλῶν τὸν ἀριθμόν, or Euseb., Vit. Constant. III. 8, where it is said of the Council of Nicaea: ἐπὶ τῆς παρούσης χορείας ἐπισκόπων μὲν πληθὺς ἦν, πεντήκοντα καὶ διακόνων ἀριθμὸν ὑπερακοντίζουσα, ἑπομένων δὲ τούτοις πρεσβυτέρων καὶ διακόνων, ἀκολούθων τε πλείστων ὅσων ἑτέρων οὐδ' ἦν ἀριθμὸς εἰς κατάληψιν). The readers were here and there in the second and third century sought to be taken into the ordo of priests and deacons, doubtless because the possibility of two ordines had not yet been thought of; then there appeared in the group psalm-singers, gravediggers, etc., without any fixed stages of rank having been formed. It is peculiarly oriental this coupling of the psalm-singer with the reader, since the fourth century. It may be considered probable that so far as the East, in the fourth century, had comprehended and embraced the thought of an ordo minor it had been influenced by the west (by Rome). On the great differences of the oriental church with regard to the ordines and the present position, in which the sub-deacons and readers really still exist, see Denzinger, *Ritus Orientalium*, Tom. I. (1863), p. 116 and fol.; Silbernagl, *Verfassung u. gegenwärtiger Bestand sämmtl. Kirchen d. Orients*, 1865, p. 2 f. and *passim*; Gass, *Symbolik d. griech. Kirchen*, 1872 (p. 277 and fol.); and the striking articles as, for example, 'Armenier,' 'Kopten,' etc., in Herzog's *Real-Encyclop.*, 2nd ed.; and in the Dictionary of Christian Biography, by Smith and Wace. The Roman Church and the western churches generally have not appointed any new classes of officers in the clergy after the middle of the third century. Thus even before Constantine there were 'fossores' in the churches (see, for example, the *Gesta apud Zenophilum*, in Routh, *l. c.* IV. p. 323), soon also 'cantores'; but they were not 'de clero,' as the exorcists, readers, and doorkeepers.

conception of a clergy of eight degrees[1] is certainly not a Christian one; but in the fundamental idea that this clergy should be neutral in the difference between high and low, rich and poor, Roman and barbarian, a Christian thought was effectively at work and therein the old world found its conqueror.

[1] I do not go any further into the various rights and duties of the higher and lower clergy (thus, in regard to marriage and church requirements) or the manner of designation, choice, appointment of the latter, as these questions do not belong to the history of the origin of the lower clergy. Still from here also there falls a light on the origin of the whole group.

SUPPLEMENTARY

It has been shown above that the appointment of the clerici minores in Rome took place, most probably in the first years of the government of the Bishop Fabian, thus soon after the year 236, and we have in this connection pointed to the assertions of the Catal. Liberianus and of the Lib. Pontificalis (of Fabian). These assertions deserve a special consideration.

The Catal. Liberianus remarks on Fabian: 'Hic regiones divisit diaconibus.' As is well-known, the few historical notices which the Catalogue contains on the events of the time of government of single popes are reliable: we find such notices only on Pius, Pontian, Fabian, Cornelius, Lucius, and Julius. We may thus accept as authentic the statement that Fabian divided the regions of the city of Rome among the deacons: that is, that he placed each region under a deacon. This is an extremely interesting piece of news, for it shows the adaptation of the church government of the Christian congregations in Rome to the civic-religious system in a most instructive manner. The regions—that is, the overseers of the regions—in Rome in the time of the Empire may be described in short thus [1]: Augustus had in place of the four old regions made fourteen new ones. For each of these regions an overseer was chosen yearly by lot. The overseers had to sanction the building of temples for the lares, and to arrange and perfect in their circles the local sacrifices. 'The Augustan overseers of the regions have, to all appearance, nothing more to do with the general town arrangements; and it appears as if this appointment, as well as the whole arrangement of the suburbs of the capital, had an overwhelmingly religious character.' So it remained—apart from an attempted alteration on the part of Domitian, as to which we have no authentic information—until the beginning of

[1] See Mommsen, *Röm. Staatsrecht*, Bd. II. 1st Abth. (1874), p. 485, and II. 2nd Abth. (1877), pp. 992 and fol., 1012 and fol., 1031 and fol.

the third century. Heliogabalus had in view, however, a new order of things, and his successor, Alexander Severus, carried it out. Of the former it is said (Vita 20): 'Voluit et per singulas urbis regiones praefectos urbi facere, et fecisset si vixisset'; of the latter (Vita 13): 'Fecit Romae curatores urbis quattuordecim, sed ex consulibus viros, quos audire negotia urbana cum praefecto urbis iussit, ita ut omnes aut magna pars adessent cum acta fierent.' Thus Alexander placed by the side of the city prefect a kind of council of fourteen consular curators appointed for the single regions of the town. It is of no importance to consider the relations they held to the old overseers, whether they took their place or worked beside them. What is new and important to us is this, that in the interest of directing and taking care of the town community the single regions received curators, a kind of under-burgomasters, who stood under the city prefect, and had to transact the town business with him. Now it is just at this time that we meet with the notice in the Catalog. Liber.: 'Fabianus regiones divisit diaconibus.' When we call to mind the scope of action allotted to the church deacons the parallel is striking; they are in a certain measure the under bishops; they have relations to the bishop just as the curatores urbis to the praefectus urbi. Thus Fabian has here followed the new municipal arrangements in his appointments; for the reverse view is, in spite of Alex. Sever., Vita 45 [1], quite improbable. The new municipal arrangements had, it appears, only a short existence: while the ecclesiastical ones remained, and have on their part contributed to such a state of things that the Roman bishop held his congregation so firmly in hand, and was so powerful in the city, that even Decius declared that the raising of an anti-Caesar in Rome would be more endurable to him than the appointment of a bishop there [2].

There were, however, in Rome fourteen regions, and the

[1] 'Ubi (Alexander) aliquos voluisset vel rectores provinciis dare vel propositos facere vel procuratores, id est rationales, ordinare, nomina eorum proponebat, hortans populum, ut si quis quid haberet criminis probaret manifestis rebus, si non probasset, subiret poenam capitis; dicebatque, grave esse, cum id Christiani et Iudaei facerent in praedicandis sacerdotibus, qui ordinandi sunt, non fieri in provinciarum rectoribus, quibus et fortunae hominum committerentur et capita.'

[2] Cypr., Ep. 55, 9.

Catal. Liber. speaks of a dividing of the regions among them. Did each deacon, perhaps, receive *two* regions? The Liber Pontif. adds to the notice of Liberianus the words: 'et fecit septem subdiaconos.' If this assertion is not to be trusted by itself, at any rate the account of Cornelius in the letter to Fabius of the year 250 is indisputable, that in Rome there were seven deacons and *seven* sub-deacons. Thus we have the fourteen overseers. Before Fabian we cannot prove the existence of sub-deacons; it is certain that Fabian divided the regions; the sub-deacons could not have risen later than the time of Fabian in Rome; at the time of the successor to Fabian the total number of deacons and sub-deacons was fourteen—thus it is exceedingly probable that *the appointment of seven sub-deacons in Rome, and with it the creation of the sub-diaconate generally was a consequence of the arrangement of Fabian, by which each region should receive an ecclesiastical curator, while, in deference to holy scripture, the number seven for the deacons was not allowed to be increased.* Even by this hypothesis the fact remains that the sub-diaconate is nothing else than the diaconate of a second order; but the occasion for its formation is now to a certain degree proved, by which the ecclesiastical government was to be settled on the same lines as the municipal.

There is no doubt also in the number of the acolytes a significance from what has been given above in the fourteen regions ($14 \times 3 = 42$), so that in each region there were three acolytes. Beyond all question[1] in later times there were acolytes for the regions. But later circumstances must not be dated back, without further consideration, into the third century, and besides the name of acolyte is not appropriate to such a meaning.

[1] See Hinschius, *System des kath. Kirchenrechts*, vol. i. pp. 322, 377. The subject of the later ecclesiastical regions and their government is not treated here.

www.ingramcontent.com/pod-product-compliance
Lightning Source LLC
Chambersburg PA
CBHW071939160426
43198CB00011B/1465